# LOUISIANA
# FAMILY LAW
## GUIDE

# LOUISIANA FAMILY LAW
## GUIDE

A Client's Guide to
Divorce, Custody, Child Support,
Spousal Support, Community Property,
and More

## BY STEPHEN RUE

**PELICAN PUBLISHING COMPANY**
Gretna 2004

*The word "Pelican" and the depiction of a pelican are trademarks
of Pelican Publishing Company, Inc., and are registered
in the U.S. Patent and Trademark Office.*

**Library of Congress Cataloging-in-Publication Data**

Rue, Stephen.
  Louisiana family law guide : a client's guide to divorce, custody, child support, spousal support, community property, and more / by Stephen Rue.
    p. cm.
Includes index.
  ISBN 1-58980-196-2 (pbk. : alk. paper) — ISBN 1-58980-192-X (hardcover : alk. paper) 1. Divorce—Law and legislation—Louisiana—Popular works. 2. Support (Domestic relations) —Louisiana—Popular works. 3. Domestic relations—Louisiana—Popular works. I. Title.

  KFL100.Z9R84 2004
  346.76301'5—dc22

                                                    2003026112

This guide is not intended or offered as advice for legal, medical, or physiological problems. Please consult a licensed attorney, health-care provider, counselor, and/or religious advisor for real legal, medical, psychological, and/or spiritual needs. The contents of this book are merely concepts to be discussed with your attorney. Every effort was made to present accurate information. The publisher and the author assume no liability associated for any errors and/or omissions. Consult your attorney regarding the applicability and accuracy of the contents presented in this book.

Printed in the United States of America

Published by Pelican Publishing Company, Inc.
1000 Burmaster Street, Gretna, Louisiana 70053

*To my family*

*To Jeannie Rue Pearson, who has been a dedicated and caring mother, teacher, and example of one who unselfishly gives unconditional love and support*

*To my uncle, J. Robert Ates, who, through the absence of my father, became my surrogate father, big brother, caring and supportive uncle, and mentor*

*To my sister Elizabeth Brennan. She is a wonderful mother to my beautiful nieces Brooke and Ashley. I am very proud of Elizabeth.*

*To the thousands of clients whom I have represented during their own legal concerns—I continue to devote my efforts, skill, and professionalism to you and your children.*

*And finally, to the children of Louisiana. I pray that through this guide your parent will gain knowledge and wisdom to be the best parent he or she can be through the divorce process and through the rest of your lives.*

# CONTENTS

# PREFACE

*Louisiana Family Law Guide* was created to assist you in under-standing, coping with, and managing your life in the context of Louisiana laws regarding divorce, child custody, child support, spousal support, community-property division, domestic abuse, and related topics.

Once you are faced with the realities of an impending divorce, you often don't have the time to read several books regarding the intricate details of divorce litigation. This book is not meant to replace a competent divorce lawyer licensed in Louisiana; however, it will be your quick and concise guide, providing you with the key concepts and knowledge necessary to defeat the normal feelings of overwhelmingness and despair. You will be shown how to promptly target your particular concerns and be directed on how to take action to protect your precious rights. Once you have obtained a comfort level with the basic principles of your concerns, this guide will provide further references to assist you in a productive dialogue with your chosen attorney.

Each of the fifty states has unique characteristics in their laws; Louisiana is no different. Of the thousands of clients who have come into one of our law offices in Louisiana, at least half of these have concerns about the strange laws of Louisiana, and most have heard antiquated vestiges that linger from the obscure Napoleonic Code.

*Louisiana Family Law Guide* will provide you an overview of the state's family law and explain the most common areas of concern. With the assistance of your family lawyer, you should have a very good grasp on what to expect and how to optimize favorable results. Each case can only be properly analyzed after considering your par-ticular circumstances and needs. I have worked diligently to provide the most recent facts as they pertain to Louisiana law and the interplay with laws of other states as well as federal legislation; however, the law is dynamic, and laws do change. Your lawyer should be able to advise you as to Louisiana's current law and how it relates to your case. I strongly recommend that you seek professional advice and do not handle your divorce without a lawyer. You may wish to consider consulting an attorney, accountant, certified financial planner, tax advisor, and other such professionals. Discuss the concepts disclosed in this book with your lawyer and consider his advice on each of the issues presented.

In this guide, I provide helpful gems gathered by representing thousands of clients. Although these concepts should not be taken as legal advice, you can take comfort knowing that thousands have benefited from understanding the foundation of Louisiana family law and from learning the lessons gleaned from my representation of many clients who have found themselves in similar positions.

I also have supplied anecdotes and illustrative quotes from various clients. Names and localities may have been changed to maintain confidentiality. The purpose of these anecdotes and quotes is to let you know that your experience is not uncommon, and you will survive the process.

Although selected Louisiana laws are provided, I recommend that you simply read them at your leisure as supplemental information and don't worry about the intricacies of interpretation of these laws. This guide provides you with practical applications of facts that will help you in understanding the process and assisting your selected attorney in the best presentation of your legal interests. If you need further advice, please do not hesitate to contact me. Good luck!

# ACKNOWLEDGMENTS

I wish to thank my longtime office manager, Jennifer Thompson, for her years of loyalty and devotion to our clients. I wish to thank my fellow attorney Raul E. Guerra, Jr., for his commitment to ensure the accuracy of this guide. Finally, I wish to thank my entire team of divorce lawyers for their aggressive and professional representation of our clients throughout Louisiana.

# LOUISIANA
# FAMILY LAW
## GUIDE

Chapter 1

# CONTROL YOUR BODY
# AND MIND

"My husband left me for another woman.
Now, the kids seem to be my sole responsibility.
I am overweight and feel totally betrayed and abandoned. I
don't know what to do. I don't know where to turn. Please help me!"
—Elizabeth B.
age 34, married, two children, real-estate agent
New Orleans, Louisiana

Simply put, a divorce and its aftermath are very emotional experiences. *Expect stress—it is very normal.*

Divorce brings concerns about children, money, property, and newfound single status. There are no Louisiana laws that directly address the emotional stress associated with the divorce process, although temporary restraining orders and injunctions can eliminate stress regarding potentially volatile confrontations with your spouse.

We should not allow our emotions to guide us to act and make decisions that are irrational and not in the best interests of our children and ourselves.

## 1. Emotions Will Arise

Realize that sad emotions will arise. Transcend your emotions and separate them from the decisions that affect your finances and your children. The more emotion becomes involved in your divorce proceeding, the longer your divorce process will likely last and the more it will cost. As you start to take control of your emotions, you also will start to gain control of your divorce proceeding. Regain inner peace and enjoy your new life. One step toward peacefulness is in knowing what you may encounter in your litigation. This guide will provide you a framework for your expectations.

You may encounter a series of emotions that many refer to as the emotional life cycle of a divorcé or divorcée:

NORMAL EMOTIONAL LIFE CYCLE
OF A DIVORCÉ OR DIVORCÉE

- Denial or surprise
- Anger
- Depression and feelings of despair
- Desires to negotiate with your spouse
- Sadness
- Acceptance and understanding
- Pursuit for further happiness

## 2. You Are Not Alone and Your Experience Is Not Unique

Remember that each year *over two million people divorce* and encounter some form of anxiety, doubt, denial, depression, loneliness, guilt, anger, sadness, overwhelmingness, forgetfulness, and/or frustration. They also may feel a sense of relief. It is unlikely that you will be able to avoid these pressures. What you can control is your body and your mind. Remember that divorce no longer carries a stigma of shame.

You are not the honoree at a Louisiana jazz funeral—you are getting divorced. Life goes on!

## 3. Divorce Statistics

We have all heard that divorce invades an alarming 50 percent of marriages. Society is beginning to look at marriage as a contract. As a result of this sterile view of this union, judges are becoming more dispassionate toward particular litigants. Today many consider divorce like going to the dentist and getting a tooth pulled. It may be painful, but it also can be quick.

Approximately 95 percent of divorce proceedings do not result in a contested trial (American Bar Association). The divorce rate hovers around 4.4 to 4.6 divorces per every 1,000 marriages. In the seventies and eighties, the divorce rate climbed from 2.5/1,000 in 1966 to highs of 5.3/1,000 in 1979 and 1981. It has leveled off since the 1981 peak.

The average length of a first marriage is 11 years. A woman remarries for an average of 7.1 years, while men remarry for an average of 7.4 years. The average duration of an American marriage is 9.8 years. The average age for a woman who marries and divorces several times is 33 for the first divorce, 39 for the second, and 42 for three or more. The average age for men of multiple divorces is 35 for the first, 42 for the second, and 46.5 for subsequent divorces.

Divorces are more prevalent during the time when men are, on average, 30-34 years old and when women are 25-29 years old. A female's divorce rate is highest between the very young ages of 15 and 19. A male's divorce rate is highest between the ages of 20 and 24.

The median age for women at the time of their first marriage is 21 years, 23.1 years for men. The median age of spouses at the time of the first marriage divorce decree is 35.1 for women and 33.2 for men.

Women start the legal proceedings in more than 90 percent of all divorces.

## 4. Your Own Emotional and Physical Well-Being Affects Your Chances of Getting Custody or Visitation of Your Children

Louisiana Civil Code article 134 lists the factors that are used to determine the child's best interest for custody and visitation decisions. Two of the factors directly involve your physical and emotional well-being.

> The court shall consider all relevant factors in determining the best interest of the child. Such factors may include:
>
> (1) The love, affection, and other emotional ties between each party and the child. . . .
>
> (7) The mental and physical health of each party.
>
> C.C. Article 134 stated in pertinent part.

Article 136 addresses an award of visitation rights to a parent and considers

> (4) The willingness of the relative to encourage a close rela tionship between the child and his parent or parents.
>
> and
>
> (5) The mental and physical health of the child and the relative.
>
> C.C. Article 136 stated in pertinent part.

## 5. Good to Yourself

Celebrate each day in your life. Take good care of yourself. Eating healthy and exercising regularly will allow you to be physically prepared for this time of inherent stress and uncertainty. Anger and bitterness eat at you if you let them. The person most hurt by your rage is you. Don't forget, don't regress, but do forgive your spouse for your own sake and for the sake of your children. This is not to say that you should forgive and reconcile, but rather, forgive for the sake of being happy. Forgive for the sake of being healthy. Forgive for the sake of moving on. Get what is just and fair to you and the children. Forgive and live. If you feel overwhelmed, consider seeking advice from a mental-health professional and/or religious and spiritual advisor. Also seek help for any substance-abuse problem. Remember that your lawyer is not a therapist. Other professionals are better equipped to handle your emotional needs. If time permits, reading books regarding divorce and related issues also will reduce your level of stress.

- It's okay to cry and express your feelings.
- Talk to *supportive* friends who do not flame the fire of your anger or grief.
- Read books that help you get through the divorce process.
- Consider joining a divorce support group.
- Exercise regularly.
- Eat healthy.
- Resist destructive temptations.
- Consult a counselor or religious advisor.
- Focus on your career or potential career.

## 6. Talk with Your Children

Take time to talk with your children and explain that you are getting a divorce. Tailor your statements to the age of the children. Emphasize that the breakup is not their fault and that your decision to divorce is made and that they cannot change it. Do not speak badly of the other parent. Frequently reassure the children that both of you are still their parents and that they are loved and will not be abandoned. Tell them that you will take care of them and keep them safe. Everything will be all right!

Chapter 2

# Your Louisiana Divorce

"What can I expect when I get a divorce?"

—Jeanine B.
age 33, married, no children, teacher
Lafayette, Louisiana

## 1. What Is a Divorce?

A divorce is a formal statement and a court's legal termination of the marriage contract between spouses. Once a party files for divorce and/or becomes divorced, that party's legal rights and obligations regarding various incidental matters change.

In Louisiana, a marriage ends upon the occurrence of one of four events:

1. the death of either spouse;
2. the issuance of a court order authorizing the spouse of a person presumed dead to remarry, as provided by law;
3. a judicial declaration of its nullity, when the marriage is relatively null; or
4. divorce.

## 2. Matters Affected by a Divorce

1. Marital status
2. Child custody and visitation
3. Child support
4. Spousal support
5. Rights for injunctive relief (restraining orders)
6. Property rights
7. Taxes
8. Credit
9. Bankruptcy

19

10. Use of the residence and other property
11. Removal of personal property
12. Use of your surname (last name)

All of the above topics will be covered in detail in this guide.

## 3. Grounds for Divorce in Louisiana

### Three Ways to Get a Divorce in Louisiana

1. Article 102 (living apart one hundred eighty days)
2. Article 103 (living separate and apart continuously for a perod of six months or more on the date the petition is filed; other grounds)
3. Louisiana Revised Statute 9:307-9 (special divorce and separation laws solely for covenant marriages)

> "I simply don't want to be married anymore. My wife and I have grown apart. What are the grounds for divorce? Do I have to claim that someone is at fault to get a divorce?"
>
> —Robert P.
> age 43, seeking a divorce, one child, architect
> Shreveport, Louisiana

## 4. The Ever-Changing Nature of Divorce Law

Divorce law has evolved to conform to the prevailing views of our time. In past decades, divorce laws were drafted to dissuade persons from divorcing. These restrictive laws were framed with the purpose of preserving the family unit. Louisiana was our parent, with the arrogant position that it knew what was best for us. Divorces were instituted based on a spouse's guilt or innocence ("fault"). Fault was a major player in the determination of alimony and apportionment of property. Along with the age of fault came the age of gender bias. This included the "tender years doctrine," which presumed that the mother should be the custodial parent of an infant or young child.

This rather-antiquated system of family "justice" created bitter court fights and lingering anger and regret.

Today, divorce in America is taking a new direction. States, including Louisiana, are no longer as stringent in their role to maintain family units. Modern legislatures are realizing America's freedom of choice, while preserving and enforcing the legal and moral parental obligation to raise and support children. As a result of this changed focus, more states are permitting divorces on grounds other than fault.

A "no-fault divorce" aids in lessening the stresses associated with torrid allegations of infidelity or intemperance. Such allegations still raise their ugly heads in battles over spousal support, child custody, and the like; however, the system is slightly more civil and less combative as a whole. Accompanying a trend toward "no-fault" divorces is the aspiring goal of the courts to be gender neutral. Although constitutionally mandated, the goal has not been fully obtained, yet progress is being made.

Within the last decade, with the emergence of stronger religious and conservative coalitions throughout Louisiana and the rest of the country, there has been, once again, a movement toward more restrictive laws regarding divorce. For example, in 1997, Louisiana enacted laws for "covenant marriages" as an alternative to traditional marriages. The designation "covenant marriage" means that Louisiana recognizes the spouses like contractual partners, and there are much more restrictive grounds for divorce and an extended time period of separation that must be satisfied prior to being eligible for the divorce. Marriage counseling also may be a prerequisite to the divorce. The vast majority of marriages in Louisiana are not covenant marriages, and unless you entered into a covenant marriage at the time of your ceremony or adopted the provisions of a covenant marriage at a later date, you should not concern yourself with the laws concerning these restrictive provisions.

As socioeconomic and political influences change, so will our divorce laws. They will evolve, whether for good or bad, based on the will of the people. Hence, you have a vital role in molding the future of our domestic life. If you have a strong view on an issue surrounding marriage and divorce, write your state and federal legislators. Find out their views on matters that affect you and your children. Advocate, or you may succumb to the will and views of others.

## 5. Louisiana's "Fault" and "No-Fault" Divorces

C.C. Art. 3521. Divorce or separation
A court of this state may grant a divorce or separation only for grounds provided by the law of this state.

All states provide a legal basis to get a divorce without the necessity of formally blaming your spouse with bad conduct. These states are typically called "no-fault states." Terms often found to describe the basis of seeking a no-fault divorce are irreconcilable differences, incompatibility, and/or irretrievable breakdown. Other no-fault trends include allowing a couple to get divorced after they have lived separate and apart for a requisite period of time, depending on the state, from six months to three years. Usually, the separation of the parties must be accompanied by the intent of the parties to permanently be separated, without reconciliation.

### No-Fault Louisiana Divorce

"My husband and I have decided to get a divorce. We have no hard feelings . . . It just did not work out. Can I get a divorce based on 'irreconcilable differences' or something like that? We don't want to throw nasty allegations at each other. We just want a divorce."

—Renata A.
age 36, seeking a divorce, no children
pharmaceutical sales representative
West Monroe, Louisiana

In Louisiana one can get divorced seeking a no-fault basis or a fault basis.

Jurisdictions that currently permit *solely* no-fault divorces include Arizona, California, Colorado, Delaware, Florida, Hawaii, Iowa, Kentucky, Michigan, Minnesota, Missouri, Montana, Nebraska, Oregon, Washington, Wisconsin, and Wyoming, and Washington, DC.

States that currently permit divorces based on no-fault and fault grounds include Alabama, Alaska, Arkansas, Connecticut, Georgia, Idaho, Illinois, Indiana, Kansas, *Louisiana*, Maine, Maryland, Massachusetts, Mississippi, New Hampshire, Nevada, New Jersey, New Mexico, New York, North Carolina, North Dakota, Ohio, Oklahoma, Pennsylvania, Rhode Island, South Carolina, South Dakota, Tennessee, Texas, Utah, Vermont, and West Virginia.

In Virginia, all divorces require proof of grounds.

Regardless of the state in which the divorce proceeding is being conducted, or the grounds used for the divorce, you must also address applicable issues of child custody, child support, spousal support, property division, and related matters.

Louisiana's primary divorce grounds are quite similar to other states:

C.C. Art. 102. Judgment of divorce; living apart one hundred eighty days prior to rule

Except in the case of a covenant marriage, a divorce shall be granted upon motion of a spouse when either spouse has filed a petition for divorce and upon proof that one hundred eighty days have elapsed from the service of the petition, or from the execution of written waiver of the service, and that the spouses have lived separate and apart continuously for at least one hundred eighty days prior to the filing of the rule to show cause.

The motion shall be a rule to show cause filed after all such delays have elapsed.

C.C. Art. 103. Judgment of divorce; other grounds
Except in the case of a covenant marriage, a divorce shall be granted on the petition of a spouse upon proof that:
(1) The spouses have been living separate and apart continuously for a period of six months or more on the date the petition is filed;
(2) The other spouse has committed adultery; or
(3) The other spouse has committed a felony and has been sentenced to death or imprisonment at hard labor.

## Fault Louisiana Divorce

Most no-fault states also provide grounds for divorce found in states that require a statement of fault.

In a divorce proceeding, a state may require you to cite reasons, in your divorce pleading, stating why you want the divorce. These states are called "fault-divorce states." In fault-divorce states, the party seeking the divorce makes allegations that the other spouse is to blame for some conduct or omission that renders a valid reason for the state to grant a divorce. The actual grounds for a "fault-related divorce" vary from state to state. In the states that permit a divorce by claiming some sort of fault, grounds for fault vary to include abandonment, adultery, attempted murder of a spouse, bigamy, conviction of a felony with imprisonment, cruel treatment (mental or physical), desertion, habitual drunkenness or intemperance, habitual use of narcotic drugs, impotency or sterility not known at the time of marriage, infection of spouse with a venereal disease, or insanity.

Louisiana has limited the grounds that a spouse may use in an attempt to claim fault as the reason for the breakup of the marriage.

### Louisiana's Fault Grounds for Divorce

1. Adultery
2. Commitment of a felony and has been sentenced to death or imprisonment at hard labor

## 6. Adultery

"My husband cheated on me years ago and I forgave him because we had small children. Now, he seems to be doing it again. Now that the children are grown, I am not going to forgive him this time. I want to divorce him based on his adultery. What evidence of adultery do I need?"

—Jennifer F.
age 55, married, adult children, teacher
Houma, Louisiana

Although adultery may appear to be a common ground used in getting a fault divorce, only 3 percent of divorces in the United States are granted on the grounds of adultery.

A common defense for the allegation of adultery is that the spouses reconciled with the intent to resume their marriage after the faithful spouse became aware of the adulterous acts of the "fallen" spouse. In many states, including Louisiana, if the parties reconcile, then the act or acts of adultery cannot be used as the fault ground for the divorce. States vary on their positions of whether a single act of intercourse after knowledge of the other party's adulterous act constitutes reconciliation. In Louisiana, courts look at the specific factual circumstances in determining whether reconciliation has occurred; unfortunately, in Louisiana there is no consistent standard used in determining whether there has been reconciliation. A new act of adultery would have to occur in order to create a new cause of action for adultery. If adultery is a potential issue in your case, talk to your attorney to understand how reconciliation may affect your litigation.

Adultery can be proven by direct evidence, such as eyewitness testimony of a reliable witness (i.e., an investigator) as well as by a videotape or photograph. Adultery is most often proven by inferential circumstantial (nondirect) evidence. In order to prove adultery by circumstantial evidence, motive and opportunity to commit adultery are crucial.

Circumstantial evidence can be found in all shapes and forms. Look at the following examples that have been used in Louisiana divorce courts:

- Paramour's telephone number on matches
- Calendar with incriminating writings

- Cellular-telephone bills
- Long-distance telephone bills
- Discarded condom wrappers
- Discarded hosiery
- Credit-card receipts and billings
- Hotel or restaurant receipts
- Lingerie that is not yours
- Personal address book
- Perfume or lipstick on shirt, other garments, or sheets (Do not wash or launder.)
- Photographs
- Sworn testimony of eye/earwitnesses
- Sworn testimony of guilty spouse
- Sworn testimony of paramour
- Telephone calls on answering machine (Save.)
- Written confessions by spouse

Most divorce cases do not require the use of a private investigator. Before you spend money for surveillance on your spouse, talk to your lawyer about the need for this expense. Furthermore, your spouse may suspect surveillance and dodge your efforts to catch him or her in the act.

### Be Aware of the Omnibus Crime Control and Safe Street Act of 1968

"I think that Ray is cheating on me. We don't make love like we used to and sometimes I walk into the room and he is talking on the phone then he abruptly hangs up. I just know that he is seeing another woman. Can I tape record all of the phone calls at my house?"

—Mary R.
age 56, considering a divorce, two adult children, housewife
Baton Rouge, Louisiana

The Omnibus Crime Control and Safe Street Act of 1968 makes it a federal crime to do any of the following acts:

Illegal Acts Regarding Listening to or Recording Telephone Calls

1. To listen in on a telephone conversation if one is not a party to the call and does not have permission to listen by at least one party to the call

2. To record a telephone call if one is not a party to the call and/or does not have permission from the party to record the call

We all have heard of people, before or during a divorce, who have recorded their spouse's telephone conversation with a lover. Because it is done all the time does not make it legal. If you currently have unauthorized recordings of telephone calls of your spouse with his or her lover, or if you feel the need to record your spouse's telephone conversations, relax, but immediately consult your Louisiana lawyer.

## 7. Special Laws Regarding Separation and Divorce of Covenant Marriages

R.S. 9:307 Divorce or separation from bed and board in a covenant marriage; exclusive grounds

A. Notwithstanding any other law to the contrary and subsequent to the parties obtaining counseling, a spouse to a covenant marriage may obtain a judgment of divorce only upon proof of any of the following:

(1) The other spouse has committed adultery.

(2) The other spouse has committed a felony and has been sentenced to death or imprisonment at hard labor.

(3) The other spouse has abandoned the matrimonial domicile for a period of one year and constantly refuses to return.

(4) The other spouse has physically or sexually abused the spouse seeking the divorce or a child of one of the spouses.

(5) The spouses have been living separate and apart continuously without reconciliation for a period of two years.

(6)(a) The spouses have been living separate and apart continuously without reconciliation for a period of one year from the date the judgment of separation from bed and board was signed.

(b) If there is a minor child or children of the marriage, the spouses have been living separate and apart continuously without reconciliation for a period of one year and six months from the date the judgment of separation from bed and board was signed; however, if abuse of a child of the marriage or a child of one of the spouses is the basis for which the judgment of separation from bed and board was obtained, then a judgment of divorce may be obtained if the spouses have been living separate and apart continuously without reconciliation for a period of one year from the date the judgment of separation from bed and board was signed.

B. Notwithstanding any other law to the contrary and subsequent to the parties obtaining counseling, a spouse to a covenant marriage may obtain a judgment of separation from bed and board only upon proof of any of the following:

(1) The other spouse has committed adultery.

(2) The other spouse has committed a felony and has been sentenced to death or imprisonment at hard labor.

(3) The other spouse has abandoned the matrimonial domicile for a period of one year and constantly refuses to return.

(4) The other spouse has physically or sexually abused the spouse seeking the divorce or a child of one of the spouses.

(5) The spouses have been living separate and apart continuously without reconciliation for a period of two years.

(6) On account of habitual intemperance of the other spouse, or excesses, cruel treatment, or outrages of the other spouse, if such habitual intemperance, or such ill-treatment is of such a nature as to render their living together insupportable.

R.S. 9:308 Separation from bed and board in covenant marriage; suit against spouse; jurisdiction, procedure, and incidental relief

A. Unless judicially separated, spouses in a covenant marriage may not sue each other except for causes of action pertaining to contracts or arising out of the provisions of Book III, Title VI of the Civil Code; for restitution of separate property; for separation from bed and board in covenant marriages, for divorce, or for declaration of nullity of the marriage; and for causes of action pertaining to spousal support or the support or custody of a child while the spouses are living separate and apart, although not judicially separated.

B. (1) Any court which is competent to preside over divorce proceedings, including the family court for the parish of East Baton Rouge, has jurisdiction of an action for separation from bed and board in a covenant marriage, if:

(a) One or both of the spouses are domiciled in this state and the ground therefor was committed or occurred in this state or while the matrimonial domicile was in this state.

(b) The ground therefor occurred elsewhere while either or both of the spouses were domiciled elsewhere, provided the person obtaining the separation from bed and board was domiciled in this state prior to the time the cause of action accrued and is domiciled in this state at the time the action is filed.

(2) An action for a separation from bed and board in a covenant marriage shall be brought in a parish where either party is domiciled, or in the parish of the last matrimonial domicile.

(3) The venue provided herein may not be waived, and a judgment of separation rendered by a court of improper venue is an absolute nullity.

C. Judgments on the pleadings and summary judgments shall not be granted in any action for separation from bed and board in a covenant marriage.

D. In a proceeding for a separation from bed and board in a covenant marriage or thereafter, a court may award a spouse all incidental relief afforded in a proceeding for divorce, including but not limited to spousal support, claims for contributions to education, child custody, visitation rights, child support, injunctive relief and possession and use of a family residence or community movables or immovables.

R.S. 9:309 Separation from bed and board in a covenant marriage; effects

A. (1) Separation from bed and board in a covenant marriage does not dissolve the bond of matrimony, since the separated husband and wife are not at liberty to marry again; but it puts an end to their conjugal cohabitation, and to the common concerns, which existed between them.

(2) Spouses who are judicially separated from bed and board in a covenant marriage shall retain that status until either reconciliation or divorce.

B. (1) The judgment of separation from bed and board carries with it the separation of goods and effects and is retroactive to the date on which the original petition was filed in the action in which the judgment is rendered, but such retroactive effect shall be without prejudice to the liability of the community for the attorney fees and costs incurred by the spouses in the action in which the judgment is rendered, or to rights validly acquired in the interim between commencement of the action and recordation of the judgment.

(2) Upon reconciliation of the spouses, the community shall be reestablished between the spouses, as of the date of filing of the original petition in the action in which the judgment was rendered, unless the spouses execute prior to the reconciliation a matrimonial agreement that the community shall not be reestablished upon reconciliation. This matrimonial agreement shall not require court approval.

(3) Reestablishment of the community under the provisions of this Section shall be effective toward third persons only upon filing notice of the reestablishment for registry in accordance with the provisions of *Civil Code Article 2332* (emphasis added). The reestablishment of the community shall not prejudice the rights of third persons validly acquired prior to filing notice of the reestablishment nor shall it affect a prior community property partition between the spouses.

## 8. No Residency Requirement in Louisiana

"I just moved here from Mississippi. Can I file for divorce in Louisiana?"

—Ernie C.
age 28, married, one child, unemployed
Monroe, Louisiana

Most states require one or both spouses to reside or be domiciled in the state for a certain length of time in order to be divorced. Some states, such as Louisiana, do not have such a residency requirement. To be "domiciled" in a state simply means that the state is considered your primary residence. Once you have established a permanent residence in Louisiana, there are no further residency requirements; however, you may have to prove in court that you have established a permanent residence in Louisiana.

The residency requirements of Louisiana and other states and provinces are provided in the appendix. Keep in mind that the state legislatures can change the length of time required to be considered a resident for divorce purposes. In fact, the requirement often does change. Check with your lawyer to see if the requirements have remained the same.

### Proving Your Residency in Louisiana

You can help your lawyer prove your Louisiana residency by showing your permanent or substantial connection to the state.

Ways You Can Assist Your Lawyer
in Proving That You Are a Louisiana Resident:

1. Get a Louisiana driver's license;
2. Send a change-of-address form to the U.S. Post Office in your former state indicating your new residential address;
3. Register to vote in Louisiana;
4. Purchase a house or rent an apartment in Louisiana; and/or
5. Any other act that establishes your intent and desire to remain in the state of Louisiana.

## 9. Incidental Matters

C.C. Art. 105 Determination of incidental matters

In a proceeding for divorce or thereafter, either spouse may request a determination of custody, visitation, or support of a minor child; support for a spouse; injunctive relief; use and occupancy of the family home or use of community movables or immovables; or use of personal property.

## 10. Have You Been Served with Louisiana Divorce or Other Court Papers?

"This morning a sheriff's deputy came to my house and handed me some court papers. It looks like my wife has filed for divorce. What do I do now?"

—Tony L.
age 34, served with a divorce petition
no children, engineer
Lake Charles, Louisiana

### Very Important Tips
If You Have Just Been Served with Divorce Papers
of Other Court Documents
1. Immediately contact an experienced family-law attorney who is licensed to practice law in Louisiana.

2. Select a competent Louisiana divorce lawyer using the recommendations found in this guide.

3. Do not sign anything without consulting with your divorce attorney.

4. Take a breath and try to relax. Do not do anything hasty or rash that may be detrimental to you in the future.

If you have been served with a divorce petition or other court documents, you have an affirmative responsibility to respond, or you may have a judgment placed against you without further notice. A "judgment by default" can be levied against you if you fail to answer within the time limits allowed by Louisiana law (Arts. 1701-2).

### C.C.P. Art. 1701 Judgment by default

A. If a defendant in the principal or incidental demand fails to answer within the time prescribed by law, judgment by default may be entered against him. The judgment may be obtained by oral motion in open court or by written motion mailed to the court, either of which shall be entered in the minutes of the court, but the judgment shall consist merely of an entry in the minutes.

B. When a defendant in an action for divorce under *Civil Code Article 103(1)* (emphasis added), by sworn affidavit, acknowledges receipt of a certified copy of the petition and waives formal citation, service of process, all legal delays, notice of trial, and appearance at trial, a judgment of default may be entered against the defendant the day on which the affidavit is filed. The affidavit of the defendant may be prepared or notarized by any notary public. The judgment may be obtained by oral motion in open court or by written motion mailed to the court, either of which shall be entered in the minutes of the court, but the judgment shall consist merely of an entry in the minutes. Notice of the signing of the final judgment as provided in Article 1913 is not required.

### C.P. Art. 1702 Confirmation of default judgment

A. A judgment of default must be confirmed by proof of the demand sufficient to establish a prima facie case. If no answer is filed timely, this confirmation may be made after two days, exclusive of holidays, from the entry of the judgment of default. When a judgment of default has been entered against a party that is in default after having made an appearance of record in the case, notice of the date of the entry of the judgment of default must be sent by certified mail by the party obtaining the judgment of default to counsel of record for the party in default, or if there is no counsel of record, to the party in default, at least seven days, exclusive of holidays, before confirmation of the judgment of default.

B. (1) When a demand is based upon a conventional obligation, affidavits and exhibits annexed thereto which contain facts sufficient to establish a prima facie case shall be admissible, self-authenticating, and sufficient proof of such demand. The court may, under the circumstances of the case, require additional evidence in the form of oral testimony before entering judgment.

(2) When a demand is based upon a delictual obligation, the testimony of the plaintiff with corroborating evidence, which may be by affidavits and exhibits annexed thereto which contain facts sufficient to establish a prima facie case, shall be admissible, self-authenticating, and sufficient proof of such demand. The court may, under the circumstances of the case, require additional evidence in the form of oral testimony before entering judgment.

(3) When the sum due is on an open account or a promissory note or other negotiable instrument, an affidavit of the correctness thereof shall be prima facie proof. When the demand is based upon a promissory note or other negotiable instrument, no proof of any signature thereon shall be required.

C. In those proceedings in which the sum due is on an open account or a promissory note, other negotiable instrument, or other conventional obligation, or a deficiency judgment derived therefrom, including those proceedings in which one or more mortgages, pledges, or other security for said open account, promissory note, negotiable instrument, conventional obligation, or deficiency judgment derived therefrom is sought to be enforced, maintained, or recognized, or in which the amount sought is that authorized by *R.S. 9:2782* (emphasis added) for a check dishonored for nonsufficient funds, a hearing in open court shall not be required unless the judge, in his discretion, directs that such a hearing be held. The plaintiff shall submit to the court the proof required by law and the original and not less than one copy of the proposed final judgment. The judge shall, within seventy-two hours of receipt of such submission from the clerk of court, sign the judgment or direct that a hearing be held. The clerk of court shall certify that no answer or other pleading has been filed by the defendant. The minute clerk shall make an entry showing the dates of receipt of proof, review of the record, and rendition of the judgment. A certified copy of the signed judgment shall be sent to the plaintiff by the clerk of court.

D. When the demand is based upon a claim for a personal injury, a sworn narrative report of the treating physician or dentist may be offered in lieu of his testimony.

E. Notwithstanding any other provisions of law to the contrary, when the demand is for divorce under *Civil Code Article 103(1)* (emphasis added), whether or not the demand contains a claim for relief incidental or ancillary thereto, a hearing in open court shall not be required unless the judge, in his discretion, directs that a hearing be held. The plaintiff shall submit to the court an affidavit specifically attesting to and testifying as to the truth of all of the factual allegations contained in the petition, and shall submit the original and not less than one copy of the proposed final judgment. If no answer or other pleading has been filed by the defendant, the judge shall, after two days, exclusive of holidays, of entry of a preliminary default, render and sign the judgment or direct that a hearing be held. The minutes shall reflect rendition and signing of the judgment.

R.S. 13:3491 Divorce under Civil Code Article 102; notice of suit

A. A notice in a divorce action under *Civil Code Article 102* (emphasis added) must be signed by the clerk of the court or his deputy issuing it with an expression of his official capacity and under the seal of his office; must be accompanied by a certified copy of the petition, exclusive of exhibits, even if made a part thereof; and must contain all of the following:

(1) The date of issuance.
(2) The title of the cause.
(3) The name of the person to whom it is addressed.
(4) The title and location of the court issuing it.
(5) Statements to the following effect:

(a) The person served is being sued for divorce by his spouse under *Civil Code Article 102* (emphasis added), and that one hundred eighty days after the service occurs or after the parties commenced living separate and apart, whichever is later, the suing spouse is entitled to file a motion for final divorce.

(b) The suing spouse will no longer be able to move for a final divorce after two years have elapsed from the date of the service.

(c) The person served is entitled to file his or her own motion for a final divorce against the suing spouse.

(d) The person served is entitled to file motions for incidental relief in the divorce proceeding, including motions for spousal support, child custody, and child support.

B. The statements required to appear in the notice shall provide substantially as follows:

### ATTENTION

YOU ARE BEING SUED FOR DIVORCE BY YOUR SPOUSE. ONE HUNDRED EIGHTY DAYS AFTER YOU RECEIVE THIS NOTICE OR ONE HUNDRED EIGHTY DAYS AFTER YOU AND YOUR SPOUSE PHYSICALLY SEPARATED, WHICHEVER OCCURRED LAST, YOUR SPOUSE MAY FILE FOR AND OBTAIN A FINAL DIVORCE.

IF YOUR SPOUSE FAILS TO FILE FOR A FINAL DIVORCE IN TWO YEARS, HE MAY NOT DO SO WITHOUT FILING NEW PAPERS AND WAITING ANOTHER ONE HUNDRED EIGHTY DAYS.

IF YOU ARE UNSURE OF WHAT TO DO AS A RESULT OF THIS NOTICE, YOU SHOULD TALK IMMEDIATELY WITH AN ATTORNEY ABOUT IT.

R.S. 13:3492 Divorce under Civil Code Article 102; notice of rule to show cause

A. A notice of a rule to show cause under *Civil Code Article 102* (emphasis added), must be signed by the clerk of the court or his deputy issuing it with an expression of his official capacity and under the seal of his office; must be accompanied by a certified copy of the motion, order and rule to show cause; and must contain all of the following:

(1) The date of issuance.
(2) The title of the cause.
(3) The name of the person to whom it is addressed.
(4) The title and location of the court issuing it.
(5) The return date, time, and place.
(6) Statements to the following effect:

(a) The person served is being directed to appear and show cause why a divorce should not be granted to his spouse.

(b) The necessity for the lapse of one hundred eighty days from service of the petition of divorce upon the person or from the date the parties commenced living separate and apart, whichever is later.

(c) The person served is entitled to appear and oppose the divorce action and to file motions for incidental relief in the divorce proceeding, including motions for spousal support, child custody, and child support.

B. The statements required to appear in the notice shall provide substantially as follows:

ATTENTION YOU ARE BEING SUED FOR FINAL DIVORCE. A JUDGMENT OF DIVORCE MAY BE RENDERED AGAINST YOU ON THE DATE SPECIFIED IN THE ATTACHED RULE TO SHOW CAUSE UNLESS YOU APPEAR AND OPPOSE THE RULE.

ONE HUNDRED EIGHTY DAYS MUST HAVE PASSED SINCE YOU OR YOUR SPOUSE RECEIVED THE FIRST NOTICE OF THE DIVORCE ACTION OR ONE HUNDRED EIGHTY DAYS AFTER YOU AND YOUR SPOUSE PHYSICALLY SEPARATED, WHICHEVER OCCURRED LAST.

YOU MAY SEEK CUSTODY OF CHILDREN, AND MONEY FOR THEIR SUPPORT AND YOUR SUPPORT, AS WELL AS OTHER RELIEF TO PROTECT YOU.

IF YOU ARE UNSURE WHAT TO DO, YOU SHOULD IMMEDI-ATELY TALK WITH AN ATTORNEY ABOUT IT.

## 11. A Legal Separation?

"Years ago, I got a divorce from my first wife and we had to go through a legal separation. Do I have to go through a separation to get a divorce under today's law?"

—Kyle S.
age 50, considering a second divorce
one adult child, stockbroker
New Iberia, Louisiana

Legal separation no longer exists in Louisiana unless you entered into a covenant marriage or adopted the marriage provisions under covenant-marriage law.

A legal separation is a court's decree and recognition that married persons are living separately while remaining married. This provides an increased opportunity for reconciliation. A legal separation and a divorce are different. If you are legally separated, you are still married, as you have not dissolved the marriage. If you are merely legally separated, you cannot remarry. If you are divorced, you can. Talk to your lawyer and see whether any of the provisions of a covenant marriage apply to you.

A legal separation may provide a period of time for you to evaluate your marriage. A legal separation also permits you to clear up any unresolved emotional conflicts.

During a legal separation under a covenant-marriage arrangement, you may be entitled to temporary spousal support, previously called "alimony pendente lite." You also may be entitled to child support and other relief.

## 12. Can You Get an Annulment in Louisiana?

> "We got married over a few months ago, but it's not working out. Can I get out of the marriage with an annulment?"
> —Janet H.
> age 23, considering an annulment
> no children, student
> Ruston, Louisiana

A marriage can only be dissolved through a divorce decree or an annulment.

A legal annulment is a court's official decree that the marriage was not valid, thus somewhat eliminating the alleged trauma or stigma of divorce. Grounds for an annulment include circumstances in which the marriage occurred due to fraud or duress or in instances of bigamy, marriage of a person under the age of consent, or marrying a close relative.

C.C. Art. 94. Absolutely null marriage

A marriage is absolutely null when contracted without a marriage ceremony, by procuration, or in violation of an impediment. A judicial declaration of nullity is not required, but an action to recognize the nullity may be brought by any interested person.

C.C. Art. 95. Relatively null marriage; confirmation
A marriage is relatively null when the consent of one of the parties to marry is not freely given. Such a marriage may be declared null upon application of the party whose consent was not free. The marriage may not be declared null if that party confirmed the marriage after recovering his liberty or regaining his discernment.

C.C. Art. 96. Civil effects of absolutely null marriage; putative marriage

An absolutely null marriage nevertheless produces civil effects in favor of a party who contracted it in good faith for as long as that party remains in good faith.

When the cause of the nullity is one party's prior undissolved marriage, the civil effects continue in favor of the other party, regardless of whether the latter remains in good faith, until the marriage is pronounced null or the latter party contracts a valid marriage.

A marriage contracted by a party in good faith produces civil effects in favor of a child of the parties.

A purported marriage between parties of the same sex does not produce any civil effects.

C.C. Art. 97. Civil effects of relatively null marriage
A relatively null marriage produces civil effects until it is declared null.

Annulments are not common because the Louisiana legislature has narrowly defined circumstances in which a legal annulment would be appropriate. Consult your attorney to see if this would be a viable or desired option for you.

Legal annulments and religious annulments are different. Consult your religious leader to determine the requirements for a religious annulment.

## 13. The Effect of Reconciliation on Your Divorce Proceeding
CC. Art. 104 Reconciliation
The cause of action for divorce is extinguished by the reconciliation of the parties.

## 14. Two-Year Abandonment of Divorce Action

C.C.P. Art. 3954 Abandonment of action

A. A divorce action instituted under *Civil Code Article 102* (emphasis added) is abandoned if the rule to show cause provided by that Article is not filed within two years of the service of the original petition or execution of written waiver of service of the original petition.

B. This provision shall be operative without formal order, but on ex parte motion of any party or other interested person, the trial court shall enter a formal order of dismissal as of the date of abandonment.

## 15. If Desired, Don't Forget to Ask for Your Name Change

"I never liked my husband's last name. Can I change it back to my maiden name?"

—Kathleen G.
age 41, divorcing, four children, social worker
Jennings, Louisiana

C.C. Art. 100. Surname of married persons
Marriage does not change the name of either spouse. However, a married person may use the surname of either or both spouses as a surname.

Once you are divorced, you may change your name and/or remarry. If you wish to return to the use of your maiden name, ask your lawyer to seek it at the time of your divorce. You can ask the court to change your name back to your maiden name, another unmarried name, or any other new name that you choose.

Your spouse cannot force you to change your married name.

You should notify all pertinent persons and companies of your name change and/or change in address and telephone number. Remember to contact all important people and places about your name change.

If Name or Address Changes, Contact
- Accountant
- Alumni associations
- Banks
- Charitable organizations
- Church
- Clubs/civic or social organizations
- Credit bureaus

- Credit-card companies
- Doctors
- Driver's license bureau
- Employer
- Financial institutions
- Frequent-flier programs
- Friends
- Health club
- Insurance agent
- Internal Revenue Service
- Landlord
- Lawyers
- Medical facilities
- Mortgage company
- Neighbors
- Post office
- Professional associations
- Registrar of voters
- Schools
- Social Security Administration
- State of Louisiana Department of Revenue
- Telephone company
- United States State Department (for name change on passport)
- Utility company

## 16. Once Divorced, Make a New Will

Once you are divorced, you should consider making a new will that accounts for your current desires as to the disposition of property at your death. Do not rely on Louisiana law to automatically disinherit your former spouse, as Louisiana laws do change over time.

# Chapter 3

# SELECT AN EXPERIENCED LOUISIANA DIVORCE LAWYER

"I see all of these lawyers' ads in the yellow pages and I've heard of several attorneys with bold nicknames like "Bulldog" and "the Witch" but who is really good? My friend suggested a lawyer that she used in her first divorce. How can I find a competent divorce lawyer that understands my needs?"

—Kelly J.
age 29, divorcing, one child, musician
Hammond, Louisiana

Choosing the right lawyer is one of the most important factors in getting successful results in your case. Most people merely use the telephone book or ask a friend for a recommendation. Their search for and investigation into choosing a lawyer ends there. If you are lucky, your spouse will use this haphazard approach.

If you have a simple uncontested divorce, then most divorce lawyers can handle your case. Simply shop for the best price from a competent lawyer licensed to practice in Louisiana.

## 1. Inquire before You Hire—Ways to Find a Good Divorce Lawyer

- Ask friends and family. (*Warning:* Do not base your decision solely on their advice. They may not have done their home work in selecting the best attorney in the area. However, word-of-mouth reputation is usually one of the best indicators of the quality of an attorney. Also, remember that no two divorce cases are identical and the results that a lawyer got for your rel ative may not be the same results that the lawyer could get for you.) Be leery of using a friend attorney for free services, as you will put a strain on the friendship.
- Ask other lawyers. If you know any lawyers, ask them whom

they would recommend and why. Remember that a personal-injury attorney may not be the best individual to represent you in a divorce proceeding.

- Ask your accountant and/or financial advisor.
- Ask your therapist and members of support groups.
- Contact the clerks in charge of the domestic dockets at your parish courthouse and ask for three recommendations. These individuals see the divorce lawyers in court on a regular basis, and if you get the right person on the telephone, he or she can tell you the good, the bad, and the ugly about the superior divorce lawyers.
- Ask mediators who practice family-law mediation.
- Ask marriage counselors who advise divorcing couples.
- Ask personnel at local battered-women's shelters (if abuse is an issue in your relationship).
- Contact the Louisiana State Bar Association at the following address:

Louisiana State Bar Association's
Directory of Family-Law Specialists
Louisiana State Bar Association
601 St. Charles Avenue
New Orleans, LA 70130
Toll-free (800) 421-LSBA (5722)
(504) 566-1600
www.LSBA.org
Statewide Lawyer Referral
and Information Service
(888) 503-5747
Local Louisiana Bar Services
Baton Rouge    (225) 344-9926
Lafayette    (337) 237-4700
Lake Charles    (337) 436-2914
New Orleans    (504) 561-8828
Shreveport    (318) 222-0720

If you wish to contact the author,
write him at the following address
and your message will be forwarded to him:
Pelican Publishing Company, Inc.
1000 Burmaster Street/P.O. Box 3110
Gretna, LA 70053

## 2. The Louisiana State Bar Association's "Helpful Hints for Working with a Lawyer"

- Ask about cost. If your problem requires more work than the initial half-hour consultation, remember to ask for the lawyer's fees in writing.
- Remember your rights. You do not have to hire the lawyer after the initial consultation; feel free to find a lawyer with whom you are comfortable. You have hired a lawyer when you agree to allow them to do more legal work for you.
- Be prepared. Bring any papers you think you may need to the first half-hour consultation. Be prepared to give the lawyer all background information. You may also want to prepare a list of questions to ask the lawyer.
- Be efficient. If you do hire an attorney, don't make unnecessary phone calls. Most lawyers charge for the time spent on the phone with a client. Keep a running list of questions; cover them in one phone call or ask them at your next scheduled appointment.
- Keep records. File any material you receive from your lawyer in one place. Your file is often the best way to answer your questions about your case.
- If you have any questions concerning any of these services, please contact the LSBA Statewide Lawyer Referral and Information Service for more information.
(Source: www.LSBA.org)

Your chosen attorney should be a professional and competent advocate.

After you have done your research by speaking with your personal and professional contacts, you should interview several potential divorce lawyers. But first, be aware that some people who are planning to go through a divorce try to eliminate their spouse's choice of an attorney.

## 3. Be Aware That Some Spouses Attempt to Neutralize Their Best Opposition by Consulting Several Divorce Lawyers

> "I am afraid that my husband is going to hire the very best lawyer in town. I would attempt to hire that lawyer myself, but I'm not sure who he will get. I think that he has two or three attorneys in mind that are well-known here in Minden."
>
> —Helen G.
> age 40, divorcing, one child, antique dealer
> Minden, Louisiana

If you anticipate a major domestic battle and you live in a community that has a limited amount of good domestic attorneys, some attorneys have recommended that you prevent your spouse from hiring a select group of these attorneys. These attorneys suggest that you find out who the very best attorneys are, not those necessarily in your spouse's anticipated price range, and set up appointments with all of them. The lawyers may charge a consultation fee. This gives you an opportunity to compare the lawyers before you make your choice. And here's the kicker . . . some case law suggests that your spouse cannot hire any attorney whom you have consulted because you previously have a professional relationship with that lawyer. This is especially effective in a small community with a mere handful of good domestic attorneys. Many lawyers suggest being certain that you pay for the consultation, but don't pay cash; use a check so you can later prove that you consulted with that lawyer on a certain date. If the lawyer originally refuses to take a consultation fee, drop a check written in his or her name or in the law firm's name for a nominal amount (i.e., $25). The chances are high that the check will be deposited in the lawyer's bank account, and your canceled check will be evidence preventing your spouse from using that attorney or anyone in that attorney's law firm.

Don't worry about what you disclose to the lawyer during the consultation. What you say is confidential, and the lawyer cannot tell the information to anyone, even if you do not hire him or her.

Louisiana law is trying to deal with this maneuver. Recent rulings do not absolutely exclude your spouse from hiring an attorney with whom you merely had a consultation.

## 4. Interview Several Attorneys

"I have used a divorce attorney for my first divorce, and I was very unhappy with the results. My wife took me to the cleaners. When I first met the lawyer, I had some doubts about his abilities, but I thought he would do a satisfactory job. I mistakenly thought that all divorce lawyers were alike. I don't plan on making that mistake again."

—Jay D.
age 37, divorcing, three children, insurance agent
New Roads, Louisiana

Most prospective clients merely go into the lawyer's office and let the lawyer take complete control over the discussion. In essence, the lawyer interviews you as if he were already your selected attorney. Turn the meeting around. First, listen to what the lawyer has to say, without prompting. This will give you a general idea of his competency level. Then take control by asking your potential lawyer the following questions (remember, you are the client and customer):

### Interview the Divorce Lawyer

1. Ask how long he has been a lawyer.
2. Ask how long he has practiced divorce law. Lawyers who do not normally handle divorce cases are more likely to make mistakes. They are also more likely to procrastinate on your case, because the work is unfamiliar to them.
3. Ask the lawyer how often he goes to trial in contested cases.
4. Ask how much of the lawyer's practice is devoted to domestic law. If the lawyer says that he devotes less than half of his time to divorce cases, then thank the attorney for his time and leave.
5. Ask the lawyer to rate himself as to his ability as a litigate on a scale from one to ten (ten being best). If the lawyer scores himself less than an eight, the honest lawyer probably does not have the confidence or competence necessary to be the type of litigator that you need. After all, if he does not haveconfidence in his own ability, how can he possibly have greater confidence in his ability to win for you? A confident attorney not only knows the law, but also challenges any attack on his client's position. The judge will sense the level of confidence and competency. In a tight decision, the extra aura of righteousness very well may be the intangible factor that allows you to have custody or a child-support award in your favor.
6. Ask the lawyer whether he will personally handle the case or will an associate be assigned the case. Make sure that you are speaking to the lawyer that you want to handle your case. It's a waste of time to interview an attorney who will not actuallybe representing you. If you are in a true battle over custody, property rights, or other vital issues, don't ever settle for second best. It's usually worth the extra money to hire the lead attorney.
7. Ask for the attorney's home, car, and/or beeper telephone numbers. Be able to contact him when you need him. Many lawyers are extremely hesitant to give their private telephone numbers; however, you should insist on a means to contact the attorney on an emergency basis. Clients often need to immediately contact their attorneys when visitation disputes arise, when one spouse refuses to return the children, etc.

8. Ask to review the retainer agreement. Don't be afraid to ask to take the retainer agreement home and study it prior to signing it.

9. Ask the attorney how he charges for his legal services and expenses. If he charges by the hour, ask at what intervals of an hour does he charge. For example, some lawyers bill for legal services on a quarter-hour basis (.25 of an hour), while others may charge by a tenth of an hour (.10 of an hour). Also, ask if he charges for any questions that you may have regarding your bill.

10. Ask the lawyer what he charges for a photocopy, a facsimile, travel, etc.

11. Ask the lawyer what other charges he expects to be incurred during the litigation, such as fees for investigators, mediators, experts, evaluators, etc. (By your numerous inquiries of your prospective attorney, you should get a good idea of the range of hourly rates that lawyers charge for services in your community.)

12. Ask how many months the lawyer would estimate the case will last.

13. Ask the attorney to give you references of at least three recent clients who are happy with his services. He should be able to contact these clients and ask them if it is all right to disclose their identity and give the prospective client their telephone numbers. You should contact the former clients and get the scoop on the attorney.

14. Ask your prospective lawyer if he will send you copies of each letter and pleading that he sends out on your behalf. It is important that you stay informed.

15. Ask the lawyer if any of the legal fees are nonrefundable.

16. Ask the lawyer if he knows all of the federal- and state-tax implications that may result from your case.

17. Ask the lawyer for the names of other good domestic lawyers whom he would recommend. This gives you a good idea of who the other good lawyers are in your area.

18. Ask the lawyer if he has payment plans and what are the methods of payment. Can you use credit cards?

19. Ask the lawyer if he or she charges interest on unpaid balances.

### After the Interview

1. Ask yourself if you can get along with your attorney. Is the attorney someone in which you can have faith? Are your personalities compatible? Trust your instincts; they are rarely wrong.

2. Ask yourself if the lawyer appears to be genuinely sensitive to your needs.

3. Did the lawyer promptly see you at the time of your scheduled appointment?
4. Ask yourself whether the lawyer gave you his or her undivided attention.
5. Be totally honest with your attorney. He cannot help you to his fullest abilities if you do not disclose the skeletons in your closet. Whatever you tell him is confidential, so go for it and tell all!
6. Provide your chosen lawyer with a copy of the completed questionnaire found in appendix A.

## 5. Keep a Record of Your Calls to Your Attorney

"I like to keep track of my time and money. I called my attorney on many occasions and seldom got a returned phone call. When I got my monthly statement for the lawyer, I was astonished to see charges for my telephone calls that went unanswered. I also received expensive charges for telephone calls that only lasted a few minutes. I am deeply offended by these business practices. If I do not get proper resolution of these billing issues, then I shall change attorneys."

—Harry L.
age 52, divorcing, one adult child
roofing-company manager
Harvey, Louisiana

Keep a telephone log of when you call your attorney and when he returns your telephone calls. In doing this, you will also be creating a document that can be used to confirm the telephone conferences charged on your billing statement.

## 6. Make Your Lawyer Promptly Return Telephone Calls

One of the greatest complaints about lawyers is that they fail to promptly return client telephone calls. Ask the attorney how promptly he returns client telephone calls. If your lawyer does not promptly return your telephone calls, send him a certified letter indicating so. Note the times and dates of each call. Also, the letter should include all inquiries that need to be addressed or facts that you need to relate to your attorney. You can expedite the process by faxing your letter to your attorney. Tell your prospective attorney that you intend to send him these letters should he not promptly return your telephone calls. Remember, the squeaky wheel gets the grease!

Good divorce attorneys are busy. Keep in mind that they are often in court, at depositions, or in conferences with other clients, and may not be available to immediately receive or return your telephone call. Indicate to the attorney that you expect to be able to talk to his secretary, paralegal, or another lawyer on your case in order to convey any message that is vital to you. A lawyer should return telephone calls within twenty-four hours. Have the lawyer pledge to you that he will return your calls within the twenty-four-hour period.

### 7. Collect Your Thoughts before You Call Your Attorney

If your attorney charges you for every telephone call that you make to him, write down and collect all of the topics that you want to discuss, then make one call.

If a lawyer charges $175 per hour and charges on each quarter of an hour (fifteen-minute intervals), a twelve-minute telephone call that addresses three issues would cost you $43.75. However, if you did not collect your thoughts and made three separate calls for each issue over the next day or two, the same twelve minutes of conversation with your lawyer would cost you $131.25.

### 8. Stay Informed

Tell your lawyer to send you copies of each correspondence and pleading that he files on your behalf. Keep a file of your case for your own review.

### 9. Watch Out for Advertised Low Prices

Be cautious about hiring a legal clinic or law firm that advertises a very low flat fee for a divorce case. Often there is an advertised fee for a very limited legal service, such as merely the divorce. The firm may be advertising the low fee to get you in the door, then it may inform you that there are additional fees for litigation of child support, custody, visitation, property rights, and other issues. If all you need is a simple uncontested divorce, these legal clinics are quite affordable and serve your limited purpose.

Once you have an idea of what the lawyer charges, then you should ask him to give you an estimate of the expected cost of the litigation. Many attorneys will not be able to answer this question with much accuracy because many factors that affect the cost of the litigation are beyond his control, such as the extent to which your spouse's attorney fights each issue as well as how much discovery he tenders to your answer.

## 10. One Lawyer Cannot Represent Both of You

"We want to save money on the divorce. Can we use one lawyer?"

—Holly K.
age 34, divorcing, no children, teacher
Bogalusa, Louisiana

A lawyer can only represent one spouse. If he would represent both spouses, then a conflict of interest would exist; a lawyer likely would not be able to serve the best interests of both parties. If your spouse insists on using one lawyer to handle your domestic case, be sure that you are the client, not your spouse. This creates a fiduciary responsibility of the lawyer to you. Ask your lawyer to inform your spouse that you are the client, not him or her.

## 11. You Are Not Wed to Your Divorce Attorney

"Last week, we went to court for a hearing and lost miserably. My lawyer was totally outgunned by my husband's attorney. I have lost faith in my lawyer's abilities. I truly believe that he was intimidated by the other lawyer. Now, I have to battle over the property. I fear that I will lose again. What advice can you give me?"

—Yvette P.
age 47, married, one child
small-business owner
Winnfield, Louisiana

When you hire your attorney, you have accomplished one of the most important acts toward the success of your case. If you are later dissatisfied with your attorney, don't hesitate to fire him and get a new one. Your prior research on attorneys will have come in handy. Hopefully, if you have done your homework properly, you will be very happy with your initial selection of an attorney.

Remember, you may terminate your attorney at any time. It is not usually wise to do so just before a scheduled hearing. On occasion, after terminating your attorney, the attorney might refuse to release your file until his bill is paid in full.

If you have followed the tips found in this book, you will have on file copies of all pleadings as the case progresses, thus you will not be put under any major duress because of the actions of your terminated attorney.

Ask your new attorney to request your file from your last one.

Having to personally fight with your old lawyer over your file merely puts unnecessary stress upon you during this naturally stressful time in your life. Let the new lawyer get the file for you.

Chapter 4

# CONTROL YOUR LEGAL FEES AND EXPENSES

"I have heard nightmares about the cost of a divorce. I don't have a lot of money but I still want to get a good divorce lawyer. Is that possible?"

—Arthur P.
age 38, married, no children, chef
Gramercy, Louisiana

You do have the power to control your legal fees, court costs, and other legal expenses. Unfortunately, money is the life's blood of your domestic case. No one wants to spend money on lawyers and related court costs and expenses. And very few consider legal costs as regular bills that must be paid on a monthly basis. Most people want to spend as little money as possible. In contested domestic disputes, the spouse who harshly restricts paying money for a good lawyer is often penny-wise and pound-foolish.

## 1. Payment of Legal Fees Can Be a Sound Financial Investment

The quality of your lawyer often is revealed by the hourly rate that he or she charges or the initial retainer fee that is required for representation. There very well may be excellent lawyers who charge minimal fees for their services. Although they may be excellent lawyers, they are clearly poor businesspersons. Get a quality lawyer who believes that the services he or she provides are worth it.

It's remarkable the return on your investment that you may receive by biting the bullet and hiring a quality lawyer. Just imagine the cash flow of a mere $250 per month in child support during the eighteen years of a minor child's life. That's $54,000! If you hire a superb lawyer who is able to get you $500 per month, your recovery totals $108,000 (not to mention other future increases in child support,

51

due to changes in a parent's income or the child's expenses). A child-support award of $750 per month totals $162,000 over the first eighteen years of your child's life. Are you willing to pay a few thousand dollars in legal fees for a 100 percent or more return on your investment in comparison to the results of an inferior attorney?

Can you afford not to hire a quality domestic attorney? On the other hand, as a payer of child support, can you afford $250, $500, or $1,000 a month more in child support over the remaining minor years of your child's life?

What is the value of the real-estate, retirement, and other valuables that you will dispute about in your divorce case? A house and retirement are usually the greatest financial investments that most people make during their lives. Do you want to put these investments in the hands of an attorney who is inferior to the attorney of your spouse? And, of course, there is no value that can be placed on your children.

## 2. Control Your Cash Flow

- Ask for an estimate of your legal expenses.
- Ask your attorney whether he or she will charge you a flat fee for all of your legal needs.
- Consider using credit cards for cash advances and/or to pay for your legal and living expenses in order to manage your cash flow.
- Create a budget.
- Consider applying for credit cards solely in your name.
- Consider opening new, separate bank accounts.
- Consider closing joint credit-card accounts.
- Write certified, return-receipt, requested letter to credit companies indicating that you are getting a divorce and that you will not be responsible for further charges on the account.
- Gather a nest egg of funds for a rainy day.
- Open a safety-deposit box.
- Ask your attorney to provide a reasonable estimate of expected court costs, service fees, expert expenses, and additional costs.
- Anticipate possible fees for experts, mediators, appraisers, DNA tests, depositions, and evaluators.
- Consider filing an In Forma Pauperis Application.
- After your case is finished, get a refund of unused court costs deposited with the clerk of court.

- Ask your attorney to seek reimbursement of attorney fees, court costs, and service fees associated with seeking past-due child support or alimony.
- Check your legal bill for errors.

## 3. A Divorce Lawyer's Fees Should Be Reasonable and He or She Should Not Charge a Contingency Fee in a Divorce Matter

The Louisiana State Bar Association's *Rules of Professional Conduct* set forth the criteria for the reasonableness of an attorney's fees. Rule 1.5 is provided, in pertinent part, as follows:

RULE 1.5 FEES

(a) A lawyer's fee shall be reasonable. The factors to be considered in determining the reasonableness of a fee include the following:

(1) The time and labor required, the novelty and difficulty of the questions involved, and the skill requisite to perform the legal service properly;

(2) The likelihood, if apparent to the client, that the acceptance of the particular employment will preclude other employment by the lawyer;

(3) The fee customarily charged in the locality for similar legal services;

(4) The amount involved and the results obtained;

(5) The time limitations imposed by the client or by the circumstances;

(6) The nature and length of the professional relationship with the client;

(7) The experience, reputation, and ability of the lawyer or lawyers performing the services; and

(8) Whether the fee is fixed or contingent.

(b) When the lawyer has not regularly represented the client, the basis or rate of the fee shall be communicated to the client, preferably in writing, before or with in a reasonable time after commencing the representation. . . .

(d) A lawyer shall not enter into an arrangement for, charge, or collect:

(1) Any fee in a domestic relations matter, the pay ment or amount of which is contingent upon the securing of a divorce or upon the amount of alimony or support, or property settlement in lieu thereof; . . .

## 4. In Forma Pauperis Application

Divorce courts throughout Louisiana have forms that you can fill out asking the court to allow you to file your domestic papers without paying filing fees up front. These forms are usually called In Forma Pauperis Applications or motions. The forms require you to report your income and expenses, as well as the various assets and liabilities that you have. If the court grants your application, you will save an average of one to two hundred dollars. You can usually obtain a copy of an In Forma Pauperis Application or motion through your attorney or through the clerk of court's office at your local courthouse. You can file this application even if you have paid for an attorney.

Some courts allow a party to pay the filing fees and service charges in monthly installments. Look into this; it can help your cash flow.

## 5. Consider Using Credit Cards for Your Legal Fees

Many attorneys take credit cards such a VISA, MasterCard, Discover, and American Express. You may have joint credit cardswith your spouse or a credit card that is solely in your name. If you use your joint credit card, check with your credit-card company; you may be told that as long as you sign the actual credit-card receipt, then your spouse likely will not be able to successfully defeat the charge. Often your spouse will be the credit-card company's primary contact, and the credit-card bill will be directed to his or her attention. You will put your spouse in a position of having to pay the billed charges, or you might jeopardize the credit rating of you both. In a worst-case scenario, you will have to pay the minimal monthly balance required by the credit-card company. The actual financial responsibility for the use of a joint credit card for your legal services may be resolved in the community-property settlement or by a separate hearing with the judge. Many spouses only have joint credit cards. Discuss with your attorney the legal and moral ramifications of using the credit card for legal services.

## 6. Buy Other Necessities with Credit Cards

"I'm short on cash right now after putting a deposit down on a new apartment. What can I do to survive until my next pay check?"

—Wendy M.
age 25, married, one child, receptionist
Harvey, Louisiana

You also may use your credit cards to buy items that you may need during your divorce case. If you have left your residence, you may need sheets, pillows, additional clothes, nonperishable foodstuffs, diapers, etc. Don't forget that most grocery stores now take credit cards.

It is often a race to use the plastic before your spouse closes the credit-card accounts. Be sure that you have secured enough valued items to get you through the potentially hard times ahead. Like a squirrel gathering nuts, be prepared for the harsh divorce winter. By buying the essential goods that you will need until you get alimony, child support, or other relief, you will have prevented your spouse from being able to use undue financial duress to force you into a less-than-favorable money settlement regarding alimony, child support, or property division.

Don't forget that someone will ultimately have to pay the credit-card bills, so judge what is most appropriate for your individual financial circumstance. You may not want to jeopardize your credit worthiness; however, sometimes a less-than-perfect credit rating is better than not eating.

## 7. Get Your Own Individual Credit Cards

"Frank used our joint American Express to pay for his attorney."
—Sandi C.
age 34, married, two children, police officer
New Orleans, Louisiana

Whether you are preparing for a future divorce or in the midst of a divorce lawsuit, apply for your own credit cards—only in your name. It is best that the credit-card accounts are opened with you using a post-office box or a confidant's residence as the mailing and billing address. These separate (nonjoint) credit cards will give you future freedom to have uninterrupted credit and provide you with greater spending flexibility. If your spouse cancels the joint accounts, you have your new accounts to protect you from unfair financial pressures from your spouse.

It often is easier to have your credit application accepted by a company while you are still married. If you are laying the ground work for a future divorce, be aware that information regarding applications and individual credit cards may be placed in a credit report that your spouse could get his or her hands on. It also is prudent not to apply to the same credit-card company that you are currently using. Your spouse could call the company about the joint account, and a credit-card company representative could inadvertently inform your spouse about the other individual account.

## 8. Consider Closing or Notifying Joint Credit-Card Accounts

"What do I do with our joint credit cards?"
—Julie M.
age 42, married, one child, public-relations specialist
Baton Rouge, Louisiana

Once you have gained the maximum benefit from the joint credit cards, notify each credit-card company and department store that you are canceling the account or will no longer be responsible for charges of the other spouse. The safest and surest method of protecting yourself from further financial exposure is to close the joint credit card. Make sure that you notify them in writing and send the letter by certified mail. Be sure to keep copies of these letters.

## 9. Get Your Credit Reports

"I have no idea how many credit cards we have. Janet has always been in charge of paying the family bills."
—William T.
age 36, married, three children, newspaper reporter
Shreveport, Louisiana

Call or write one or more credit-reporting bureaus to get a full record of you and your spouse's credit history. You may find information regarding debt/credit of which you were not aware.

The three main credit-reporting bureaus are listed here:

EQUIFAX       1-800-685-1111
EXPERIAN      1-888-397-3742
TRANS UNION 1-800-916-8800

## 10. Reserve Money for Attorney Fees and Other Expenses

"I do not have enough money to get divorced right now. What do I do?"
—Denise F.
age 31, married, one child, clothing salesperson
Alexandria, Louisiana

Reserve enough money for a nest egg of cash necessary to pay attorney fees and other necessary expenses. Discuss with your attorney the likely amount of support that you may receive from your spouse, if any, which would supplement this amount.

A separate safety-deposit box at a new bank is an excellent place to keep these funds from being taken from you by your spouse.

## 11. Don't Get Paid with "Old Money," and Pay with "Old Money"

> "Shouldn't I leave my money in the bank account so that he can pay all of the bills?"
>
> —Erin A.
> age 28, married, one child, unemployed
> Kenner, Louisiana

Halloween can come once or twice a month if you have the shocking experience of being paid child support or alimony with money that was quickly seized by your spouse from a prior joint bank account ("old money"). Likewise, the paying spouse has a greater ability to pay his or her obligations if he uses the "old money."

The goal of the recipient of the funds is to be paid with money recently earned by the payer ("new money") versus the funds from both spouses' prior savings ("old money"). Whether the payment is a trick or a treat often depends on where the money came from in the first place. The wisdom of having control of the funds is ever more apparent upon reflection of this principle.

## 12. Taking Money from Joint Bank Accounts

Many couples simply agree to split the funds found in bank accounts. While in other cases, a rush to the bank may be the only action that prevents you from being at the financial mercy of your spouse. History has proven that many spouses empty the joint bank accounts at the peril of the other spouse. Many attorneys suggest you look at the checking-account register and ensure that there is enough money to cover previously written checks, then remove the balance of the money after discussing with your attorney the legal and moral implications of such actions. Many judges will consider any preemptive strike at taking joint funds as prepayment of support, while others will find that it is a matter to be resolved in the division of marital assets. Should you place funds into a new bank account, solely in your name, many suggest using a different bank, as many bank clerks are not consistent on maintaining confidentiality when a spouse inquires about other accounts at the bank that you as a couple have been using in the past.

### 13. Get Refund on Unused Court Cost Deposited with the Clerk of Court After Case Is Finished

Usually, your initial filing fees are a deposit for the initial pleadings and for future filings. Once the domestic case is over its major battles, a vast majority of lawyers and clients forget to inquire with the clerk of court's office as to whether any filing fees are unused. These excess funds usually can be refunded to you. Simply ask the clerk of court's office for their procedure on obtaining a refund of these unused filing fees.

### 14. Anticipate Possible Fees for Experts, Mediators, Appraisers, DNA Tests, Depositions, and Evaulators

"I paid the attorney fees and court costs. What other expenses can I expect?"

—Ashley R.
age 33, married, two children, real-estate agent
Gonzales, Louisiana

It is not uncommon for many domestic cases to require additional costs for experts, mediators, appraisers, evaluators, DNA paternity tests, and/or depositions. Ask your attorney whether any of these costs are expected. Additionally, ask him to provide you with an estimate of these costs. Many times a lawyer can give you a good sense on when these expenses will have to be paid. Knowledge that these expenses exist will enable you to better budget and manage your cash flow.

### 15. Reimbursement of Attorney Fees, Court Costs, and Service Fees Associated with Seeking Past-Due Child Support or Spousal Support

"My ex has not paid child support for the last three months. Now I have to pay a lawyer to make him pay."

—Latesha O.
age 31, divorced, two children, office manager
Bossier City, Louisiana

Most states, including Louisiana, allow you to get reimbursed for the attorney fees, court costs, and service fees that were expended by a spouse seeking past-due child support or alimony. This general rule only applies when there is a prior judgment awarding the spouse child support or alimony. Unfortunately, in many cases, the court will order an amount of attorney-fee reimbursement that is less than what the seeking spouse has actually expended. Ask your attorney to request the court to order the other spouse to pay the actual attorney fees paid by you.

## 16. Check Your Legal Bill for Errors

Always check your legal bill. Attorneys' support staffs usually produce your statement, and errors can occur. Insist that your lawyer send you a statement of legal services, itemizing his work and the related expenses, on a monthly basis. Never hesitate to question a charge. A good attorney should welcome your billing inquires.

Chapter 5

# GET POSSESSION OF CHILDREN AND PROPERTY

"I know that there are many things to do, but I don't know what to do first."

—Paula G.
age 44, married, one child, flight attendant
Kenner, Louisiana

## 1. Get Possession

In a divorce case, possession of children and property is everything. Get and keep the physical custody of your children, money, documents, and property. Safeguard everyone and everything. You must protect your monetary assets during a divorce. You and your spouse have conflicting financial interests.

## 2. Children

"There is no way that I would allow my husband to take my little boy and girl from me."

—Adelle P.
age 27, married, two children, nurse
Baton Rouge, Louisiana

Without a court order indicating which parent has temporary physical custody of the children, both parents have equal rights to the children. If you want custody of your children, go get your children. If you have possession of your children, keep them. Immediately have your attorney file a motion asking for the temporary custody of your children and a restraining order preventing your spouse from taking them without your written permission.

C.C. Art. 131 Court to determine custody

In a proceeding for divorce or thereafter, the court shall award custody of a child in accordance with the best interest of the child.

C.C. Art. 132 Award of custody to parents

If the parents agree who is to have custody, the court shall award custody in accordance with their agreement unless the best interest of the child requires a different award.

In the absence of agreement, or if the agreement is not in the best interest of the child, the court shall award custody to the parents jointly; however, if custody in one parent is shown by clear and convincing evidence to serve the best interest of the child, the court shall award custody to that parent.

C.C.P. Art. 3945. Incidental order of temporary child custody; injunctive relief; exceptions

A. The injunctive relief afforded either party to an action for divorce or other proceeding which includes a provision for the temporary custody of a minor child shall be governed by the additional provisions of this Article.

B. An ex parte order of temporary custody of a minor child shall not be granted unless:

(1) It clearly appears from specific facts shown by a verified petition or by supporting affidavit that immediate and irreparable injury will result to the child before the adverse party or his attorney can be heard in opposition.

(2) The applicant's attorney certifies to the court, in writing, either:

(a) The efforts which have been made to give the adverse party reasonable notice of the date and time such order is being presented to the court.

(b) The reasons supporting his claim that notice should not be required.

C. An ex parte order of temporary custody shall:

(1) Expire by operation of law within fifteen days of signing of the order; however, the order may be extended for good cause shown at any time before its expiration for one period not exceeding ten days.

(2) Provide specific provisions for temporary visitation by the

adverse party of not less than forty-eight hours during the fifteen-day period, unless the verified petition or supporting affidavit clearly demonstrates that immediate and irreparable injury will result to the child as a result of such visitation.

(3) Be endorsed with the date on which the ex parte order is signed and the date and hour of the rule to show cause.

D. The rule to show cause why the respondent should not be awarded the custody, joint custody, or visitation of the child shall be assigned for hearing not more than fifteen days after signing of the ex parte order of temporary custody.

E. Any ex parte order not in compliance with the provisions of this Article is not enforceable, and is null and void.

F. In the event an ex parte order of temporary custody is denied, the court shall specifically allocate between the parents the time which the child shall spend with each parent, unless immediate and irreparable injury will result to the child.

G. The provisions of this Article do not apply to any order of custody of a child requested in a verified petition alleging the applicability of the Domestic Abuse Assistance Act, R.S. 46:2131 et seq., Children's Code Article 1564 et seq., or the Post-Separation Family Violence Relief Act, *R.S. 9:361* (emphasis added) et seq.

## 3. Property and Sentimental Items

Take possession of all personal, separate, and community property including any sentimental items that are not the sole separate property of your spouse. Your possession will aid in the prevention of the secretness, alienation, or destruction of these items.

C.C. Art. 2341 Separate property.

The separate property of a spouse is his exclusively. It comprises: property acquired by a spouse prior to the establishment of a community property regime; property acquired by a spouse with separate things or with separate and community things when the value of the community things is inconsequential in comparison with the value of the separate things used; property acquired by a spouse by inheritance or donation to him individually; damages awarded to a spouse in an action for breach of contract against the other spouse or for the loss sustained as a result of fraud or bad faith in the management of community property by the other spouse; damages or other indemnity awarded to a spouse in connection with the management of his separate property; and things acquired by a spouse as a result of a voluntary partition of the community during the existence of a community property regime.

C.C. Art. 2338 Community property.

The community property comprises: property acquired during the existence of the legal regime through the effort, skill, or industry of either spouse; property acquired with community things or with community and separate things, unless classified as separate property under Article 2341; property donated to the spouses jointly; natural and civil fruits of community property; damages awarded for loss or injury to a thing belonging to the community; and all other property not classified by law as separate property.

C.C. Art. 2340 Presumption of community.

Things in the possession of a spouse during the existence of a regime of community of acquets and gains are presumed to be community, but either spouse may prove that they are separate property.

C.C. Art. 3526. Termination of community; movables and Louisiana immovables acquired by a spouse while domiciled in another state

Upon termination of the community, or dissolution by death or by divorce of the marriage of spouses either of whom is domiciled in this state, their respective rights and obligations with regard to immovables situated in this state and movables, wherever situated, that were acquired during the marriage by either spouse while domiciled in another state shall be determined as follows:

(1) Property that is classified as community property under the law of this state shall be treated as community property under that law; and

(2) Property that is not classified as community property under the law of this state shall be treated as the separate property of the acquiring spouse. However, the other spouse shall be entitled, in value only, to the same rights with regard to this property as would

be granted by the law of the state in which the acquiring spouse was domiciled at the time of acquisition.

C.C. Art. 2346 Management of community property.

Each spouse acting alone may manage, control, or dispose of community property unless otherwise provided by law.

C.C. Art. 2369.3. Duty to preserve; standard of care

A spouse has a duty to preserve and to manage prudently former community property under his control, including a former community enterprise, in a manner consistent with the mode of use of that property immediately prior to termination of the community regime. He is answerable for any damage caused by his fault, default, or neglect.

A community enterprise is a business that is not a legal entity.

## 4. Pets

"My schnauzer and two Persians are my children. I have had Fritzy since he was a puppy. I've had Chops and Suey for four years."

—Laura S.
age 27, no children, one dog, two cats
computer consultant
Monroe, Louisiana

Despite popular sentiment, in Louisiana pets are property. If you want your pets, keep them. When you hire an attorney, tell him of your concerns regarding your pets. The facts regarding how you acquired them are very important.

## 5. Money

"We have thousands of dollars in a joint checking account. We also have several credit cards in both of our names."

—Carla N.
age 36, no children, television-station sales
Lake Charles, Louisiana

Get cash from all available sources. Make sure enough money is kept in accounts to pay for previously written checks. Also speak to your attorney, C.P.A., and certified financial planner about other legal, tax, and financial consequences.

## 6. The House/Apartment and Furnishings

"My home is beautiful. The renovation has been a labor of love. It's part of me. I've painstakingly found the most beautiful pieces to complement the decor. The house is my home—my daughter's home. I want to do everything that I can do to keep it."

—Robin E.
age 36, one child, housewife
Chalmette, Louisiana

If you want possession of your house or apartment, remain there. If you are battered or otherwise abused, immediately refer to the chapter on abuse for further insights.

R.S. 9:374 Possession and use of family residence or community movables or immovables

A. When the family residence is the separate property of either spouse, after the filing of a petition for divorce or in conjunction therewith, the spouse who has physical custody or has been awarded temporary custody of the minor children of the marriage may petition for, and a court may award to that spouse, after a contradictory hearing, the use and occupancy of the family residence pending the partition of the community property or one hundred eighty days after termination of the marriage, whichever occurs first. In these cases, the court shall inquire into the relative economic status of the spouses, including both community and separate property, and the needs of the children, and shall award the use and occupancy of the family residence to the spouse in accordance with the best interest of the family. The court shall consider the granting of the occupancy of the family home in awarding spousal support.

B. When the family residence is community property or the spouses own community movables or immovables, after or in conjunction with the filing of a petition for divorce or for separation of property in accordance with Civil Code Article 2374 (emphasis added), either spouse may petition for, and a court may award to one of the spouses, after a contradictory hearing, the use and occupancy of the family residence and use of community movables or immovables to either of the spouses pending further order of the court. In these cases, the court shall inquire into the relative economic status of the spouses, including both community and separate property, and the needs of the children, if any, and shall award the use and occupancy of the family residence and the use of any community movables or immovables to the spouse in accordance with the best interest of the family. If applicable, the court shall consider the granting of the occupancy of the family home and the use of community movables or immovables in awarding spousal support.

C. A spouse who uses and occupies or is awarded by the court the use and occupancy of the family residence pending either the termination of the marriage or the partition of the community property in accordance with the provisions of R.S. 9:374(A) or (B) shall not be liable to the other spouse for rental for the use and occupancy, unless otherwise agreed by the spouses or ordered by the court.

D. The court may determine whether the family home is separate or community property in the contradictory hearing authorized under the provisions of this Section.

E.(1) In a proceeding for divorce or thereafter, upon request of either party, where a community property regime existed, a summary proceeding may be undertaken by the trial court within sixty days of filing, allocating the use of community property, including monetary assets, bank accounts, savings plans, and other divisible movable property pending formal partition proceeding, pursuant to R.S. 9:2801 (emphasis added).

(2) Upon court order, each spouse shall provide the other a complete accounting of all community assets subsequent to said allocation and in compliance with Civil Code Article 2369.3 (emphasis added), providing the duty to preserve and prudently manage community property.

(3) The court shall determine allocation of community assets after considering:

(a) The custody of the children and exclusive possession of the house.

(b) The total community assets.

(c) The need of one spouse for funds to maintain a household prior to formal partition.

(d) The need of a spouse to receive legal representation during the course of the divorce proceeding.

### Be the Queen or King of the Castle

After consulting with your attorney, consider changing the locks of your house or apartment. Be sure to get the approval of your lawyer, because in many states, such as Louisiana, to prohibit a spouse from entering his or her own house/apartment without a court order may be considered constructive abandonment.

### Don't Get Locket Out of Your House/Apartment

If your spouse changes the locks at your house or apartment, immediately call your attorney, your spouse, and the police to see if your spouse has a legal right to prohibit you from being in your house/apartment.

Ask your lawyer to file a motion seeking a restraining order against your spouse from locking you out of your residence.

## 7. Inventory Everything

You can prevent trying to rely solely on your memory by inventorying your property. Once you have a good inventory of these items, consider photographing and/or videotaping them. Additionally, get a friend to view all of the items and provide the date and his or her initials next to each item inspected so that the friend later may testify as a witness to the existence and condition of your property, should the property disappear.

When listing all of your financial records, including credit-card accounts, car titles, and insurance policies, be sure to be as specific as possible by listing the account number and account balances at the time that you make your list. Get the originals or copies of all documents.

You may use the forms found in appendix A to assist you in this inventory process. As an additional mental reminder, use the following list to assist you in your quest to locate, inventory, possess, and/or photocopy.

### Documents and Things
#### to Locate, Inventory, Possess, and/or Copy

Gather documents and things regarding you, your spouse, and your children as to the following:

**Income information:**
• Paychecks
• Payroll stubs

- Federal and state income-tax returns and refunds
- Cash-register receipts
- Receipt records
- Severance pay
- "Golden parachute" retirement plans
- Documents evidencing any company or employer reimburse mentfor entertainment, travel, automobile, and/or other expenses
- Other employment benefits, such as sick pay, vacation pay, bonuses, health-club and country-club memberships, and frequent-flier programs
- Records regarding rental income
- Scholastic and vocational diplomas, awards, and/or degrees

**Investment information:**
- Stocks, bonds, mutual funds, promissory notes, options, certificates of deposit, purchase agreements, and other investments
- Deferred, retirement, and/or savings plans, such as IRAs, 401(k)s, profit sharing, and stock options
- Financial statements, balance sheets, profit and loss statements, and income statements
- Trust agreements
- Custodial accounts

**Bank records:**
- Checkbook registers
- Canceled checks
- Savings accounts
- Christmas-club accounts
- Loan applications
- Documents in safety-deposit boxes
- Bank accounts: checking, savings, money-market, and line-of-credit accounts

**Insurance information:**
- Insurance policies—whether life, health, auto, disability, or other

**Cars, boats, motorcycles, motor homes, trailers, and airplanes:**
- Titles and registrations
- Keys
- Actual vehicles
- Appraisals on all vehicles

**Marriage-related documents:**
- Present and prior marriage licenses, divorce papers, adoption papers

- Inheritance documents, judgments regarding child support
- Prenuptial, postnuptial agreements

**Real-estate and furniture:**
- Titles or deeds to all property
- Appraisals of property
- Evaluations of furniture, furnishings, etc.
- Time-share unit's agreements
- Household furniture and furnishings receipts

**Other business records:**
- Articles of incorporation, initial and annual reports, minute books, stockholder subscriptions, partnership agreements, and other documentation concerning the financial condition of any legal entity in which your spouse has or had a legal or equitable interest

**Medical records:**
- Health records
- Counseling and/or psychological evaluations of any party to this litigation and/or of the minor child
- Medical-insurance cards
- Dental and orthodontic records
- Prescriptions

**Evidence of other monthly expenses:**
- All current invoices/bills
- Housing (rent or mortgage payment note)
- Property insurance and taxes
- Premises/yard maintenance and repair
- Condominium charges
- Furniture payments
- Household supplies and repairs
- Utilities
- Electricity
- Gas
- Water
- Telephone
- Home
- Beeper
- Cable
- Food
- Groceries
- Meals eaten out/including work lunches
- Automobile/transportation
- Car note

- Gasoline
- Car maintenance
- Parking
- Other transportation expenses
- Clothing
- Average new purchases/replacements
- Dry cleaning and laundry
- Personal and grooming (haircuts/nails)
- Education
- School/lessons/tutoring
- Books
- Miscellaneous education expenses
- Day care/baby-sitting
- Pet/pet supplies
- Maid
- Union dues
- Recreation
- Gifts, donations, religious tithes
- Vacation
- Other debts

**Miscellaneous documents and things:**
- Jewelry
- Artwork
- Antiques and collectibles
- Birth certificates
- Passports/visas/green cards
- Vaccination records

## 8. Your Financial Figures Are Your Friends

"My husband is the manager of our family owned nursery business. We review all of the books on a monthly basis. The company bookkeeper pays all of the company bills. I pay our personal monthly bills."

—Catherine W.
age 37, married, two children
physician and co-owner of nursery
Bossier City, Louisiana

If your spouse is not anticipating your move toward a divorce, then methodically and discreetly get originals or copies of all financial records regarding your spouse's business affairs and income, as well as both of your expenses. Safeguard these documents with your attorney or a confidant or in a new safety-deposit box at a new bank.

## 9. Get Information from Computers

Make a backup tape or diskette of the information on your computer. Give the tape and/or diskette to your attorney. Also consider making a printout of any particularly revealing data.

## 10. Get Possession of All Documents You Will Need to Prepare Your Taxes

> "He has always prepared the state and federal tax returns."
> —Faye W.
> age 48, married, one child, jeweler
> River Ridge, Louisiana

Accumulate all documents you will need to prepare your taxes.

## 11. Videotape and/or Photograph Each Room of Your House/Apartment

> "I am leaving my husband and moving out of the apartment this weekend. I don't have a place to move the furniture."
> —Tammy T.
> age 22, married, no children, unemployed
> Ruston, Louisiana

If you videotape the furniture, appliances, and other valuable items in the house, then you have proof of the items that were in the dwelling on a certain date. A quick tip is to videotape the first page of your local newspaper, showing its publication date, and also keep the copy of that first page to show proof of the earliest date on which the video could have been made. If any of the items disappear after your physical separation from the spouse, then the court may require the other spouse to account for the missing items.

## 12. File Ex Parte Motions

> "I have taken the money out of our checking account. I've put the money in my separate safety deposit box at my new bank. Tomorrow I am changing the locks on the house while Richard is at work. My daughter is going to stay at my mother's house tomorrow night."
> —Aimee C.
> age 28, married, one child
> court reporter
> Covington, Louisiana

Often the test on who gets the immediate possession of children, money, homes, and property depends on who wins the race to the courthouse and files ex parte motions. These pleadings permit you to get the possession of children and things or injunctions under certain circumstances without an initial court hearing. Talk to your attorney about what circumstances may apply for you.

C.C.P. Art. 3601. Injunction, grounds for issuance; preliminary injunction; temporary restraining order

An injunction shall issue in cases where irreparable injury, loss, or damage may otherwise result to the applicant, or in other cases specifically provided by law; provided, however, that no court shall have jurisdiction to issue, or cause to be issued, any temporary restraining order, preliminary injunction, or permanent injunction against any state department, board or agency, or any officer, administrator or head thereof, or any officer of the State of Louisiana in any suit involving the expenditure of public funds under any statute or law of this state to compel the expenditure of state funds when the director of such department, board or agency, or the governor shall certify that the expenditure of such funds would have the effect of creating a deficit in the funds of said agency or be in violation of the requirements placed upon the expenditure of such funds by the legislature.

During the pendency of an action for an injunction the court may issue a temporary restraining order, a preliminary injunction, or both, except in cases where prohibited, in accordance with the provisions of this Chapter.

Except as otherwise provided by law, an application for injunctive relief shall be by petition.

Chapter 6

# PATERNITY

"My baby was born last month. Now my estranged husband says that she is not his child and he refuses to help out financially. What can I do to get help?"

—Susan B.
age 22, married, one child, waitress
Opelousas, Louisiana

## 1. Paternity

A prerequisite to the establishment of child custody or support is the determination of paternity and maternity. In most cases, the matter is not disputed, and both parents have their names on the child's birth certificate. However, in a growing number of cases, the paternity of the child is in dispute. The majority of the time, the biological mother is trying to prove that a certain man is the biological father of a child. In other instances, the presumed father is in doubt of his paternity because of reservations about the mother's fidelity. Regardless of the reason, the matter may come into dispute. When it does, the Louisiana legislature and courts have created a body of law and testing procedures to deal with these concerns.

## 2. Time Is of the Essence When Establishing or Disavowing Paternity

Whether you wish to establish or disavow paternity, the time allowed to bring the matter before a court is passing (it may have already passed). Immediately seek your attorney's assistance if paternity or maternity is an issue.

## 3. Louisiana Classifications of Children

In Louisiana, children are either legitimate or illegitimate

(Louisiana Civil Code Article 178). "Legitimate children are those who are either born or conceived during marriage or who have been legitimated as provided hereafter" (Louisiana Civil Code Article 179). "Illegitimate children are those who are conceived and born out of marriage" (Louisiana Civil Code Article 180). The classification of illegitimate children may be changed to legitimate through legal proceedings (Louisiana Revised Statute Article 9: 46 and 9:391).

## 4. Louisiana's Laws of Presumption of Paternity

Most states, including Louisiana, have enacted laws that provide that if a couple is married during the conception or birth of a child, then the couple is presumed to be the biological parents of the child. Since the chief goal of these laws is to establish paternity, Louisiana addresses this issue in terms of the husband being the father of the child. The Louisiana law provides a "rebut table presumption," in which the parent can go to court, within a limited time period, and attempt to prove that he is not the parent of the child.

Other states have a narrower stance on paternity/maternity. These state laws provide that if a couple is married during the conception or birth of a child, then it is conclusive that the couple are the parents of the child.

Whether rebut table presumptions or conclusive presumptions exist, the states have taken the parental policy of making it difficult to make a child illegitimate.

In Louisiana, if a couple is not married, no presumption regarding paternity is applicable.

## 5. The Husband Is Presumed to Be the Father; the Presumption Is Rebuttable

C.C. Art. 184. Presumed paternity of husband.

The husband of the mother is presumed to be the father of all children born or conceived during the marriage.

C.C. Art. 185. Presumption of paternity, date of birth

A child born less than three hundred days after the dissolution of the marriage is presumed to have been conceived during the marriage. A child born three hundred days or more after the dissolution of the marriage is not presumed to be the child of the husband.

C.C. Art. 186. Presumption of paternity, negation.

The husband of the mother is not presumed to be the father of the child if another man is presumed to be the father.

## 6. Proof of Paternity

1. Birth certificate (Art. 193)
2. Evidence of reputation that the child has been consistenly considered as a child born during the marriage (Art. 194)
3. Evidence of reputation sufficient to establish material facts such as:
    "a. That such individual has always been called by the surname of the father from whom he pretends to be born;
    b. That the father treated him as his child, and that he provided as such for his education, maintenance and settlement in life;
    c. That he has constantly been acknowledged as such in the world;
    d. That he has been acknowledged as such within the family (Art. 195)."
4. Written or oral evidence (Art. 196)
5. Formal or informal acknowledgment of child before or after marriage to the mother (Art. 198)
6. The alleged father's signature on a notarized act of acknowledgment (Art. 200)
7. Evidence of hospital bills (R.S. 9:394)
8. Genetic testing—DNA (R.S. 9:394)
9. Blood sample (R.S. 398.2)
10. Father's written act of acknowledgment (Art. 110 and R.S. 9:392)

## 7. Genetic Testing (DNA) Is the Mother of All Proof

R.S. 9:394 Evidence of hospital bills and tests in paternity action

> In an action to establish paternity, originals or certified copies of bills for pregnancy, childbirth, and genetic testing shall be admissible as an exception to the hearsay rule and shall be prima facie evidence that the amounts reflected on the bills were incurred for such services or testing on behalf of the child. Extrinsic evidence of authenticity of the bills, or their duplicates, as a condition precedent to admissibility shall not be required.

Science has advanced to such a point that most of the guesswork is taken out of a paternity dispute. Genetic DNA testing has become the norm for disputed paternity cases. Each state has established a threshold (percentage requirement) for genetic test results in which a rebut table or conclusive presumption of paternity is created if the probability of paternity is equal to or greater than a threshold percentage (i.e., alleged father's probability of being the child's biological father is a 99 percent likelihood according to DNA test results).

DNA testing can be accomplished as early as nine to ten weeks of pregnancy. Tests can be run on the fetus through chorionic villus sampling (CVS). Although rarely used, this technique is available and may be valuable in assisting your attorney in seeking the establishment of paternity at the earliest time allowed by state law.

## 8. Appointment of attorney in disavowal actions

C.C. Art. 5091.1. Appointment of attorney in disavowal actions

> In any action to disavow paternity, the judge shall appoint an attorney to represent the child whose status is at issue, and the attorney so appointed shall not represent any other party in the litigation.

## 9. Action to Disavow

Article 187 provides the burden of proof necessary for a husband to disavow the paternity of a child.

Evidence Often Used to Disavow Paternity
1. Negative blood tests.
2. Unmatched DNA prints.
3. Sterility.
4. Physical impossibility because of location during the time of conception.
5. Any other scientific or medical evidence which thcourt may deem relevant under the circumstances (Art. 187).

A husband may lose his right to disavow paternity.

C.C. Art. 188. Husband's loss of right to disavowal

A man who marries a pregnant woman and who knows that she is pregnant at the time of the marriage cannot disavow the paternity of such child born of such pregnancy. However, if the woman has acted in bad faith and has made a false claim of fatherhood to the marrying spouse, he may disavow paternity provided that he proves such bad faith on the part of the mother, and he proves by a preponderance of the evidence that the child is not his. If another man is presumed to be the father, however, then the provisions of Article 186 apply. The husband also cannot disavow paternity of a child born as the result of artificial insemination of the mother to which he consented.

## 10. There Is a Time Limit for a Husband to Disavow

Art. 189. Time limit for disavowal by the husband

A suit for disavowal of paternity must be filed within one year after the husband learned or should have learned of the birth of the child; but, if the husband for reasons beyond his control is not able to file suit timely, then the time for filing suit shall be suspended during the period of such inability.

Nevertheless, the suit may be filed within one year from the date the husband is notified in writing that a party in interest has asserted that the husband is the father of the child, if the husband lived continuously separate and apart from the mother during the three hundred days immediately preceding the birth of the child.

## 11. Lying Under Oath in a Paternity Case

Whoever intentionally falsely swears in a paternity case may be fined up to five hundred dollars, or imprisoned for up to six months, or both (R.S. 9:125.1).

## 12. Time Limit to Disavow and Time to Establish Paternity

"I had three children with my ex and have been paying child support for the last four years. Last week, my ex confessed that the youngest child is probably not mine. Can I prove that I am not the boy's biological father? I only want to pay her if he is my child."

—Johnny C.
age 34, divorced, three children
specialty advertising
Kenner, Louisiana

States have established narrow time limits (usually less than one year from birth) for a father to attempt to legally disavow a child. Again, the policy is intended to prevent the child from becoming legally illegitimate, regardless as to whether the husband is the father. On the other hand, states have established much broader time frames to allow the establishment of paternity. In many states, after a child reaches the "age of majority," he has another one to five years to seek the establishment of paternity.

Chapter 7

# CUSTODY AND VISITATION

"The kids are my babies. I'm the mother and my children should stay with me. I should be awarded custody of my two sons."
—Stacy W.
age 32, divorcing, two children, housewife
Baton Rouge, Louisiana

"I have been there for my boys since they were born. Just because I'm a man doesn't mean that I should not get custody of my children. Stacy is not a better parent than I am."
—Wayne W.
age 35, divorcing, two children, physician
Baton Rouge, Louisiana

## 1. Best Advice: Be a Good Parent!

Although "be a good parent" seems like obvious advice, many parents lose sight of this primary responsibility while in the throws of an emotional and otherwise trying legal-custody battle.

### Quick Facts

There are 11.5 million American, divorced, custodial parents, comprised of 9.9 million women and 1.6 million men (U.S. Census Bureau).

According to national statistics, for each divorce decree granted, an average of one minor child (under the age of eighteen) is involved (0.9 per divorce decree). Thus, under the current divorce rate, more than one million children are directly affected by a divorce each year (1,075,000).

Throughout America, mothers are awarded sole custody of their children 71 percent of the time. Joint custody awards occur 15.5 percent of the time. Fathers receive the sole-custody award 8.5 percent of the time. And friends and other relatives receive custody in 5 percent of all custody decrees.

## 2. What Is Custody?

Custody can be defined in terms of physical possession or in terms of legal responsibilities. It may be temporary or permanent; joint, shared, or sole; and legal and/or physical.

## 3. Legal Custody and Physical Custody

The heart and soul of legal custody lies in the ability of a parent to make crucial decisions regarding the child, including the day-to-day decisions of child rearing. Physical custody, as the term suggests, is the actual physical possession and control of the child.

C.C. Art. 131. Court to determine custody

In a proceeding for divorce or thereafter, the court shall award custody of a child in accordance with the best interest of the child.

C.C. Art. 132. Award of custody to parents

If the parents agree who is to have custody, the court shall award custody in accordance with their agreement unless the best interest of the child requires a different award.

In the absence of agreement, or if the agreement is not in the best interest of the child, the court shall award custody to the parents jointly; however, if custody in one parent is shown by clear and convincing evidence to serve the best interest of the child, the court shall award custody to that parent.

C.C.P. Art. 3945. Incidental order of temporary child custody; injunctive relief; exceptions

A. The injunctive relief afforded either party to an action for divorce or other proceeding which includes a provision for the temporary custody of a minor child shall be governed by the additional provisions of this Article.

B. An ex parte order of temporary custody of a minor child shall not be granted unless:

(1) It clearly appears from specific facts shown by a verified petition or by supporting affidavit that immediate and irreparable injury will result to the child before the adverse party or his attorney can be heard in opposition.

(2) The applicant's attorney certifies to the court, in writing, either:

(a) The efforts which have been made to give the adverse party reasonable notice of the date and time such order is being presented to the court.

(b) The reasons supporting his claim that notice should not be required.

C. An ex parte order of temporary custody shall:

(1) Expire by operation of law within fifteen days of signing of the order; however, the order may be extended for good cause shown at any time before its expiration for one period not exceeding ten days.

(2) Provide specific provisions for temporary visitation by the adverse party of not less than forty-eight hours during the fifteen-day period, unless the verified petition or supporting affidavit clearly demonstrates that immediate and irreparable injury will result to the child as a result of such visitation.

(3) Be endorsed with the date on which the ex parte order is signed and the date and hour of the rule to show cause.

D. The rule to show cause why the respondent should not be awarded the custody, joint custody, or visitation of the child shall be assigned for hearing not more than fifteen days after signing of the ex parte order of temporary custody.

E. Any ex parte order not in compliance with the provisions of this Article is not enforceable, and is null and void.

F. In the event an ex parte order of temporary custody is denied, the court shall specifically allocate between the parents the time which the child shall spend with each parent, unless immediate and irreparable injury will result to the child.

G. The provisions of this Article do not apply to any order of custody of a child requested in a verified petition alleging the applicability of the Domestic Abuse Assistance Act, R.S. 46:2131 et seq., *Children's Code Article 1564 et seq.*, or the Post-Separation Family Violence Relief Act, *R.S. 9:361* (emphasis added) et seq.

## 4. Temporary Custody

Temporary custody (also referred to as "provisional custody") generally means that the person possessing temporary/provisional custody has legal possession and control of a child until a court rules otherwise or until an event occurs that would trigger a change or termination in custody (i.e., the child reaching the age of majority, the child being emancipated, etc.). The child will live with a particular parent while the court proceedings are underway. Getting temporary custody has great advantages, as temporary custody often leads to permanent custody.

### Getting Temporary Custody

As previously stated, your immediate and continued physical possession and custody of your children will significantly increase your chances of getting permanent custody. If at all possible, do the following:

1. Keep the kids!
2. Stay in your house with your children.
3. Get a court order of temporary custody, pending the custody trial.

This is often a race to the courthouse, so do it now!

### If You Possess the Children, Continue the Trial Date; If You Don't, Press for a Quick Trial Date

If you have an order of temporary custody, it is to your advantage to prolong the date of the custody trial, which determines the permanent custody arrangements. Judges do not like to disturb the status quo of the children's existence. The continuity of the children's living environment is an important factor in the ultimate custody determination. Remember that when the children are accustomed to the neighborhood of friends, certain schools, and churches, a judge will be hesitant to usurp then from the familiar living arrangements. Hence, ask your attorney to file for a continuance of the custody trial date.

If you are on the other side of the temporary-custody fence, in which case you do not have the physical custody of the children, ask your attorney to expedite a trial date. Have the attorney emphasize to the judge that any undue delays in trying the custody issues shall be unfairly prejudicial to your case.

The bottom line is that temporary custody often leads to permanent custody!

## 5. Permanent Custody

Permanent custody means, as the name suggests, a continued possession and control of a child after the custody matter has been resolved in court or agreed upon by the parties.

## 6. Joint Custody

R.S. 9:335. Joint custody decree and implementation order

A. (1) In a proceeding in which joint custody is decreed, the court shall render a joint custody implementation order except for good cause shown.

(2) (a) The implementation order shall allocate the time periods during which each parent shall have physical custody of the child so that the child is assured of frequent and continuing contact with both parents.

(b) To the extent it is feasible and in the best interest of the child, physical custody of the children should be shared equally.

(3) The implementation order shall allocate the legal authority and responsibility of the parents.

B. (1) In a decree of joint custody the court shall designate a domiciliary parent except when there is an implementation order to the contrary or for other good cause shown.

(2) The domiciliary parent is the parent with whom the child shall primarily reside, but the other parent shall have physical custody during time periods that assure that the child has frequent and continuing contact with both parents.

(3) The domiciliary parent shall have authority to make all decisions

affecting the child unless an implementation order provides otherwise. All major decisions made by the domiciliary parent concerning the child shall be subject to review by the court upon motion of the other parent. It shall be presumed that all major decisions made by the domiciliary parent are in the best interest of the child.

C. If a domiciliary parent is not designated in the joint custody decree and an implementation order does not provide otherwise, joint custody confers upon the parents the same rights and responsibilities as are conferred on them by the provisions of Title VII of Book I of the Civil Code.

R.S. 9:336. Obligation of joint custodians to confer

Joint custody obligates the parents to exchange information concerning the health, education, and welfare of the child and to confer with one another in exercising decision-making authority

# 7. Shared Custody

R.S. 9:315.9. Effect of shared custodial arrangement

A.(1) "Shared custody" means a joint custody order in which each parent has physical custody of the child for an approximately equal amount of time.

(2) If the joint custody order provides for shared custody, the basic child support obligation shall first be multiplied by one and one-half and then divided between the parents in proportion to their respective adjusted gross incomes.

(3) Each parent's theoretical child support obligation shall then be cross multiplied by the actual percentage of time the child spends with the other party to determine the basic child support obligation based on the amount of time spent with the other party.

(4) Each parent's proportionate share of work-related net child care costs and extraordinary adjustments to the schedule shall be added to the amount calculated under Paragraph (3) of this Subsection.

(5) Each parent's proportionate share of any direct payments ordered to be made on behalf of the child for net child care costs,

the cost of health insurance premiums, extraordinary medical expenses, or other extraordinary expenses shall be deducted from the amount calculated under Paragraph (3) of this Subsection.

(6) The parent owing the greater amount of child support shall owe to the other parent the difference between the two amounts as a child support obligation. The amount owed shall not be higher than the amount which that parent would have owed if he or she were a domiciliary parent.

B. Worksheet B reproduced in *R.S. 9:315.20* (emphasis added), or a substantially similar form adopted by local court rule, shall be used to determine child support in accordance with this Subsection.

## 8. Split Custody

R.S. 9:315.10. Effect of split custodial arrangement

A. (1) "Split custody" means that each party is the sole custodial or domiciliary parent of at least one child to whom support is due.

(2) If the custody order provides for split custody, each parent shall compute a total child support obligation for the child or children in the custody of the other parent, based on a calculation pursuant to this Section.

(3) The amount determined under Paragraph (2) of this Subsection shall be a theoretical support obligation owed to each parent.

(4) The parent owing the greater amount of child support shall owe to the other parent the difference between the two amounts as a child support obligation.

B. Worksheet A reproduced in *R.S. 9:315.20* (emphasis added), or a substantially similar form adopted by local court rule, shall be used by each parent to determine child support in accordance with this Section.

## 9. Sole Custody

Sole custody is more readily seen in cases in which one parent is found to be neglectful, abusive, or mentally/physically incapable of taking care of a child. Sole custody is also found by consent of the parents.

## 10. Custody to a Nonparent

C.C. Art. 133. Award of custody to person other than a parent; order of preference

If an award of joint custody or of sole custody to either parent would result in substantial harm to the child, the court shall award custody to another person with whom the child has been living in a wholesome and stable environment, or otherwise to any other person able to provide an adequate and stable environment.

## 11. "Best Interest of Child" Standard

The ultimate criteria used in determining which parent gets primary custody of a child is the court's evaluation of what is in the best interest of the minor child. In general terms, the "best interest test" inquires into the safety, health, happiness, and well-being of the child.

A child's relationship with both parents is very important to the child's future. Children who do not have an active relationship with a parent are more likely to commit crimes, do poorly in school, drop out of school, and have greater psychological health concerns.

### Sincerely Act in the Best Interest of Your Children

If you are truly a good parent, you are going to want what is best for your children. The best-interest test is the pivotal legal standard used in custody disputes. The court will inquire into the quality of your relationship with your children, as well as the emotional, spiritual, educational, and health needs of each child. The court also will weigh the positive and negative attributes of each parent.

The most impressive characteristic of a parent, which transcends all other aspects of custody determinations, is whether a parent is sincerely acting in the best interest of his or her child.

C.C. Art. 134. Factors in determining child's best interest

The court shall consider all relevant factors in determining the best interest of the child. Such factors may include:

(1) The love, affection, and other emotional ties between each party and the child.

(2) The capacity and disposition of each party to give the child love, affection, and spiritual guidance and to continue the education and rearing of the child.

(3) The capacity and disposition of each party to provide the child with food, clothing, medical care, and other material needs.

(4) The length of time the child has lived in a stable, adequate environment, and the desirability of maintaining continuity of that environment.

(5) The permanence, as a family unit, of the existing or proposed custodial home or homes.

(6) The moral fitness of each party, insofar as it affects the welfare of the child.

(7) The mental and physical health of each party.

(8) The home, school, and community history of the child.

(9) The reasonable preference of the child, if the court deems the child to be of sufficient age to express a preference.

(10) The willingness and ability of each party to facilitate and encourage a close and continuing relationship between the child and the other party.

(11) The distance between the respective residences of the parties.

(12) The responsibility for the care and rearing of the child previously exercised by each party.

## 12. Factors Used in Determining Custody and Visitation Rulings in Louisiana

"How can I prove that I should get custody of my children?"
—Kim T.
age 30, divorcing, two children, commercial artist
Shreveport, Louisiana

Other often-unspoken or unconstitutional variables that influence a judge's custody decision include the following:

1. The gender of the child and parent (maternal/paternal preferences)
2. The age of the child and parent
3. The sexual preference of the parent
4. The significant other(s) of a parent (i.e., new spouse, boyfriend, girlfriend, other relatives, etc.)
5. The criminal and/or driving record of a parent
6. The race of the child and parent
7. The religious orientation of a parent
8. The temporary custody arrangements currently in effect
9. Keeping children together
10. The work schedules of the parents
11. The financial resources of a parent
12. The alcohol or drug abuse of a parent
13. The history of neglect or abuse of a parent
14. Which parent lives in the state, county (parish), and city ("home cooking!")

## 13. Your Child's Preference

"When my boy was young, I thought that he should live with his mother so I let her have custody. Now Steve is fourteen years old and has indicated that he would prefer to live with me and my new wife. Does Steve's preference to live with me count?"
—Clifton L.
age 37, divorced and remarried
one child from first marriage, attorney
Algiers, Louisiana

One of the most commonly asked questions that lawyers receive in custody disputes is whether the child's preference will be considered by the judge. There is no set age for a minor child to testify; however, if your child is mature, a judge might allow him to testify in open court or in the judge's chambers.

The judge may consider your child's maturity, intelligence, willingness to testify, emotional stability, and susceptibility to being bribed or unduly persuaded ("brainwashed").

Children may testify against the "better" parent because of the lack of discipline and rules of the other parent, the bribes of the other parent, or one parent's lies about the other. Children often change their minds on a regular basis. It is not surprising to see that a child tells each parent, in private, that he or she wishes to reside with that parent.

Having the child testify can be very stressful on the child and may lead to psychological problems, such as guilt regarding having to choose one parent over the other. You should first ask yourself whether your child should provide any testimony. Please be very cautious about bringing your children to court. The event can be very traumatic.

As a rule of thumb, most children thirteen or older will be allowed to testify as to their preferences and any other material facts that they have observed. Often a child's preference is revealed to the judge through the report of an evaluator. The child talks to the evaluator, and this information is often related to the judge and is often a significant factor in the evaluator's custody recommendation to the court. Usually, children under thirteen years old can tell their preference to the evaluator.

Custodial mothers are more likely than custodial fathers to have never been married. Custodial fathers are more likely to be currently married than their female counterparts, and both parents are equally likely to have been divorced or separated.

Generally, fathers with custody are older than mothers with custody. Approximately 46 percent of custodial fathers are over forty years old. Only 11 percent of custodial fathers are thirty years old or younger. Custodial fathers have more education than the average custodial mother. Men with custody are twice as likely to have a college degree (National Center for Health Statistics).

Children with fathers who are actively involved in their school lives receive improved grades and are less likely to fail a grade and/or be expelled.

The judge will consider your involvement in the child's life. Become very involved in your child's life.

For each child, who is the following person after you in your child's life? What is your relationship with this person? How can you develop a better relationship with that person? Will he or she be a good witness for your custody case?

## 14. Closed Custody Hearing Available

C.C. Art. 135. Closed custody hearing

A custody hearing may be closed to the public.

## 15. Visitation Rights

C.C. Art. 136. Award of visitation rights

A. A parent not granted custody or joint custody of a child is entitled to reasonable visitation rights unless the court finds, after a hearing, that visitation would not be in the best interest of the child.

B. Under extraordinary circumstances, a relative, by blood or affinity, or a former stepparent or stepgrandparent, not granted custody of the child may be granted reasonable visitation rights if the court finds that it is in the best interest of the child. In determining the best interest of the child, the court shall consider:

(1) The length and quality of the prior relationship between the child and the relative.

(2) Whether the child is in need of guidance, enlightenment, or tutelage which can best be provided by the relative.

(3) The preference of the child if he is determined to be of sufficient maturity to express a preference.

(4) The willingness of the relative to encourage a close relationship between the child and his parent or parents.

(5) The mental and physical health of the child and the relative.

C. In the event of a conflict between this Article and *R.S. 9:344* (emphasis added) or 345, the provisions of the statute shall supersede those of this Article.

Important Potential Witnesses in a Custody Dispute

- •Teachers
- • Day-care providers/baby-sitter/nanny
- • Coaches
- • Doctors
- • Dentist
- • Priest/pastor/rabbi/spiritual leader
- • Neighbors
- • Child's best friends

- Boy scout/cub scout/girl scout/brownie leaders
- School principal
- PTA members
- Sunday-school teachers
- Guidance counselor
- Relatives actively involved in child's life
- Other persons actively involved in child's life
- Police officers summoned to any domestic dispute
- Housekeeper
- Psychiatrist/sociologist/social worker
- School nurse
- Instructors of extracurricular activities

## 16. Find Out Who Is the Primary Caretaker of Your Child

"How can I show that I am my daughter's primary caretaker?"
—Elizabeth R.
age 40, divorcing, one child, casino executive
New Orleans, Louisiana

An excellent way to assist your attorney and the judge is to establish which parent is actively involved in the day-to-day activities of your child's life. Ask yourself, and tell your attorney, who does (or doesn't do) the following tasks:

Factors in Determining Who Is the Primary Caregiver

- Who wakes up your child?
- Who bathes your child?
- Who grooms your child?
- Who dresses your child?
- Who buys the groceries for your child?
- Who prepares the meals/cooks for your child?
- Who buys your child's clothing?
- Who buys your child's books and uniforms?
- Who takes your child to and from school and/or day care?
- Who prepares the school lunches for your child?
- Who takes your child to and from extracurricular activities?
- Who coaches or attends the extracurricular activities of your child?
- Who participates in the boy-scout or girl-scout activities of your child?

- Who attends the PTA meetings?
- Who takes your child to the doctor?
- Who takes your child to the dentist or orthodontist?
- Who keeps the medical records?
- Who stays home from work in order to take care of your sick child?
- Who takes your child to church or synagogue?
- Who takes your child to Sunday school?
- Who assists your child with his or her homework?
- Who attends parent/teacher conferences?
- Who monitors what your child watches on television or at the movies?
- Who changes the diapers?
- Who toilet trains your child?
- Who disciplines your child?
- Who knows your child's friends?
- Who speaks to your child's guidance counselor?
- Who cleans your child's house or bedroom?
- Who cleans your child's clothes?
- Who tucks your child into bed at night?
- Who reads your child bedtime stories?
- Who keeps the house safe for your child?
- Who takes your child to birthday parties?
- Who takes the child trick or treating?
- Who regularly communicates with your child?
- Who has custody of any other siblings?
- What else do you do for your child?

Keep receipts and documents regarding all of the foregoing activities. While loving and helping your child, you will inevitably incur expenses, receive receipts, receive documents, and take photographs. These documents and things can assist you in proving your active participation in your child's life.

## 17. Soul-Search and Do a Personal Inventory and Assessment or Why You Want Custody

"I hurt my back at work. Now they have me on social security disability. I really want to have custody of my daughter, but I'm in pain all of the time and I truly wonder if I can take care of her."

—Murray A.
age 32, divorcing, one child
disabled worker
Alexandria, Louisiana

By answering above questions in section 16, you will be able to come to grips with your actual involvement in your child's life. If you score yourself high on your personal involvement with your child, then you should move to the next inquiry as to why you want the primary physical custody of your child.

If you scored yourself low or less involved in the day-to-day activities of your child's life, be honest with yourself and evaluate what is in the best interest of your child.

Regardless of how you scored yourself or your spouse, as a parent, please revisit your shortcomings and evaluate how you can become more involved. This constructive criticism and the acting upon it should compel you to be a better parent and significantly improve your chances of becoming the primary custodial parent of your child.

## 18. Write a Detailed Letter to Your Attorney That Describes Attributes and Shortcomings of Both Parents

By writing a detailed letter to your attorney that describes the attributes and shortcomings of both parents, you will be able to force yourself to soul-search, and you will assist your attorney in preparing the custody case and resolving the matter in the best interest of the children. Be sure to write on the top of each sheet and on each side of the letter that the letter is addressed to your attorney and is a "CONFIDENTIAL ATTORNEY-CLIENT COMMUNICATION AND WORK PRODUCT." By so describing the letter, you may prevent your spouse from using the letter against you if he or she gets his or her hands on the correspondence. Once completed, give the letter to your attorney.

Correct your bad habits. We all have bad habits. Realize and work on them.

## 19. Go to Co-Parenting Classes

A child is often the victim and pawn in a couple's emotionally charged turmoil. Co-parenting courses are designed to bring parents back to the core of their responsibility to love, communicate with, and take care of their child. Another goal of co-parenting classes is to emphasize the important fact that although a couple no longer will be husband and wife they will remain parents of that child. Creating a level of harmony is important for the sake of the child. Go to a co-parenting course. Every parent can be enriched by the experience.

R.S. 9:306. Seminar for divorcing parents

A. Upon an affirmative showing that the facts and circumstances of the particular case before the court warrant such an order, a court exercising jurisdiction over family matters may require the parties in a custody or visitation proceeding to attend and complete a court-approved seminar designed to educate and inform the parties of the needs of the children.

B. If the court chooses to require participation in such a seminar, it shall adopt rules to accomplish the goals of Subsection A of this Section, which rules shall include but not be limited to the following:

(1) Criteria for evaluating a seminar provider and its instructors.

(2) Criteria to assure selected programs provide and incorporate into the provider's fee structure the cost of services to indigents.

(3) The amount of time a participant must take part in the program, which shall be a minimum of three hours but not exceed four hours nor shall the costs exceed twenty-five dollars per person.

(4) The time within which a party must complete the program.

C. For purposes of this Section, "instructor" means any psychiatrist, psychologist, professional counselor, social worker licensed under state law, or in any parish other than Orleans, means a person working with a court- approved, nonprofit program of an accredited university created for educating divorcing parents with children. All instructors must have received advanced training in instructing co-parenting or similar seminars.

D. The seminar shall focus on the developmental needs of children, with emphasis on fostering the child's emotional health. The seminar shall be informative and supportive and shall direct people desiring additional information or help to appropriate resources. The course content shall contain but not be limited to the following subjects:

(1) The developmental stages of childhood, the needs of children at different ages, and age appropriate expectations of children.

(2) Stress indicators in children adjusting to divorce, the grief process, and avoiding delinquency.

(3) The possible enduring emotional effects of divorce on the child.

(4) Changing parental and marital roles.

(5) Recommendations with respect to visitation designed to enhance the child's relationship with both parents.

(6) Financial obligations of child rearing.

(7) Conflict management and dispute resolution.

E. Nonviolent acts or communications made during the seminar, which are otherwise relevant to the subject matter of a divorce, custody, or visitation proceeding, are confidential, not subject to disclosure, and may not be used as evidence in favor of or against a participant in the pending proceeding. This rule does not require the exclusion of any evidence otherwise discoverable merely because it is presented or otherwise made during the seminar.

## 20. Know When and What to Tell Your Children

It is a difficult thing to tell your children that you are divorcing. No matter how hard, it must be done. Once the decision has been made to divorce, the children should be told. If possible, both parents should talk with the children together. The meeting with the children should be an honest discussion of your separation. Emphasize that the breakup is not their fault and that the decision to divorce is made and they cannot change it. Do not degrade or cast blame or fault on the other parent. Frequently reassure the children that both of you are still their parents and that they are loved and will not be abandoned. Tell them that you will take care of them and keep them safe.

After you have comforted and reassured your children, inform them, as well as you can, of the proposed living arrangements.

If one parent is absent and/or not willing to cooperate in a joint meeting with the children, speak to your children with the same honest love and affection. Continually remember to divorce yourself from your emotions and not degrade or blame the other parent in the presence of the children.

Anticipate that, regardless of how well your discussions with your children have gone, they will likely experience some feelings of abandonment, fear, guilt, and despair. It is natural. Perhaps the best advice is to continue to communicate with your children. Tell and show them that they are loved. To some degree, they too are going through stress of the divorce process.

## 21. Do Not Underestimate the Maternal Preference

"Do I even have a chance to get custody of my children? I hear that the mother always gets the kids."
—Robert S.
age 27, divorcing, two children
computer sales
Covington, Louisiana

In the seventies, gender-based presumptions in the law were declared unconstitutional by the United States Supreme Court, *Orr v. Orr*, 440 US 268 (1979). Prior to this decision, the "tender years doctrine," which provided that the mother should have custody of infants and toddlers in their tender years, was routinely cited as the basis of custody decisions. Mothers had to be found unfit to lose custody of their very young children.

Judges throughout the nation are slowly coming into the twenty-first century. Unfortunately, gender bias still exits. For generations, young children, regardless of their age, were thought to be best served by being with their mothers. Various psychological and sociological studies have varied results on what is in the best interest of child based on his or her gender and age. Many courts provide preferences toward fathers for male children in their teens. As the maternal/paternal debate races on, children are being placed with significant consideration given to the gender of the parent. The best way to overcome gender bias hurdles is to show the court your overwhelming involvement in your child's life.

## 22. Mediation

Many courts require mediation in a custody dispute. Please refer to the "Mediation and Arbitration" chapter.

R.S. 9:332. Custody or visitation proceeding; mediation

A. The court may order the parties to mediate their differences in a custody or visitation proceeding. The mediator may be agreed upon by the parties or, upon their failure to agree, selected by the court. The court may stay any further determination of custody or visitation for a period not to exceed thirty days from the date of issuance of such an order. The court may order the costs of mediation to be paid in advance by either party or both parties jointly. The court may apportion the costs of the mediation between the parties if agreement is reached on custody or visitation. If mediation concludes without agreement between the parties, the costs of mediation shall be taxed as costs of court. The costs of mediation shall be subject to approval by the court.

B. If an agreement is reached by the parties, the mediator shall prepare a written, signed, and dated agreement. A consent judgment incorporating the agreement shall be submitted to the court for its approval.

C. Evidence of conduct or statements made in mediation is not admissible in any proceeding. This rule does not require the exclusion of any evidence otherwise discoverable merely because it is presented in the course of mediation. Facts disclosed, other than conduct or statements made in mediation, are not inadmissible by virtue of first having been disclosed in mediation.

R.S. 9:333. Duties of mediator

A. The mediator shall assist the parties in formulating a written, signed, and dated agreement to mediate which shall identify the controversies between the parties, affirm the parties' intent to resolve these controversies through mediation, and specify the circumstances under which the mediation may terminate.

B. The mediator shall advise each of the parties participating in the mediation to obtain review by an attorney of any agreement reached as a result of the mediation prior to signing such an agreement.

C. The mediator shall be impartial and has no power to impose a solution on the parties.

R.S. 9:334. Mediator qualifications

A. In order to serve as a qualified mediator under the provisions of this Subpart, a person shall:

(1)(a) Possess a college degree and complete a minimum of forty hours of general mediation training and twenty hours of specialized training in the mediation of child custody disputes; or

(b) Hold a license or certification as an attorney, psychiatrist, psychologist, social worker, marriage and family counselor, professional counselor, or clergyman and complete a minimum of sixteen hours of general mediation training and twenty hours of specialized training in the mediation of child custody disputes.

(2) Complete a minimum of eight hours of co-mediation training under the direct supervision of a mediator who is qualified in accordance with the provisions of Paragraph (3) of this Subsection, and who has served a minimum of fifty hours as a dispute mediator.

(3) Mediators who prior to August 15, 1997, satisfied the provisions of Paragraph (1) of this Subsection and served a minimum of fifty hours as a child custody dispute mediator are not required to complete eight hours of co- mediation training in order to serve as a qualified mediator and are qualified to supervise co-mediation training as provided in Paragraph (2) of this Subsection.

(4) Have served as a Louisiana district, appellate, or supreme court judge for at least ten years, have completed at least twenty hours of specialized mediation training in child custody disputes, and no longer be serving as a judge.B. The training specified in Paragraph A(1) above shall include instruction as to the following:

(1) The Louisiana judicial system and judicial procedure in domestic cases.

(2) Ethical standards, including confidentiality and conflict of interests.

(3) Child development, including the impact of divorce on development.

(4) Family systems theory.

(5) Communication skills.

(6) The mediation process and required document execution.

C. A dispute mediator initially qualified under the provisions of this Subpart shall, in order to remain qualified, complete a minimum of twenty hours of clinical education in dispute mediation every two calendar years.

D. Upon request of the court, a mediator shall furnish satisfactory evidence of the following:

(1) Educational degrees, licenses and certifications.(2) Compliance with qualifications established by this Subpart.(3) Completion of clinical education.

E. The Louisiana State Bar Association, Alternative Dispute Resolution Section, may promulgate rules and regulations governing dispute mediator registration and qualifications, and may establish a fee not to exceed one hundred dollars for registration sufficient to cover associated costs.

## 23. Custody/Visitation Evaluations—Get Experts and Use Tests

Make sure that the evaluator interviews the children, the parents, and any other person who can shed light on your attributes as a parent, your spouse's deficits as a parent, or your child's needs. The failure to request that the evaluator interview third parties is often a tragic flaw that can affect the evaluator's custody recommendation. Use your list of favorable witnesses that you outlined in Your Personal Profile, found in appendix A.

R.S. 9:331. Custody or visitation proceeding; evaluation by mental health professional

A. The court may order an evaluation of a party or the child in a custody or visitation proceeding for good cause shown. The evaluation shall be made by a mental health professional selected by the parties or by the court. The court may render judgment for costs of the evaluation, or any part thereof, against any party or parties, as it may consider equitable.

B. The court may order a party or the child to submit to and cooperate in the evaluation, testing, or interview by the mental health professional. The mental health professional shall provide the court and the parties with a written report. The mental health professional shall serve as the witness of the court, subject to cross-examination by a party.

R.S. 9:331.1 Drug testing in custody or visitation proceeding

The court for good cause shown may, after a contradictory hearing, order a party in a custody or visitation proceeding to submit to specified drug tests and the collection of hair, urine, tissue, and blood samples as required by appropriate testing procedures within a time period set by the court. The refusal to submit to the tests may be taken into consideration by the court. The provisions of *R.S. 9:397.2* (emphasis added) and 397.3(A), (B), and (C) shall govern the admissibility of the test results. The fact that the court orders a drug test and the results of such test shall be confidential and shall not be admissible in any other proceedings. The court may render judgment for costs of the drug tests against any party or parties, as it may consider equitable.

## 24. Prepare for a Potential Visit from the Department of Social Services or a Court-Appointed Evaluator

In many custody disputes in which a private-sector evaluator is not used, the Department of Social Services, also referred to in many states as Family Services, provides a social worker who conducts interviews of the parents, children, and other relevant parties. The social worker also may visit your house to inspect your living environment. Make sure that your house is clean and tidy. Traces that you are a member of the local cult or paramilitary group should be removed.

## 25. Watch Out for Undue Influences in the Evaluation Process

Some attorneys and/or parents attempt to unfairly influence the evaluation process by attempting to select or recommend an evaluator who may be prone to side with a particular gender or a particular attorney. Ask your attorney to inquire into the past personal and professional relationships between the opposing attorney and the evaluator.

Another grave concern in the evaluation process is the tendency of many parents to lie about the other parent in an attempt to gain favor with the evaluator. If you believe that your spouse might stoop to such despicable tactics, anticipate any potential lies and provide the evaluator with evidence, including other witnesses who would impeach your spouse's false statements. If your spouse is caught in a lie, you can gain a significant advantage.

## 26. Find Out the Track Record of the Evaluator

If you reasonably believe that the evaluator is unfairly biased toward the other side, ask your lawyer to request that the evaluator send copies of all correspondences to or from any attorney or party in your case.

## 27. Consider Getting an Independent Expert/Evaluator

If you reasonably believe that the evaluator's bias is overwhelming, ask your attorney to seek appointment of another evaluator. If the court refuses, your attorney can request that another evaluation be conducted by a privately retained expert. This may be very expensive; however, in a hotly contested custody battle, your own expert evaluator could make all the difference.

## 28. If the Odds Are Stacked Against You, Ask That Various Tests Be Conducted

Many psychological tools are now available to custody evaluators. These tests are used to evaluate whether a parent has any significant psychological disorders or personality flaws that would substantially interfere with parenting.

The MMPIT (Minnesota Multiphase Personality Inventory Test) is widely used to objectively diagnose various personality traits and abnormalities of parents and children, which can assist an evaluator in a custody evaluation. Without going into the details of each test, it is important to know that most psychological tests involve the evaluator's administration of the test and his or her subjective scoring and interpretation.

Tests on the children also can be used to see whether the child has any emotional, behavioral, or learning disorders that need to be addressed. Psychiatrists, sociologists, and social workers conduct various tests that are used to evaluate behavior patterns and characteristics of children.

## 29. Both Parents Are Entitled to Receive Medical and School Records

Pursuant to the U.S. Family Educational Rights and Privacy Act, either parent, whether custodial or noncustodial, is entitled to full access of his or her child's school records. Upon request, noncustodial parents are allowed to receive written documents normally sent to the custodial parent, such as grades/report cards and notices of parent/teacher conferences.

Additionally, insist on being notified if any health or medical conditions arise concerning your children.

R.S. 9:351. Access to records of child

Notwithstanding any provision of law to the contrary, access to records and information pertaining to a minor child, including but not limited to medical, dental, and school records, shall not be denied to a parent solely because he is not the child's custodial or domiciliary parent.

Have a provision in the court order/custody plan stating that your child shall not be placed in any school or camp without a court order or without your written permission.

## 30. If the Other Parent Has a Drug or Alcohol Problem, Ask the Court to Conduct Random Drug Tests and/or Order That the Addicted Parent Go to Alcoholics Anonymous or Narcotics Anonymous

It is beneficial to all concerned for a parent to seek assistance with his or her drug or alcohol problem. It is also important that the judge address the problem because of the potentially devastating results that could occur if the substance abuse is left unattended.

Additionally, bringing to the court's attention the legitimate substance-abuse problems of the other parent gives you a competitive advantage in the custody dispute.

Ask your attorney to seek injunctions prohibiting your spouse from drinking, being intoxicated, and/or using drugs in the presence of the children.

## 31. In Cases of Substance Abuse, Insist on Supervised Visitation

> "I am not letting my child around Jeff until he gets off the alcohol."
>
> —Debra H.
> age 26, divorcing, one child
> real-estate agent
> Lake Charles, Louisiana

When your spouse has a substance-abuse problem, the health and welfare of your children are in jeopardy. Your attorney should request the court to restrict the other parent's visitation privileges to supervised visitation, if not to terminate visitation.

The person supervising the visitation should be trustworthy and reliable. Courts frequently order supervised visitation and believe that the children are being adequately protected. Too often, the person ordered to supervise the visitation is irresponsible and/or is not even present at the time of the visitation sessions. Insist on a responsible party to conduct the supervision of the visitation.

### Restrictions on Visitation

R.S. 9:341. Restriction on visitation

A. Whenever the court finds by a preponderance of the evidence that a parent has subjected his or her child to physical abuse, or sexual abuse or exploitation, or has permitted such abuse or exploitation of the child, the court shall prohibit visitation between the abusive parent and the abused child until such parent proves that visitation would not cause physical, emotional, or psychological damage to the child. Should visitation be allowed, the court shall order such restrictions, conditions, and safeguards necessary to minimize any risk of harm to the child. All costs incurred in compliance with the provisions of this Section shall be borne by the abusive parent.

B. When visitation has been prohibited by the court pursuant to Subsection A, and the court subsequently authorizes restricted visitation, the parent whose visitation has been restricted shall not remove the child from the jurisdiction of the court except for good cause shown and with the prior approval of the court.

R.S. 9:342. Bond to secure child custody or visitation order

For good cause shown, a court may, on its own motion or upon the motion of any party, require the posting of a bond or other security by a party to insure compliance with a child visitation order and to indemnify the other party for the payment of any costs incurred.

## 32. Return of Child Kept in Violation of Custody and Visitation Order

R.S. 9:343. Return of child kept in violation of custody and visitation order

A. Upon presentation of a certified copy of a custody and visitation rights order rendered by a court of this state, together with the sworn affidavit of the custodial parent, the judge, who shall have jurisdiction for the limited purpose of effectuating the remedy provided by this Section by virtue of either the presence of the child or litigation pending before the court, may issue a civil warrant directed to law enforcement authorities to return the child to the custodial parent pending further order of the court having jurisdiction over the matter.

B. The sworn affidavit of the custodial parent shall include all of the following:

(1) A statement that the custody and visitation rights order is true and correct.

(2) A summary of the status of any pending custody proceeding.

(3) The fact of the removal of or failure to return the child in violation of the custody and visitation rights order.

(4) A declaration that the custodial parent desires the child returned.

### 33. Visitation Rights for Grandparents and Siblings

"My son divorced his wife and now, I never get to see my grandchild. Is there anything that I can do?"

—Lloyd G.
age 66, grandfather, retired electrician
New Orleans, Louisiana

Custody is seldom awarded to grandparents when one or more of the parents are alive. Most states will allow grandparents the opportunity to file for custody or visitation. In the evaluation process of grandparent custody/visitation requests, the courts will turn to the "best interest of the child" standard, as well as look at the general preference to award custody to the parents.

The basic ways that grandparents get legal custody of children are as follows:

1. One or both parents have died
2. One or both parents are incarcerated
3. One or both parents have substance-abuse problems
4. One or both parents have been neglectful and/or abusive

Grandparent visitation can be quite beneficial to a child—if the grandparent does not play mind games with the child in an attempt to brainwash the child into taking sides with a particular parent or grandparent.

Courts will review the appropriateness of grandparent custody or visitation on a case-by-case basis. Most courts do recognize the importance of an extended family and the advantages of positive role models.

R.S. 9:344. Visitation rights of grandparents and siblings

A. If one of the parties to a marriage dies, is interdicted, or incarcerated, and there is a minor child or children of such marriage, the parents of the deceased, interdicted, or incarcerated party without custody of such minor child or children may have reasonable visitation rights to the child or children of the marriage during their minority, if the court in its discretion finds that such visitation rights would be in the best interest of the child or children.

B. When the parents of a minor child or children live in concubinage and one of the parents dies, or is incarcerated, the parents of the deceased or incarcerated party may have reasonable visitation rights to the child or children during their minority, if the court in its discretion finds that such visitation rights would be in the best interest of the child or children.

C. If one of the parties to a marriage dies or is incarcerated, the siblings of a minor child or children of the marriage may have reasonable visitation rights to such child or children during their minority if the court in its discretion finds that such visitation rights would be in the best interest of the child or children.

D. If the parents of a minor child or children of the marriage are legally separated or living apart for a period of six months, the grandparents or siblings of the child or children may have reasonable visitation rights to the child or children during their minority, if the court in its discretion find that such visitation rights would be in the best interest of the child or children.

## 34. Appointment of an Attorney to Represent Child in Custody or Visitation Proceedings

R.S. 9:345. Appointment of attorney in child custody or visitation proceedings

A. In any child custody or visitation proceeding, the court, upon its own motion, upon motion of any parent or party, or upon motion of the child, may appoint an attorney to represent the child if, after a contradictory hearing, the court determines such appointment would be in the best interest of the child. In determining the best interest of the child, the court shall consider:

(1) Whether the child custody or visitation proceeding is exceptionally intense or protracted.

(2) Whether an attorney representing the child could provide the court with significant information not otherwise readily available or likely to be presented to the court.

(3) Whether there exists a possibility that neither parent is capable of providing an adequate and stable environment for the child.

(4) Whether the interests of the child and those of either parent, or of another party to the proceeding, conflict.

(5) Any other factor relevant in determining the best interest of the child.

B. The court shall appoint an attorney to represent the child if, in the contradictory hearing, any party presents a prima facie case that a parent or other person caring for the child has sexually, physically, or emotionally abused the child or knew or should have known that the child was being abused.

C. The order appointing an attorney to represent the child shall serve as his enrollment as counsel of record on behalf of the child.

D. Upon appointment as attorney for the child, the attorney shall interview the child, review all relevant records, and conduct discovery as deemed necessary to ascertain facts relevant to the child's custody or visitation.

E. The appointed attorney shall have the right to make any motion and participate in the custody or visitation hearing to the same extent as authorized for either parent.

F. Any costs associated with the appointment of an attorney at law shall be apportioned among the parties as the court deems just, taking into consideration the parties' ability to pay. When the parties' ability to pay is limited, the court shall attempt to secure proper representation without compensation.

## 35. Be Careful if Your Spouse's Lawyer Is Fired

On occasion a person will fire his lawyer and instruct him to immediately withdraw from the court record, in order to avoid being served pleadings and orders through the attorney. If you have concerns that your spouse may fire his attorney, ask your lawyer to request the sheriff to serve both the attorney and the other parent.

## 36. What to Do if the Other Parent Denies You Access to Your Children

The best action is to anticipate a problem before it arises so that your lawyer can address the possibility with the court. Hopefully, admonitions and restraining orders can be placed to prevent the denial of access to your children. If all else fails, the following are potential actions:

1. File a motion for visitation.
2. File a motion to have the other parent held in contempt of court if a prior order exists awarding you custody/visitation.

3. Seek a reduction or suspension in child support until the other parent obeys the custody/visitation order.
4. File a motion to modify the prior custody/visitation order.
5. File a motion for sole custody.
6. File a motion seeking the other party to post a bond to ensure your custody/visitation rights.
7. Ask your attorney for other advice.
8. Seek assistance from law-enforcement officers to enforce a custody/visitation order.

Regrettably, sometimes there are reasons to deny access (i.e., for abuse, neglect, and/or substance-abuse problems that affect the children). Courts, counselors, child-protection agencies, battered-women shelters, and law-enforcement agencies are prepared to deal with these problems.

## 37. Specify the Visitation Rights

When working on a visitation plan for both parents, it is usually a great error to simply allow for "reasonable" or "liberal" visitation. A custody and visitation plan or order that contains this language is one that does not address the real-world problems of visitation disputes. If the term "reasonable" is used in the visitation plan, the parent seeking the visitation is subject to the whims of the primary custodial parent. What is reasonable to one parent may be quite unreasonable to the other.

The best way to avoid the nightmares that can exist with a lazy visitation plan is to insist on specified visitation. A visitation plan that explicitly identifies the dates and times of visitation will not be subject to the whims of one parent or the interpretation of either parent.

Checklist to Assist in Creating a Visitation Schedule

- Birthdays
- Christmas Eve/day/holiday
- Graduations
- Grandparent events/other relative-related special occasions
- Easter day/holiday
- Extracurricular activities
- Hanukkah
- Father's Day
- Halloween
- Fourth of July
- Labor Day

- Mardi Gras
- Memorial Day
- Mother's Day
- New Year's Eve/Day
- Sporting events
- Thanksgiving Day/holiday
- Spring break
- Summer vacation
- Other dates or occasions that have special meanings

### Maximize Your Visitation Rights

A child has the general right to continue his relationship with both parents. Parents seeking visitation should consider maximizing their specified dates of visitation. Remember to design a visitation plan that will be compatible with your work schedule.

Your imagination may be the limit to what days you may seek. Consider the following:

1. Any holiday recognized by your local, state, or federal government
2. Ask a florist—they have holidays for everything under the sun!

## 38. Formally Agree on Cost Arrangements Involved with Visitation and Travel

Often parties agree to visitation schedules without having a formal agreement as to who pays the cost of any travel involved. Have a written agreement and/or order that sets forth the financial responsibilities associated with any travel involved in the visitation process.

## 39. Allowing Visitation Creates a Free Baby-Sitter

"We divorced two years ago. I love taking care of my daughter, but I have to admit, it's hard and I can use a break sometime. I used to be so angry at Peter that I did not want to give him any more visitation than I had to. After time, I realized that I was not being fair to him or my daughter so things have changed. With my new flexibility, I've learned that I can now go out on a date and not feel bad about it."

—Amanda T.
age 36, divorced, one child
marketing executive
River Ridge, Louisiana

Many people who are in a heated, contested custody or visitation dispute often forget that allowing visitation allows for a free baby-sitter. The thirst for your spouse's blood often clouds your view of your future needs and desires. Months down the road, you may want a break from your children to go to the beach or take a vacation with a new lover.

## 40. Get More Visitation and Pay Less Child Support

In most states, child-support guidelines and schedules are based on the parent receiving visitation having average visitation rights, such as having the children on alternating weekends, alternating major holidays, and several weeks during the summer. If you receive visitation rights that are greater than the visitation rights normally given by the court, ask your lawyer to seek a decrease in your child-support obligation, as you are incurring expenses in support of your children when they are in your custody that were not envisioned by the child-support schedule.

## 41. If the Other Parent Does Not Use His or Her Visitation Rights, Ask for More Child Support and/or Payment for Baby-Sitting

Again, if your child-support guidelines envision average visitation, and the other parent is not taking the children during his scheduled visitation days, then ask your attorney to seek an increase in child support for the extra days and nights that you have custody of your children. An alternative is to ask the court to order the other parent to pay or reimburse for extra food, utilities, and day-care or baby-sitting expenses incurred because he did not pick up the children pursuant to the visitation plan.

Most courts will not compel a parent to exercise his visitation rights; however, a court is much more likely to award you money for the extra expenses incurred because of your unanticipated cost of keeping the children when the other parent should have.

## 42. If Your Child Does Not Want to See the Other Parent, Inform Your Attorney and the Court

Frequently, children do not wish to have visitation with the non-custodial parent. When this occurs, immediately inform your attorney. Whether or not your child's hesitancy has any valid basis may ultimately be determined by the judge. By informing your attorney of the problem, and allowing him to inform the court, you have diminished the chances that the court would sanction you for interfering in the other parent's visitation rights. If you do not inform your attorney of the problem, then the other parent might allege that you are persuading your child to resist visitation. Let the court and/or the court's evaluator get to the heart of the problem.

### 43. Insist on Addresses and Telephone Numbers and Maximize Telephone Access

The parent with the physical custody of the children may attempt to prohibit or restrict your physical or telephone access to your children. Insist that you have the addresses and telephone numbers of each place where the children will be residing. Additionally, you may wish to have an agreement on the minimum and maximum telephone calls the noncustodial parent can have with the children. A court order delineating the agreement will assist in eliminating future problems.

If the parents are cooperative, reasonable open access to the children is preferable.

### 44. Know When to Request a Modification of Visitation Rights

The custodial parent may wish to request a change in the visitation schedule if the other parent routinely refuses to honor the visitation plan and/or refuses to return the child at the designated time and place.

### 45. Watch Out for "Custody Blackmail"

"She won't let me see the kids unless I agree to pay her more child support and alimony."

—Paul Z.
age 38, divorcing, two children, farmer
Franklin, Louisiana

As stated in the spousal- and child-support chapters of this book, be aware of any attempts on the part of your spouse to threaten a custody battle when he or she really does not want physical custody but merely seeks financial advantage in another area of dispute. These threats of a custody battle are often used in a hidden or blatant agenda to force a spouse to make monetary concessions. If this occurs, speak to your attorney about it.

### 46. Relocation of Children

R.S. 9:355.3. Notice of proposed relocation of child to other parent

A. A parent entitled to primary custody of a child shall notify the other parent of a proposed relocation of the child's principal residence as required by *R.S. 9:355.4* (emphasis added).

B. If both parents have equal physical custody of a child, a parent shall notify the other parent of a proposed relocation of the child's principal residence as required by *R.S. 9:355.4* (emphasis added).

C. In the absence of a court order or express written agreement confected by the parties which designates the principal residence of a child, a parent shall notify the other parent of a proposed relocation of the child's principal residence as required by *R.S. 9:355.4* (emphasis added).

R.S. 9:355.4. Mailing notice of proposed relocation address

A. Notice of a proposed relocation of the principal residence of a child shall be given by registered or certified mail, return receipt requested, to the last known address of the parent no later than either:

(1) The sixtieth day before the date of the intended move or proposed relocation.

(2) The tenth day after the date that the parent knows the information required to be furnished by Subsection B of this Section, if the parent did not know and could not reasonably have known the information in sufficient time to comply with the sixty-day notice, and it is not reasonably possible to extend the time for relocation of the child.

B. The following information, if available, shall be included with the notice of intended relocation of the child:

(1) The intended new residence, including the specific address, if known.

(2) The mailing address, if not the same.

(3) The home telephone number, if known.

(4) The date of the intended move or proposed relocation.

(5) A brief statement of the specific reasons for the proposed relocation of a child, if applicable.

(6) A proposal for a revised schedule of visitation with the child.

C. A parent required to give notice of a proposed relocation shall have a continuing duty to provide the information required by this Section as that information becomes known.

R.S. 9:355.5. Court authorization to relocate

A parent seeking to relocate the principal residence of a child shall not, absent consent, remove the child pending resolution of dispute, or final order of the court, unless the parent obtains a temporary order to do so pursuant to *R.S. 9:355.10* (emphasis added).

R.S. 9:355.6. Failure to give notice of relocation or relocation without court authorization

The court may consider a failure to provide notice of a proposed relocation of a child or relocation without court authorization as provided by *R.S. 9:355.3* and *355.4* (emphasis added) as:

(1) A factor in making its determination regarding the relocation of a child.

(2) A basis for ordering the return of the child if the relocation has taken place without notice or court authorization.

(3) Sufficient cause to order the parent seeking to relocate the child to pay reasonable expenses and attorney fees incurred by the person objecting to the relocation.

R.S. 9:355.7. Failure to object to notice of proposed relocation

The primary custodian of a child or a parent who has equal physical custody may relocate the principal residence of a child after providing notice as provided by *R.S. 9:355.3* and *355.4* (emphasis added), unless the parent entitled to notice initiates a proceeding seeking a temporary or permanent order to prevent the relocation within twenty days after the receipt of the notice.

R.S. 9:355.8. Objection to relocation of child

A. A parent must initiate a summary proceeding objecting to a proposed relocation of the principal residence of a child within twenty days after receipt of notice and seek a temporary or permanent order to prevent the relocation.

B. Upon request of a copy of notice of objection, the court may promptly appoint an independent mental health expert to render a determination as to whether the proposed relocation is in the best interest of the child.

R.S. 9:355.9. Priority for temporary and final hearing

A hearing on either a temporary or permanent order permitting or restricting relocation shall be accorded appropriate priority on the court's docket.

R.S. 9:355.10. Temporary order

A. The court may grant, after a notice of objection has been filed, a temporary order allowing a parent to relocate.

B. The court, upon the request of the moving parent, may hold a limited evidentiary hearing on the proposed relocation but may not grant court authorization to remove the child on an ex parte basis.

C. If the court issues a temporary order authorizing a parent to relocate with the child, the court may not give undue weight to the temporary relocation as a factor in reaching its final determination.

D. If temporary relocation of a child is permitted, the court may require the parent relocating the child to provide reasonable security guaranteeing that the court ordered visitation with the child will not be interrupted or interfered with by the relocating parent or that the relocating parent will return the child if court authorization for the removal is denied at the final hearing.

R.S. 9:355.11. Proposed relocation not basis for modification

Providing notice of a proposed relocation of a child shall not constitute a change of circumstance warranting a change of custody. Moving without prior notice or moving in violation of a court order may constitute a change of circumstances warranting a modification of custody.

R.S. 9:355.12. Factors to determine contested relocation
In reaching its decision regarding a proposed relocation, the court shall consider the following factors:

(1) The nature, quality, extent of involvement, and duration of

the child's relationship with the parent proposing to relocate and with the non-relocating parent, siblings, and other significant persons in the child's life.

(2) The age, developmental stage, needs of the child, and the likely impact the relocation will have on the child's physical, educational, and emotional development, taking into consideration any special needs of the child.

(3) The feasibility of preserving the relationship between the non-relocating parent and the child through suitable visitation arrangements, considering the logistics and financial circumstances of the parties.

(4) The child's preference, taking into consideration the age and maturity of the child.

(5) Whether there is an established pattern of conduct of the parent seeking the relocation, either to promote or thwart the relationship of the child and the non-relocating party.

(6) Whether the relocation of the child will enhance the general quality of life for both the custodial parent seeking the relocation and the child, including but not limited to financial or emotional benefit or educational opportunity.

(7) The reasons of each parent for seeking or opposing the relocation.

(8) Any other factors affecting the best interest of the child.

R.S. 9:355.13. Burden of proof

The relocating parent has the burden of proof that the proposed relocation is made in good faith and is in the best interest of the child.

R.S. 9:355.14. Posting security

If relocation of a child is permitted, the court may require the parent relocating the child to provide reasonable security guaranteeing that the court ordered visitation with the child will not be interrupted or interfered with by the relocating party.

R.S. 9:355.15. Application of factors at initial hearing

If the issue of relocation is presented at the initial hearing to determine custody of and visitation with a child, the court shall apply the factors set forth in *R.S. 9:355.12* (emphasis added) in making its initial determination.

R.S. 9:355.16. Sanctions for unwarranted or frivolous proposal to relocate child or objection to relocation

A. After notice and a reasonable opportunity to respond, the court may impose a sanction on a parent proposing a relocation of the child or objecting to a proposed relocation of a child if it determines that the proposal was made or the objection was filed:

(1) To harass the other parent or to cause unnecessary delay or needless increase in the cost of litigation.

(2) Without being warranted by existing law or based on a frivolous argument.

(3) Based on allegations and other factual contentions which have no evidentiary support nor, if specifically so identified, could not have been reasonably believed to be likely to have evidentiary support after further investigation.

B. A sanction imposed under this Section shall be limited to what is sufficient to deter repetition of such conduct or comparable conduct by others similarly situated. The sanction may consist of, or include, directives of a nonmonetary nature, an order to pay a penalty to the court, or, if imposed on motion and warranted for effective deterrence, an order directing payment to the movant of some or all of the reasonable attorney fees and other expenses incurred as a direct result of the violation.

R.S. 9:355.17. Continuing jurisdiction

If the court grants authorization to relocate, the court may retain continuing, exclusive jurisdiction of the case after relocation of the child as long as the non-relocating parent remains in the state.

Chapter 8

# CHILD SUPPORT

## 1. Background and Statistics

The purpose of a child-support award is to provide financial assistance for a child based on the average monthly expenses associated with that child. The child-support award should be based on the proportionate income or earning capacity of the parents.

Each state has implemented child-support guidelines to assist the courts with a means of calculating what is legislatively presumed to be sufficient for the child's needs and fair relative to the parents' earnings.

### Quick Facts

Only 6.2 million (approximately half) of the 11.5 million custodial parents have a child-support award or agreement. Mothers receive child support awards at a higher rate than fathers. Annually, over 5 million custodial parents live without any award of child support from the other parent. Reasons for not seeking a child-support award include the custodial parent not wanting child support and the other parent not being able to afford to pay child support. Approximately one-third of the 5 million parents without child-support awards decided not to seek child support. Statistics from 1996 show that a mere 67 percent (or $11.9 billion dollars) of the $17.7 billion dollars of child support due to custodial parents is paid (U.S. Census Bureau).

Only half of custodial parents who have an order or agreement for child support receive payment in full. Unfortunately, approximately 25 percent of all custodial parents receive only partial payment. Worst of all, another 25 percent of custodial parents don't receive any child support at all.

Approximately, 90 percent of fathers who have joint custody pay

119

child support, while 80 percent of fathers who receive visitation pay child support (U. S. Census Bureau; American Bar Association).

State prosecutors report that approximately 2 to 5 percent of their child-support cases involve mothers who owe past-due child support (American Bar Association).

Before a child-support order can be made, paternity/maternity must be established. Paternity is discussed in chapter 6.

## 2. Standard of Living

### Quick Facts

Mothers who receive child support have a lower annual income, average $18,144 per year, than their male counterparts, who have an average income of $33,579 per year. Less than 5 percent of divorced or separated women raising children of the marriage receive alimony. Approximately 42 percent receive child support, and the average amount received by them is approximately $125 per child, per month (U.S. Census Bureau).

A widely cited study discovered that a year after a divorce, the standard of living of women and children drops by an average 73 percent, while men's standard of living actually increases an average of 42 percent. (Lenore Weitzman, "The Economics of Divorce: Social and Economic Consequences of Property, Alimony, and Child Support Awards," *UCLA Law Review* 28:1181, 1245 [1981].) Approximately one-third of all female-headed families with children live in poverty.

C.C. Art. 141. Child support; authority of court

In a proceeding for divorce or thereafter, the court may order either or both of the parents to provide an interim allowance or final support for a child based on the needs of the child and the ability of the parents to provide support.

The court may award an interim allowance only when a demand for final support is pending.

C.C. Art. 142. Modification or termination of child support award

An award of child support may be modified if the circumstances of the child or of either parent materially change and shall be terminated upon proof that it has become unnecessary.

C.C. Art. 227. Parental support and education of children.

Fathers and mothers, by the very act of marrying, contract together the obligation of supporting, maintaining, and educating their children.

C.C. Art. 3501.1. Actions for arrearages of child support

An action to make executory arrearages of child support is subject to a liberative prescription of ten years.

## 3. Child-Support Models

There are two basic models for child support:

1. Fixed child-support payments that have no provisions for future modifications
2. Escalator Clause/variable child-support payments that periodically change proportionate to actual changes in the parents' income, the consumer price index (CPI), or some other variable

## 4. Child-Support Guidelines

Federal law requires each state to create child-support guidelines (42 USC 667). Child-support guidelines presume that parents with similar incomes should be required to pay relatively equal amounts in child support. Likewise, a further goal of the implementation of child-support guidelines is to prevent large variability in the child-support awards under similar circumstances. Unfortunately, our national and state systems are seriously flawed, as they operate under a false premise that people can accurately calculate child-support figures and that parents will not misrepresent their income and/or earning capacity. If one haphazardly implements Louisiana's child-support guidelines, it could result in significant danger, as one's child may suffer financially from the miscalculations and misrepresentations. The only key to safeguard you and your child from such neglect and abuse is to know the pitfalls and to benefit from the knowledge that you will gain from the following information.

Guidelines for Determination of Child-Support Obligation

R.S. 9:315. Economic data and principles; definitions

A. Basic principles. The premise of these guidelines as well as the provisions of the Civil Code is that child support is a continuous obligation of both parents, children are entitled to share in the current income of both parents, and children should not be the economic victims of divorce or out-of- wedlock birth. The economic data underlying these guidelines, which adopt the Income Shares Model, and the guideline calculations attempt to simulate the percentage of parental net income that is spent on children in intact families incorporating a consideration of the expenses of the parties, such as federal and state taxes and FICA taxes. While the legislature acknowledges that the expenditures of two-household divorced, separated, or non-formed families are different from intact family households, it is very important that the children of this state not be forced to live in poverty because of family disruption and that they be afforded the same opportunities available to children in intact families, consisting of parents with similar financial means to those of their own parents.

B. Economic data.

(1) The Incomes Shares approach to child support guidelines incorporates a numerical schedule of support amounts. The schedule provides economic estimates of child-rearing expenditures for various income levels and numbers of children in the household. The schedule is composed of economic data utilizing a table of national averages adjusted to reflect Louisiana's status as a low-income state and to incorporate a self-sufficiency reserve for low-income obligors to form the basic child support obligation.

(2) In intact families, the income of both parents is pooled and spent for the benefit of all household members, including the children. Each parent's contribution to the combined income of the family represents his relative sharing of household expenses. This same income sharing principle is used to

determine how the parents will share a child support award.

C. Definitions. As used in this Part:

(1) "Adjusted gross income" means gross income, minus amounts for preexisting child support or spousal support obligations paid to another who is not a party to the proceedings, or on behalf of a child who is not the subject of the action of the court.

(2) "Combined adjusted gross income" means the combined adjusted gross income of both parties.

(3) "Extraordinary medical expenses" means uninsured expenses over one hundred dollars for a single illness or condition. It includes but is not limited to reasonable and necessary costs for orthodontia, dental treatment, asthma treatment, physical therapy, uninsured chronic health problems, and professional counseling or psychiatric therapy for diagnosed mental disorders.

(4) "Gross income" means:

(a) The income from any source, including but not limited to salaries, wages, commissions, bonuses, dividends, severance pay, pensions, interest, trust income, annuities, capital gains, social security benefits, workers' compensation benefits, unemployment insurance benefits, disability insurance benefits, and spousal support received from a preexisting spousal support obligation;

(b) Expense reimbursement or in-kind payments received by a parent in the course of employment, self-employment, or operation of a business, if the reimbursements or payments are significant and reduce the parent's personal living expenses. Such payments include but are not limited to a company car, free housing, or reimbursed meals; and

(c) Gross receipts minus ordinary and necessary expenses required to produce income, for purposes of income from self-employment, rent, royalties, proprietorship of a business, or joint ownership or a partnership or closely held corporation. "Ordinary and necessary expenses" shall not include amounts allowable by the Internal Revenue Service for the accelerated component of depreciation expenses or investment tax credits or any other business expenses determined by the court to be inappropriate for determining gross income for purposes of calculating child support.

(d) As used herein, "gross income" does not include:

(i) Child support received, or benefits received from public assistance programs, including Family Independence Temporary Assistance Plan, supplemental security income, food stamps, and general assistance.

(ii) Per diem allowances which are not subject to federal income taxation under the provisions of the Internal Revenue Code.

(iii) Extraordinary overtime including but not limited to income attributed to seasonal work regardless of its percentage of gross income when, in the court's discretion, the inclusion thereof would be inequitable to a party.

(5) "Health insurance premiums" means the actual amount paid by a party for providing health insurance on behalf of the child. It does not include any amount paid by an employer or any amounts paid for coverage of any other persons. If more than one dependent is covered by health insurance which is paid through a lump-sum dependent-coverage premium, and not all of such dependents are the subject of the guidelines calculation, the cost of the coverage shall be prorated among the dependents covered before being applied to the guidelines.

(6) "Income" means:

(a) Actual gross income of a party, if the party is employed to full capacity; or

(b) Potential income of a party, if the party is voluntarily unemployed or underemployed. A party shall not be deemed voluntarily unemployed or underemployed if he or she is absolutely unemployable or incapable of being employed, or if the unemployment or underemployment results through no fault or neglect of the party.

(c) The court may also consider as income the benefits a party derives from expense-sharing or other sources; however, in determining the benefits of expense-sharing, the court shall not consider the income of another spouse, regardless of the legal regime under which the remarriage exists, except to the extent that such income is used directly to reduce the cost of a party's actual expenses.

(7) "Net child care costs" means the reasonable costs of child care incurred by a party due to employment or job search, minus the value of the federal income tax credit for child care.

## 5. Rebuttable Presumption

Louisiana law creates a "legal fiction," as it presumes that the guidelines represent the child-support financial requirements of an average Louisiana parent. The presumption that the guidelines are appropriate for your children's support is rebuttable, whereby allowing a deviation from the guidelines in cases in which there is proof of special financial needs not anticipated in the guideline formulation.

R.S. 9:315.1. Rebuttable presumption; deviation from guidelines by court; stipulations by parties

A. The guidelines set forth in this Part are to be used in any proceeding to establish or modify child support filed on or after October 1, 1989. There shall be a rebuttable presumption that the amount of child support obtained by use of the guidelines set forth in this Part is the proper amount of child support.

B. The court may deviate from the guidelines set forth in this Part if their application would not be in the best interest of the child or would be inequitable to the parties. The court shall give specific oral or written reasons for the deviation, including a finding as to the amount of support that would have been required under a mechanical application of the guidelines and the particular facts and circumstances that warranted a deviation from the guidelines. The reasons shall be made part of the record of the proceedings.

C. In determining whether to deviate from the guidelines, the court's considerations may include:
(1) That the combined adjusted gross income of the parties is not within the amounts shown on the schedule in *R.S. 9:315.19* (emphasis added).

(a) If the combined adjusted gross income of the parties is less than the lowest sum shown on the schedule, the court shall determine an amount of child support based on the facts of the case, except that the amount awarded shall not be less than the minimum child support provided in *R.S. 9:315.14* (emphasis added).

(b) If the combined adjusted gross income of the parties exceeds the highest sum shown on the schedule, the court shall determine an amount of child support as provided in *R.S. 9:315.13(B)* (emphasis added).

(2) The legal obligation of a party to support dependents who are not the subject of the action before the court and who are in that party's household.

(3) That in a case involving one or more families, consisting of children none of whom live in the household of the non-custodial or nondomiciliary parent but who have existing child support orders (multiple families), the court may use its discretion in setting the amount of the basic child support obligation, provided it is not below the minimum fixed by *R.S. 9:315.14* (emphasis added), if the existing child support orders reduce the noncustodial or nondomiciliary parent's

income below the lowest income level on the schedule contained in *R.S. 9:315.19* (emphasis added).

(4) The extraordinary medical expenses of a party, or extraordinary medical expenses for which a party may be responsible, not otherwise taken into consideration under the guidelines.

(5) An extraordinary community debt of the parties.

(6) The need for immediate and temporary support for a child when a full hearing on the issue of support is pending but cannot be timely held. In such cases, the court at the full hearing shall use the provisions of this Part and may redetermine support without the necessity of a change of circumstances being shown.

(7) The permanent or temporary total disability of a spouse to the extent such disability diminishes his present and future earning capacity, his need to save adequately for uninsurable future medical costs, and other additional costs associated with such disability, such as transportation and mobility costs, medical expenses, and higher insurance premiums.

(8) Any other consideration which would make application of the guidelines not in the best interest of the child or children or inequitable to the parties.

D. The court may review and approve a stipulation between the parties entered into after the effective date of this Part as to the amount of child support to be paid. If the court does review the stipulation, the court shall consider the guidelines set forth in this Part to review the adequacy of the stipulated amount and may require the parties to provide the court with the income statements and documentation required by *R.S. 9:315.2* (emphasis added).

## 6. Calculation of Basic Child Support

The first step in determining appropriate child support is to calculate the basic child-support obligation as determined by using the guidelines and worksheet. Other child-care expenses may be added to this figure, while other deductions can be made as well.

R.S. 9:315.2. Calculation of basic child support obligation

A. Each party shall provide to the court a verified income statement showing gross income and adjusted gross income, together with documentation of current and past earnings. Spouses of the parties shall also provide any relevant information with regard to the source of payments of household expenses upon request of the court or the opposing party, provided such request is filed in a reasonable time prior to the hearing. Failure to timely file the request shall not be grounds for a continuance. Suitable documentation of current earnings shall include but not be limited to pay stubs, employer statements, or receipts and expenses if self-employed. The documentation shall include a copy of the party's most recent federal tax return. A copy of the statement and documentation shall be provided to the other party.

B. If a party is voluntarily unemployed or underemployed, his or her gross income shall be determined as set forth in *R.S. 9:315.11* (emphasis added).

C. The parties shall combine the amounts of their adjusted gross incomes. Each party shall then determine by percentage his or her proportionate share of the combined amount. The amount obtained for each party is his or her percentage share of the combined adjusted gross income.

D. The court shall determine the basic child support obligation amount from the schedule in *R.S. 9:315.19* (emphasis added) by using the combined adjusted gross income of the parties and the number of children involved in the proceeding, but in no event shall the amount of child support be less than the amount provided in *R.S. 9:315.14* (emphasis added).

E. After the basic child support obligation has been established, the total child support obligation shall be determined as hereinafter provided in this Part.

## 7. Ask for Contributions for "Extras"

In order to ensure that each parent is financially responsible for his proportionate share of all child-related expenses, instruct your attorney to seek contributions for the other parent's proportionate share of all insurance deductibles, copayments, and payments not covered by insurance. These "extra" expenses can quickly add up. Don't let these dollars slip through the hands that help your child:

- medical expenses/medical insurance
- dental expenses/dental insurance
- extraordinary medical expenses (orthodontic/psychiatric/counseling/miscellaneous health-related expenses)
- day-care expenses
- tuition/educational expenses
- extraordinary nonmedical-related expenses

## 8. Net Child-Care Costs

Net child-care costs are an addition to the basic child-support obligation, as calculated pursuant to Louisiana Revised Statute 9:315.3:

R.S. 9:315.3. Net child care costs; addition to basic obligation

Net child care costs shall be added to the basic child support obligation. The net child care costs are determined by applying the Federal Credit for Child and Dependent Care Expenses provided in Internal Revenue Form 2441 to the total or actual child care costs.

## 9. Get Day Care

Day care is a common and important expense that can significantly add to a parent's child-support obligation. Inquire with your attorney as to whether day-care expenses are included in the basic child-support award or whether you should request it as an additional child-related expense.

The actual day-care expense incurred is usually under the discretion of the primary domiciliary parent. That parent usually chooses the day-care facility and resulting costs.

## 10. Ask the Court for Participation in the Decision Regarding which Day-Care Facility Is Used

By assisting in the choice of the day-care facility, you also participate in cost control.

## 11. Replace Day Care with Your Care or That of Relatives

A parent may be able to significantly decrease the day-care expense by asking relatives to baby-sit. Grandparents and adult siblings often are more than willing to assist with this supervision. Your own physical care of your child can decrease the cost of day care. Ask for the "right of first refusal" of having the physical possession of the child in events when the child would otherwise be at the day-care center or with a baby-sitter.

A parent may argue that having relatives provide baby-sitting services is inferior to a day-care facility, as the day-care center may allow the child to gain socialization skills.

## 12. Place Child in Chosen Day-Care Facility Prior to Court Date

Judges are quite hesitant to remove a child from a day-care facility once the child has commenced attending the center. Many attorneys believe that it is prudent to register and put your child into a day-care facility prior to the child-support and/or custody trial date, as the parent shall be able to show stability in the child's life and provide evidence of actual day-care expenses. If a parent does not have the child previously registered in and/or attending a day-care facility, then the other parent will have a greater chance to impeach the need for day care and gain an advantage in choosing what type of day care and the expense.

## 13. Health Insurance Premiums

### Quick Facts

Only about 40 percent of child-support awards include medical insurance benefits. Unfortunately, another 31 percent of those parents who were ordered to provide health insurance for their children failed or refused to provide it. Of the noncustodial parents who were not ordered to provide health insurance, 18 percent provided such insurance without an order (U.S. Census Bureau).

Medical and dental expenses associated with your child should be included in the calculation and implementation of a child-support award and related child-care obligations. All orthodontic, psychiatric, and health-related needs of your child should be brought to the attention of your attorney.

If you anticipate certain future expenses for your child that have not yet arisen, ask your attorney to seek provisions in the child-support order that compel the other parent to pay for a proportionate share of these expenses as they arise. This will prevent you from having to pay your attorney to go back into court at a later date to seek this relief.

Health-care-insurance premiums also are added or subtracted from the basic child-care obligation depending on which parent pays for the health insurance. It is important to provide your attorney with a breakdown of the premium allocated to each child by the insurance provider or employer.

> R.S. 9:315.4. Health insurance premiums; addition to basic obligation
>
> In any child support case, the court may order one of the parties to enroll or maintain an insurable child in a health benefits plan, policy, or program. In determining which party should be required to enroll the child or to maintain such insurance on behalf of the child, the court shall consider each party's individual, group, or employee's health insurance program, employment history, and personal income and other resources. The cost of health insurance premiums incurred on behalf of the child shall be added to the basic child support obligation.

## 14. Extraordinary Medical Expenses

Extraordinary medical expenses are those incurred under circumstances of special medical treatment of a child. Louisiana courts consider extraordinary medical expenses to commence when those special medical treatments cost over $100 a month or $1,000 a year. Hence, it is important to request your attorney to ask the court or the opposing party for an order of support that includes an allocation of the special medical expenses under $100 per month; otherwise, one parent may get stuck with paying the $89 monthly asthma medication expense without contribution from the other parent. Make your attorney acutely aware of any such special medial and/or pharmacy expenses.

R.S. 9:315.5. Extraordinary medical expenses; addition to basic obligation

By agreement of the parties or order of the court, extraordinary medical expenses incurred on behalf of the child shall be added to the basic child support obligation.

## 15. Other Extraordinary Expenses

Other extraordinary expenses generally include expenses for tuition, books, supplies, educational transportation, and activities of a extracurricular nature. Such expenses are largely subject to the discretion of the court.

Like day care, school tuition is an expense that can be quite costly. Inquire with your attorney as to your rights associated with school expenses. Your attorney should ask for the other parent's contribution toward tuition, school-loan interest payments, uniforms, school books, supplies, and extracurricular school expenses.

Judges generally have the discretion to determine whether a parent should be obligated to pay the additional expense for a child to attend a private or parochial school instead of a public school. Many judges require a parent to prove that the child has a special need that would require the child to attend the private or parochial school. Yet, judges are reluctant to remove a child who already attends the private or parochial school. The court will look to the "best interest of the child" standard. Continuity of the child's life is very important.

### Quick Facts

Thirty four percent of America's three- and four-year-olds are enrolled in nursery schools (U.S. Census Bureau).

R.S. 9:315.6. Other extraordinary expenses; addition to basic obligation

By agreement of the parties or order of the court, the following expenses incurred on behalf of the child may be added to the basic child support obligation:

(1) Expenses of tuition, registration, books, and supply fees required for attending a special or private elementary or secondary school to meet the needs of the child.

(2) Any expenses for transportation of the child from one party to the other.

## 16. Entering into a Consent Agreement and Order Whereby the Parents Agree to Pay for College Education

Although it may not be otherwise enforceable in Louisiana, if both parents are agreeable to the general child-support provisions, it may be a good time to propose an agreement regarding the payment of your child's college education. If both parents enter into such an agreement and it is converted into a judgment of the court, it may be enforceable at a later date. There does not appear to be any harm in trying to get an agreement that benefits the future of your child.

## 17. Deductions for Income of the Child

Although deductions have been made for a child who has been working, remember that there should not be a deduction on this basis if the child has earned the income while being enrolled as a full-time student.

R.S. 9:315.7. Deductions for income of the child

A. Income of the child that can be used to reduce the basic needs of the child may be considered as a deduction from the basic child support obligation.

B. The provisions of this Section shall not apply to income earned by a child while a full-time student, regardless of whether such income was earned during a summer or holiday break.

C. The provisions of this Section shall not apply to benefits received by a child from public assistance programs, including but not limited to Family Independence Temporary Assistance Programs (FITAP), food stamps, or any means-tested program.

## 18. Calculation of Total Child Support

*It is not recommended that you try to calculate your own child-support figures.* In my many years of law practice, I have found that most of my clients who have attempted to calculate their own figures generally come up with an incorrect figure over 90 percent of the time. I have encountered many an attorney who does not regularly practice family law and makes these mistakes. Hence, I recommend that you confer with your attorney, provide the information, and let him or her make the calculations. The calculation is too important to allow for a mistake. The *Louisiana Family Law Guide* provides you with the schedule and worksheets, but please be on guard that mistakes in calculation are quite common. Let your attorney do the work for you.

R.S. 9:315.8. Calculation of total child support obligation; worksheet

A. The total child support obligation shall be determined by adding together the basic child support obligation amount, the net child care costs, the cost of health insurance premiums, extraordinary medical expenses, and other extraordinary expenses.

B. A deduction, if any, for income of the child shall then be subtracted from the amount calculated in Subsection A. The remaining amount is the total child support obligation.

C. Each party's share of the total child support obligation shall then be determined by multiplying his or her percentage share of combined adjusted gross income times the total child support obligation.

D. The party without legal custody or nondomiciliary party shall owe his or her total child support obligation as a money judgment of child support to the custodial or domiciliary party, minus any court-ordered direct payments made on behalf of the child for work-related net child care costs, health insurance premiums, extraordinary medical expenses, or extraordinary expenses provided as adjustments to the schedule.

E. "Joint Custody" means a joint custody order that is not shared custody as defined in *R.S. 9:315.9* (emphasis added).

(1) In cases of joint custody, the court shall consider the

period of time spent by the child with the nondomiciliary party as a basis for adjustment to the amount of child support to be paid during that period of time.

(2) If under a joint custody order, the person ordered to pay child support has physical custody of the child for more than seventy-three days, the court may order a credit to the child support obligation. A day for the purposes of this Paragraph shall be determined by the court; however, in no instance shall less than four hours of physical custody of the child constitute a day.

(3) In determining the amount of credit to be given, the court shall consider the following:

(a) The amount of time the child spends with the person to whom the credit would be applied.

(b) The increase in financial burden placed on the person to whom the credit would be applied and the decrease in financial burden on the person receiving child support.

(c) The best interests of the child and what is equitable between the parties.

(4) The burden of proof is on the person seeking the credit pursuant to this Subsection.

(5) Worksheet A reproduced in *R.S. 9:315.20* (emphasis added), or a substantially similar form adopted by local court rule, shall be used to determine child support in accordance with this Subsection.

## 19. Effect of Shared Custodial Arrangement

If you have a joint-custody order, wherein you have the physical custody approximately 50 percent of the time, then it likely will be defined as having "shared custody." Under a shared-custody order, Worksheet B, provided later in this chapter, is used in the child-support calculation.

R.S. 9:315.9. Effect of shared custodial arrangement

A. (1) "Shared custody" means a joint custody order in which each parent has physical custody of the child for an approximately equal amount of time.

(2) If the joint custody order provides for shared custody, the basic child support obligation shall first be multiplied by one and one-half and then divided between the parents in proportion to their respective adjusted gross incomes.

(3) Each parent's theoretical child support obligation shall then be cross multiplied by the actual percentage of time the child spends with the other party to determine the basic child support obligation based on the amount of time spent with the other party.

(4) Each parent's proportionate share of work-related net child care costs and extraordinary adjustments to the schedule shall be added to the amount calculated under Paragraph (3) of this Subsection.

(5) Each parent's proportionate share of any direct payments ordered to be made on behalf of the child for net child care costs, the cost of health insurance premiums, extraordinary medical expenses, or other extraordinary expenses shall be deducted from the amount calculated under Paragraph (3) of this Subsect2ion.

(6) The parent owing the greater amount of child support shall owe to the other parent the difference between the two amounts as a child support obligation. The amount owed shall not be higher than the amount which that parent would have owed if he or she were a domiciliary parent.

B. Worksheet B reproduced in *R.S. 9:315.20* (emphasis added), or a substantially similar form adopted by local court rule, shall be used to determine child support in accordance with this Subsection.

## 20. Effect of Split Custodial Arrangement

If you have a sole-custody order or are the domiciliary parent of at least one child, then it likely will be defined as having "split custody" for purposes of the child-support calculation. Under a split-custody order, Worksheet A, provided later in this chapter, is used in the child-support calculation.

R.S. 9:315.10. Effect of split custodial arrangement

A. (1) "Split custody" means that each party is the sole custodial or domiciliary parent of at least one child to whom support is due.

(2) If the custody order provides for split custody, each parent shall compute a total child support obligation for the child or children in the custody of the other parent, based on a calculation pursuant to this Section.

(3) The amount determined under Paragraph (2) of this Subsection shall be a theoretical support obligation owed to each parent.

(4) The parent owing the greater amount of child support shall owe to the other parent the difference between the two amounts as a child support obligation.

B. Worksheet A reproduced in *R.S. 9:315.20* (emphasis added), or a substantially similar form adopted by local court rule, shall be used by each parent to determine child support in accordance with this Section.

## 21. Voluntarily Unemployed or Underemployed Party

It is quite common for a parent to try to alleviate the financial child-support burden by losing a job, working less hours, manipulating the timing of bonuses and raises, and the like for the primary purpose of establishing a lower gross income and thus paying less child support. The courts and the Louisiana legislature have recognized this problem. Louisiana Revised Statute 9:315.11 addresses this common tactic. The courts are allowed to impute income on a parent who voluntarily becomes unemployed or underemployed. In other words, the court will calculate the payer parent's income at a level determined to be appropriate had the parent not become voluntarily unemployed or underemployed. One of the best ways to prove voluntary unemployment is through the testimony of coworkers and employers, as well as through payroll records.

R.S. 9:315.11. Voluntarily unemployed or underemployed party

If a party is voluntarily unemployed or underemployed, child support shall be calculated based on a determination of his or her income earning potential, unless the party is physically or mentally incapacitated, or is caring for a child of the parties under the age of five years.

## 22. Second Jobs and Overtime

R.S. 9:315.12. Second jobs and overtime

The court may consider the interests of a subsequent family as a defense in an action to modify an existing child support order when the obligor has taken a second job or works overtime to provide for a subsequent family. However, the obligor bears the burden of proof in establishing that the additional income is used to provide for the subsequent family.

## 23. Amounts Not Set Forth in or Exceeding the Schedule

R.S. 9:315.13. Amounts not set forth in or exceeding schedule

A. If the combined adjusted gross income of the parties falls between two amounts shown in the schedule contained in *R.S. 9:315.19* (emphasis added), the basic child support obligation shall be based on an extrapolation between the two amounts.

B. If the combined adjusted gross income of the parties exceeds the highest level specified in the schedule contained in *R.S. 9:315.19* (emphasis added), the court shall use its discretion in setting the amount of the basic child support obligation in accordance with the best interest of the child and the circumstances of each parent as provided in *Civil Code Article 141* (emphasis added), but in no event shall it be less than the highest amount set forth in the schedule.

R.S. 9:315.14. Mandatory minimum child support award

In no event shall the court set an award of child support less than one hundred dollars, except in cases involving shared or split custody as provided in *R.S. 9:315.9* (emphasis added) and 315.10.

## 24. Schedule for Child Support

R.S. 9:315.18. Schedule; information

A. The amounts set forth in the schedule in R.S. 9:315.19 (emphasis added) presume that the custodial or domiciliary party has the right to claim the federal and state tax dependency deductions and any earned income credit. However, the claiming of dependents for federal and state income tax purposes shall be as provided in Subsection B of this Section.

B. (1) The non-domiciliary party whose child support obligation is equal to or greater than fifty percent and equal to or less than seventy percent of the total child support obligation shall be entitled to claim the federal and state tax dependency deductions if, after a contradictory motion, the judge finds both of the following:

(a) No arrearages are owed by the obligor.

(b) The right to claim the dependency deductions or, in the case of multiple children, a part thereof, would substantially benefit the non- domiciliary party without significantly harming the domiciliary party.

(2) The child support order shall:

(a) Specify the years in which the party is entitled to claim such deductions.

(b) Require the domiciliary party to timely execute all forms required by the Internal Revenue Service authorizing the non-domiciliary party to claim such deductions.

C. The non-domiciliary party whose child support obligation exceeds seventy percent of the total child support obligation shall be entitled to claim the federal and state tax dependency deductions every year if no arrearages are owed by the obligor.

D. The party who receives the benefit of the exemption for such tax year shall not be considered as having received payment of a thing not due if the dependency deduction allocation is not maintained by the taxing authorities.

LA-R.S. 9:315.19 Schedule for support *(See page 142.)*

## 25. Watch for Manipulation of the Numbers

Unfortunately, many lawyers may add two plus two and come up with three.

There are no national or statewide criteria for determining how much a person earns. Likewise, there are no uniform standards regarding what period of time should be used to examine a parent's income. Many jobs are cyclical—such as construction, lawn care, Christmas-tree sales, etc. Hence, the more cyclical the business, the more important it is to have an examination of income over a twelve-month or greater period of time. Some courts will look at the income over several years. Tax returns may give insight as to whether a parent is manipulating his or her income.

## 26. Check the Calculation of Each Parent's Income

Be leery of anyone who quickly estimates and/or calculates what the other parent makes in an average month. People have wide and diverse payment methods. Many people get paid by the hour, by the week, by the job, every two weeks, or with overtime, or they get reimbursed for travel expenses and/or have expense accounts, etc.

Since child-support guidelines provide formulas for calculations based on average actual income and/or earning capacity, the time period from which the average is taken becomes critical.

For example, if parent one ("Huey P.") earned the following income for the last year and one-half, depending upon the time period used to determine his average monthly income and/or earning capacity, the calculator could create significantly varied results.

Huey P.'s "Declared" Income

| Last year: | January | $3,000.00 |
|---|---|---|
| | February | 3,000.00 |
| | March | 3,000.00 |

| | |
|---|---|
| April | 3,000.00 |
| May | 3,000.00 |
| June | 3,000.00 |
| July | 3,000.00 |
| August | 3,000.00 |
| September | 3,000.00 |
| October | 3,000.00 |
| November | 3,000.00 |
| December | 3,000.00 |
| Bonus (paid in December) | 6,000.00 |
| This year: January | 2,000.00 |
| February | 2,000.00 |
| March | 2,000.00 |
| April | 2,000.00 |
| May | 2,000.00 |
| June | 2,000.00 |

According to the above example, Huey P. made $42,000 last year. If your attorney did not discover that Huey P. made a $6,000 bonus, then he or she may incorrectly believe that Huey P.'s income last year was only $36,000. Additionally, if your attorney only calculated Huey P.'s average income based on his recent pay stub for the current year, your attorney would assume that Huey P. made an average of only $2,000 per month.

If your attorney calculates Huey P.'s income based on last year's income of $42,000, Huey P.'s average monthly declared income would be $3,500.

If your attorney calculates Huey P.'s income based on the last eighteen months, Huey P.'s average monthly declared income would be $3,000.

As you can see from the above example, lawyers can use the figures that are available (through proper discovery) and come up with entirely different answers to the question of what a parent's monthly income is.

Have a talk with your attorney and ask how the declared income of each parent is being calculated.

Instruct your attorney to subpoena the other parent's federal tax returns (and W-2 and/or 1099) for the past several years, as well as the payroll records and personnel files from his employer(s).

(Sample questions: Did your attorney know that the other parent. would receive a bonus and reimbursement for travel expenses at the

The schedule of support to be used for determining the basic child support obligation is as follows:

## LOUISIANA CHILD SUPPORT GUIDELINE SCHEDULE OF BASIC CHILD SUPPORT OBLIGATIONS

| COMBINED ADJUSTED MONTHLY GROSS INCOME | ONE CHILD | TWO CHILDREN (TOTAL) | THREE CHILDREN (TOTAL) | FOUR CHILDREN (TOTAL) | FIVE CHILDREN (TOTAL) | SIX OR MORE CHILDREN (TOTAL) |
|---|---|---|---|---|---|---|
| 600.00 | 100 | 100 | 100 | 100 | 100 | 100 |
| 650.00 | 102 | 103 | 104 | 106 | 107 | 108 |
| 700.00 | 136 | 138 | 139 | 141 | 142 | 144 |
| 750.00 | 165 | 172 | 174 | 176 | 178 | 179 |
| 800.00 | 174 | 206 | 208 | 211 | 213 | 215 |
| 850.00 | 182 | 240 | 243 | 245 | 248 | 251 |
| 900.00 | 189 | 274 | 277 | 280 | 283 | 286 |
| 950.00 | 197 | 305 | 310 | 313 | 317 | 320 |
| 1000.00 | 203 | 315 | 339 | 342 | 346 | 350 |
| 1050.00 | 210 | 325 | 367 | 371 | 375 | 379 |
| 1100.00 | 216 | 335 | 396 | 400 | 405 | 409 |
| 1150.00 | 222 | 345 | 425 | 429 | 434 | 439 |
| 1200.00 | 229 | 354 | 444 | 458 | 463 | 468 |
| 1250.00 | 235 | 364 | 456 | 487 | 493 | 498 |
| 1300.00 | 241 | 374 | 469 | 516 | 522 | 528 |
| 1350.00 | 248 | 384 | 481 | 542 | 551 | 557 |
| 1400.00 | 254 | 394 | 494 | 556 | 581 | 587 |
| 1450.00 | 260 | 404 | 506 | 570 | 610 | 617 |
| 1500.00 | 267 | 414 | 519 | 584 | 637 | 646 |
| 1550.00 | 273 | 424 | 531 | 598 | 653 | 676 |
| 1600.00 | 281 | 435 | 545 | 614 | 670 | 717 |
| 1650.00 | 288 | 446 | 560 | 630 | 688 | 736 |
| 1700.00 | 295 | 458 | 574 | 647 | 705 | 755 |
| 1750.00 | 303 | 469 | 588 | 663 | 723 | 774 |
| 1800.00 | 310 | 481 | 603 | 679 | 741 | 792 |
| 1850.00 | 317 | 492 | 617 | 695 | 758 | 811 |
| 1900.00 | 325 | 503 | 631 | 711 | 776 | 830 |
| 1950.00 | 331 | 513 | 643 | 724 | 790 | 846 |
| 2000.00 | 337 | 522 | 655 | 737 | 805 | 861 |
| 2050.00 | 343 | 532 | 667 | 751 | 819 | 877 |
| 2100.00 | 349 | 541 | 679 | 764 | 834 | 892 |
| 2150.00 | 355 | 551 | 691 | 778 | 849 | 908 |
| 2200.00 | 361 | 561 | 703 | 792 | 864 | 924 |
| 2250.00 | 368 | 570 | 715 | 805 | 878 | 940 |

| 2300.00 | 374 | 580 | 727 | 819 | 893 | 956 |
|---------|-----|-----|------|------|------|------|
| 2350.00 | 380 | 590 | 739 | 832 | 908 | 972 |
| 2400.00 | 386 | 600 | 751 | 846 | 923 | 988 |
| 2450.00 | 392 | 609 | 763 | 860 | 938 | 1004 |
| 2500.00 | 399 | 619 | 776 | 873 | 953 | 1020 |
| 2550.00 | 405 | 629 | 788 | 887 | 968 | 1035 |
| 2600.00 | 411 | 638 | 800 | 901 | 983 | 1051 |
| 2650.00 | 417 | 648 | 812 | 914 | 998 | 1067 |
| 2700.00 | 424 | 658 | 824 | 928 | 1013 | 1083 |
| 2750.00 | 430 | 668 | 836 | 942 | 1028 | 1099 |
| 2800.00 | 436 | 677 | 848 | 955 | 1042 | 1115 |
| 2850.00 | 442 | 687 | 860 | 969 | 1057 | 1131 |
| 2900.00 | 448 | 697 | 872 | 983 | 1072 | 1147 |
| 2950.00 | 455 | 706 | 885 | 996 | 1087 | 1163 |
| 3000.00 | 461 | 716 | 897 | 1010 | 1102 | 1179 |
| 3050.00 | 467 | 726 | 909 | 1024 | 1117 | 1195 |
| 3100.00 | 473 | 736 | 921 | 1037 | 1132 | 1211 |
| 3150.00 | 479 | 745 | 933 | 1051 | 1147 | 1227 |
| 3200.00 | 486 | 755 | 945 | 1065 | 1162 | 1243 |
| 3250.00 | 492 | 765 | 957 | 1078 | 1177 | 1259 |
| 3300.00 | 498 | 774 | 969 | 1092 | 1192 | 1275 |
| 3350.00 | 504 | 784 | 981 | 1106 | 1206 | 1291 |
| 3400.00 | 510 | 794 | 994 | 1119 | 1221 | 1307 |
| 3450.00 | 517 | 804 | 1006 | 1133 | 1236 | 1323 |
| 3500.00 | 523 | 813 | 1018 | 1146 | 1251 | 1339 |
| 3550.00 | 529 | 823 | 1030 | 1160 | 1266 | 1355 |
| 3600.00 | 535 | 833 | 1042 | 1174 | 1281 | 1371 |
| 3650.00 | 542 | 842 | 1054 | 1187 | 1296 | 1387 |
| 3700.00 | 548 | 852 | 1066 | 1201 | 1311 | 1402 |
| 3750.00 | 554 | 862 | 1078 | 1215 | 1326 | 1418 |
| 3800.00 | 560 | 872 | 1090 | 1228 | 1341 | 1434 |
| 3850.00 | 566 | 881 | 1103 | 1242 | 1356 | 1450 |
| 3900.00 | 573 | 891 | 1115 | 1256 | 1371 | 1466 |
| 3950.00 | 579 | 901 | 1127 | 1269 | 1385 | 1482 |
| 4000.00 | 585 | 910 | 1139 | 1283 | 1400 | 1498 |
| 4050.00 | 590 | 919 | 1149 | 1295 | 1414 | 1512 |
| 4100.00 | 596 | 927 | 1160 | 1307 | 1427 | 1526 |
| 4150.00 | 601 | 936 | 1170 | 1319 | 1440 | 1540 |
| 4200.00 | 607 | 944 | 1181 | 1331 | 1452 | 1553 |
| 4250.00 | 612 | 953 | 1191 | 1343 | 1465 | 1567 |
| 4300.00 | 618 | 961 | 1202 | 1355 | 1478 | 1581 |
| 4350.00 | 623 | 970 | 1212 | 1367 | 1491 | 1595 |
| 4400.00 | 629 | 978 | 1223 | 1379 | 1504 | 1609 |
| 4450.00 | 634 | 987 | 1234 | 1391 | 1517 | 1623 |
| 4500.00 | 640 | 995 | 1244 | 1403 | 1530 | 1637 |

| | | | | | |
|---|---|---|---|---|---|
| 4550.00 | 645 | 1003 | 1255 | 1415 | 1543 | 1650 |
| 4600.00 | 651 | 1012 | 1265 | 1426 | 1556 | 1664 |
| 4650.00 | 656 | 1020 | 1276 | 1438 | 1569 | 1678 |
| 4700.00 | 662 | 1029 | 1286 | 1450 | 1582 | 1692 |
| 4750.00 | 667 | 1037 | 1297 | 1462 | 1595 | 1706 |
| 4800.00 | 673 | 1046 | 1307 | 1474 | 1608 | 1720 |
| 4850.00 | 678 | 1054 | 1318 | 1486 | 1621 | 1734 |
| 4900.00 | 684 | 1063 | 1328 | 1498 | 1634 | 1747 |
| 4950.00 | 689 | 1071 | 1339 | 1510 | 1647 | 1761 |
| 5000.00 | 695 | 1079 | 1349 | 1522 | 1660 | 1775 |
| 5050.00 | 700 | 1088 | 1360 | 1534 | 1673 | 1789 |
| 5100.00 | 706 | 1096 | 1370 | 1545 | 1686 | 1803 |
| 5150.00 | 711 | 1105 | 1381 | 1557 | 1699 | 1817 |
| 5200.00 | 717 | 1113 | 1391 | 1569 | 1712 | 1831 |
| 5250.00 | 722 | 1122 | 1402 | 1581 | 1725 | 1844 |
| 5300.00 | 728 | 1130 | 1413 | 1593 | 1738 | 1858 |
| 5350.00 | 733 | 1139 | 1423 | 1605 | 1751 | 1872 |
| 5400.00 | 738 | 1146 | 1432 | 1616 | 1763 | 1884 |
| 5450.00 | 743 | 1153 | 1441 | 1626 | 1774 | 1896 |
| 5500.00 | 748 | 1160 | 1450 | 1636 | 1785 | 1908 |
| 5550.00 | 752 | 1167 | 1459 | 1646 | 1796 | 1920 |
| 5600.00 | 757 | 1175 | 1468 | 1657 | 1807 | 1932 |
| 5650.00 | 762 | 1182 | 1478 | 1667 | 1819 | 1944 |
| 5700.00 | 767 | 1189 | 1487 | 1677 | 1830 | 1956 |
| 5750.00 | 771 | 1196 | 1496 | 1687 | 1841 | 1968 |
| 5800.00 | 776 | 1203 | 1505 | 1698 | 1852 | 1979 |
| 5850.00 | 781 | 1211 | 1514 | 1708 | 1863 | 1991 |
| 5900.00 | 785 | 1218 | 1523 | 1718 | 1875 | 2003 |
| 5950.00 | 790 | 1225 | 1532 | 1728 | 1886 | 2015 |
| 6000.00 | 795 | 1232 | 1541 | 1739 | 1897 | 2027 |
| 6050.00 | 800 | 1240 | 1550 | 1749 | 1908 | 2039 |
| 6100.00 | 804 | 1247 | 1559 | 1759 | 1919 | 2051 |
| 6150.00 | 809 | 1254 | 1568 | 1769 | 1931 | 2063 |
| 6200.00 | 814 | 1261 | 1577 | 1780 | 1942 | 2075 |
| 6250.00 | 819 | 1269 | 1587 | 1790 | 1953 | 2087 |
| 6300.00 | 823 | 1276 | 1596 | 1800 | 1964 | 2099 |
| 6350.00 | 828 | 1283 | 1605 | 1810 | 1975 | 2111 |
| 6400.00 | 833 | 1290 | 1614 | 1820 | 1987 | 2123 |
| 6450.00 | 838 | 1297 | 1623 | 1831 | 1998 | 2135 |
| 6500.00 | 842 | 1305 | 1632 | 1841 | 2009 | 2147 |
| 6550.00 | 847 | 1312 | 1641 | 1851 | 2020 | 2159 |
| 6600.00 | 852 | 1319 | 1650 | 1861 | 2031 | 2171 |
| 6650.00 | 857 | 1326 | 1659 | 1872 | 2043 | 2183 |
| 6700.00 | 861 | 1334 | 1668 | 1882 | 2054 | 2195 |
| 6750.00 | 866 | 1341 | 1677 | 1892 | 2065 | 2207 |

| | | | | | | |
|---|---|---|---|---|---|---|
| 6800.00 | 871 | 1348 | 1687 | 1902 | 2076 | 2219 |
| 6850.00 | 875 | 1355 | 1696 | 1913 | 2087 | 2231 |
| 6900.00 | 879 | 1361 | 1703 | 1921 | 2096 | 2240 |
| 6950.00 | 883 | 1366 | 1710 | 1928 | 2105 | 2249 |
| 7000.00 | 886 | 1372 | 1717 | 1936 | 2113 | 2259 |
| 7050.00 | 889 | 1378 | 1725 | 1944 | 2122 | 2268 |
| 7100.00 | 893 | 1383 | 1732 | 1951 | 2130 | 2277 |
| 7150.00 | 896 | 1389 | 1739 | 1959 | 2139 | 2286 |
| 7200.00 | 900 | 1394 | 1746 | 1967 | 2147 | 2295 |
| 7250.00 | 903 | 1400 | 1753 | 1974 | 2156 | 2305 |
| 7300.00 | 906 | 1406 | 1760 | 1982 | 2164 | 2314 |
| 7350.00 | 910 | 1411 | 1767 | 1990 | 2173 | 2323 |
| 7400.00 | 913 | 1417 | 1774 | 1997 | 2181 | 2332 |
| 7450.00 | 916 | 1422 | 1781 | 2005 | 2189 | 2342 |
| 7500.00 | 920 | 1428 | 1788 | 2013 | 2198 | 2351 |
| 7550.00 | 923 | 1434 | 1795 | 2020 | 2206 | 2360 |
| 7600.00 | 927 | 1439 | 1802 | 2028 | 2215 | 2369 |
| 7650.00 | 930 | 1445 | 1809 | 2036 | 2223 | 2378 |
| 7700.00 | 933 | 1450 | 1816 | 2043 | 2232 | 2388 |
| 7750.00 | 937 | 1456 | 1824 | 2051 | 2240 | 2397 |
| 7800.00 | 940 | 1462 | 1831 | 2059 | 2243 | 2406 |
| 7850.00 | 944 | 1467 | 1838 | 2066 | 2246 | 2409 |
| 7900.00 | 947 | 1473 | 1845 | 2069 | 2249 | 2412 |
| 7950.00 | 950 | 1478 | 1852 | 2072 | 2252 | 2415 |
| 8000.00 | 954 | 1484 | 1859 | 2075 | 2255 | 2418 |
| 8050.00 | 957 | 1490 | 1866 | 2078 | 2258 | 2421 |
| 8100.00 | 960 | 1493 | 1871 | 2081 | 2261 | 2424 |
| 8150.00 | 962 | 1497 | 1875 | 2084 | 2264 | 2427 |
| 8200.00 | 965 | 1501 | 1880 | 2087 | 2267 | 2430 |
| 8250.00 | 967 | 1505 | 1882 | 2090 | 2270 | 2433 |
| 8300.00 | 970 | 1509 | 1884 | 2093 | 2273 | 2436 |
| 8350.00 | 972 | 1512 | 1886 | 2096 | 2276 | 2439 |
| 8400.00 | 975 | 1516 | 1888 | 2099 | 2279 | 2442 |
| 8450.00 | 977 | 1520 | 1890 | 2102 | 2282 | 2445 |
| 8500.00 | 980 | 1523 | 1892 | 2105 | 2285 | 2448 |
| 8550.00 | 982 | 1526 | 1894 | 2108 | 2288 | 2451 |
| 8600.00 | 985 | 1529 | 1896 | 2111 | 2291 | 2454 |
| 8650.00 | 987 | 1532 | 1898 | 2114 | 2294 | 2457 |
| 8700.00 | 990 | 1535 | 1900 | 2117 | 2297 | 2460 |
| 8750.00 | 992 | 1538 | 1902 | 2120 | 2300 | 2463 |
| 8800.00 | 995 | 1541 | 1904 | 2123 | 2303 | 2466 |
| 8850.00 | 997 | 1544 | 1906 | 2126 | 2306 | 2469 |
| 8900.00 | 1000 | 1547 | 1908 | 2129 | 2309 | 2472 |
| 8950.00 | 1003 | 1550 | 1910 | 2132 | 2312 | 2475 |
| 9000.00 | 1005 | 1553 | 1912 | 2135 | 2315 | 2478 |

| | | | | | | |
|---|---|---|---|---|---|---|
| 9050.00 | 1008 | 1556 | 1914 | 2138 | 2318 | 2481 |
| 9100.00 | 1011 | 1559 | 1916 | 2141 | 2321 | 2484 |
| 9150.00 | 1013 | 1562 | 1918 | 2144 | 2324 | 2487 |
| 9200.00 | 1016 | 1565 | 1920 | 2147 | 2327 | 2490 |
| 9250.00 | 1019 | 1568 | 1922 | 2150 | 2330 | 2493 |
| 9300.00 | 1022 | 1571 | 1924 | 2153 | 2333 | 2496 |
| 9350.00 | 1024 | 1574 | 1926 | 2156 | 2336 | 2499 |
| 9400.00 | 1028 | 1577 | 1928 | 2159 | 2339 | 2502 |
| 9450.00 | 1033 | 1580 | 1930 | 2162 | 2342 | 2505 |
| 9500.00 | 1038 | 1583 | 1932 | 2165 | 2345 | 2508 |
| 9550.00 | 1043 | 1586 | 1934 | 2168 | 2348 | 2511 |
| 9600.00 | 1048 | 1589 | 1936 | 2171 | 2351 | 2514 |
| 9650.00 | 1053 | 1592 | 1938 | 2174 | 2354 | 2517 |
| 9700.00 | 1058 | 1595 | 1940 | 2177 | 2357 | 2520 |
| 9750.00 | 1063 | 1598 | 1942 | 2180 | 2360 | 2523 |
| 9800.00 | 1068 | 1601 | 1944 | 2183 | 2363 | 2526 |
| 9850.00 | 1073 | 1604 | 1946 | 2186 | 2366 | 2529 |
| 9900.00 | 1078 | 1607 | 1948 | 2189 | 2369 | 2532 |
| 9950.00 | 1083 | 1610 | 1950 | 2192 | 2372 | 2535 |
| 10000.00 | 1088 | 1613 | 1952 | 2195 | 2375 | 2538 |
| 10050.00 | 1095 | 1615 | 1954 | 2197 | 2377 | 2540 |
| 10100.00 | 1102 | 1617 | 1956 | 2199 | 2379 | 2542 |
| 10150.00 | 1109 | 1619 | 1958 | 2201 | 2381 | 2544 |
| 10200.00 | 1115 | 1621 | 1960 | 2203 | 2383 | 2546 |
| 10250.00 | 1119 | 1623 | 1962 | 2205 | 2385 | 2548 |
| 10300.00 | 1123 | 1625 | 1964 | 2207 | 2387 | 2550 |
| 10350.00 | 1127 | 1630 | 1966 | 2209 | 2389 | 2552 |
| 10400.00 | 1131 | 1636 | 1968 | 2211 | 2391 | 2554 |
| 10450.00 | 1135 | 1642 | 1970 | 2213 | 2393 | 2556 |
| 10500.00 | 1138 | 1647 | 1972 | 2215 | 2395 | 2558 |
| 10550.00 | 1142 | 1653 | 1974 | 2217 | 2397 | 2560 |
| 10600.00 | 1146 | 1659 | 1976 | 2219 | 2399 | 2562 |
| 10650.00 | 1150 | 1665 | 1978 | 2221 | 2400 | 2564 |
| 10700.00 | 1154 | 1670 | 1982 | 2223 | 2402 | 2566 |
| 10750.00 | 1158 | 1676 | 1984 | 2225 | 2404 | 2568 |
| 10800.00 | 1162 | 1682 | 1986 | 2227 | 2406 | 2570 |
| 10850.00 | 1166 | 1687 | 1988 | 2229 | 2408 | 2572 |
| 10900.00 | 1170 | 1693 | 1994 | 2231 | 2410 | 2574 |
| 10950.00 | 1174 | 1698 | 2001 | 2233 | 2412 | 2576 |
| 11000.00 | 1178 | 1704 | 2008 | 2235 | 2414 | 2578 |
| 11050.00 | 1182 | 1710 | 2014 | 2237 | 2416 | 2582 |
| 11100.00 | 1186 | 1715 | 2021 | 2239 | 2421 | 2590 |
| 11150.00 | 1190 | 1721 | 2027 | 2241 | 2429 | 2599 |
| 11200.00 | 1194 | 1727 | 2034 | 2248 | 2436 | 2607 |
| 11250.00 | 1197 | 1732 | 2041 | 2255 | 2444 | 2616 |

| | | | | | | |
|---|---|---|---|---|---|---|
| 11300.00 | 1201 | 1738 | 2047 | 2262 | 2452 | 2624 |
| 11350.00 | 1205 | 1744 | 2054 | 2270 | 2460 | 2632 |
| 11400.00 | 1209 | 1749 | 2061 | 2277 | 2468 | 2641 |
| 11450.00 | 1213 | 1755 | 2067 | 2284 | 2476 | 2649 |
| 11500.00 | 1217 | 1760 | 2073 | 2291 | 2483 | 2657 |
| 11550.00 | 1220 | 1765 | 2079 | 2298 | 2491 | 2665 |
| 11600.00 | 1224 | 1771 | 2085 | 2304 | 2498 | 2673 |
| 11650.00 | 1228 | 1776 | 2092 | 2311 | 2505 | 2681 |
| 11700.00 | 1231 | 1781 | 2098 | 2318 | 2513 | 2689 |
| 11750.00 | 1235 | 1786 | 2104 | 2325 | 2520 | 2696 |
| 11800.00 | 1239 | 1791 | 2110 | 2331 | 2527 | 2704 |
| 11850.00 | 1242 | 1797 | 2116 | 2338 | 2535 | 2712 |
| 11900.00 | 1246 | 1802 | 2122 | 2345 | 2542 | 2720 |
| 11950.00 | 1249 | 1807 | 2128 | 2352 | 2549 | 2728 |
| 12000.00 | 1253 | 1812 | 2134 | 2358 | 2557 | 2735 |
| 12050.00 | 1257 | 1818 | 2140 | 2365 | 2564 | 2743 |
| 12100.00 | 1260 | 1823 | 2147 | 2372 | 2571 | 2751 |
| 12150.00 | 1264 | 1828 | 2153 | 2379 | 2578 | 2759 |
| 12200.00 | 1268 | 1833 | 2159 | 2385 | 2586 | 2767 |
| 12250.00 | 1271 | 1838 | 2165 | 2392 | 2593 | 2775 |
| 12300.00 | 1275 | 1844 | 2171 | 2399 | 2600 | 2782 |
| 12350.00 | 1278 | 1849 | 2177 | 2406 | 2608 | 2790 |
| 12400.00 | 1282 | 1854 | 2183 | 2412 | 2615 | 2798 |
| 12450.00 | 1286 | 1859 | 2189 | 2419 | 2622 | 2806 |
| 12500.00 | 1289 | 1864 | 2195 | 2426 | 2630 | 2814 |
| 12550.00 | 1293 | 1870 | 2202 | 2433 | 2637 | 2822 |
| 12600.00 | 1297 | 1875 | 2208 | 2439 | 2644 | 2829 |
| 12650.00 | 1300 | 1880 | 2214 | 2446 | 2652 | 2837 |
| 12700.00 | 1304 | 1885 | 2220 | 2453 | 2659 | 2845 |
| 12750.00 | 1307 | 1891 | 2226 | 2460 | 2666 | 2853 |
| 12800.00 | 1311 | 1896 | 2232 | 2466 | 2674 | 2861 |
| 12850.00 | 1315 | 1901 | 2238 | 2473 | 2681 | 2869 |
| 12900.00 | 1318 | 1906 | 2244 | 2480 | 2688 | 2876 |
| 12950.00 | 1322 | 1911 | 2250 | 2487 | 2696 | 2884 |
| 13000.00 | 1326 | 1917 | 2257 | 2493 | 2703 | 2892 |
| 13050.00 | 1329 | 1922 | 2263 | 2500 | 2710 | 2900 |
| 13100.00 | 1333 | 1927 | 2269 | 2507 | 2718 | 2908 |
| 13150.00 | 1336 | 1932 | 2275 | 2514 | 2725 | 2916 |
| 13200.00 | 1340 | 1937 | 2281 | 2520 | 2732 | 2923 |
| 13250.00 | 1344 | 1943 | 2287 | 2527 | 2740 | 2931 |
| 13300.00 | 1347 | 1948 | 2293 | 2534 | 2747 | 2939 |
| 13350.00 | 1351 | 1953 | 2299 | 2541 | 2754 | 2947 |
| 13400.00 | 1355 | 1958 | 2305 | 2547 | 2761 | 2955 |
| 13450.00 | 1358 | 1964 | 2312 | 2554 | 2769 | 2963 |
| 13500.00 | 1362 | 1969 | 2318 | 2561 | 2776 | 2970 |

| | | | | | | |
|---|---|---|---|---|---|---|
| 13550.00 | 1365 | 1974 | 2324 | 2568 | 2783 | 2978 |
| 13600.00 | 1369 | 1979 | 2330 | 2574 | 2791 | 2986 |
| 13650.00 | 1373 | 1984 | 2336 | 2581 | 2798 | 2994 |
| 13700.00 | 1376 | 1990 | 2342 | 2588 | 2805 | 3002 |
| 13750.00 | 1380 | 1995 | 2348 | 2595 | 2813 | 3010 |
| 13800.00 | 1384 | 2000 | 2354 | 2601 | 2820 | 3017 |
| 13850.00 | 1387 | 2005 | 2360 | 2608 | 2827 | 3025 |
| 13900.00 | 1391 | 2011 | 2367 | 2615 | 2835 | 3033 |
| 13950.00 | 1394 | 2016 | 2373 | 2622 | 2842 | 3041 |
| 14000.00 | 1398 | 2021 | 2379 | 2629 | 2849 | 3049 |
| 14050.00 | 1402 | 2026 | 2385 | 2635 | 2857 | 3057 |
| 14100.00 | 1405 | 2031 | 2391 | 2642 | 2864 | 3064 |
| 14150.00 | 1409 | 2037 | 2397 | 2649 | 2871 | 3072 |
| 14200.00 | 1413 | 2042 | 2403 | 2656 | 2879 | 3080 |
| 14250.00 | 1416 | 2047 | 2409 | 2662 | 2886 | 3088 |
| 14300.00 | 1420 | 2052 | 2415 | 2669 | 2893 | 3096 |
| 14350.00 | 1423 | 2057 | 2422 | 2676 | 2901 | 3104 |
| 14400.00 | 1427 | 2063 | 2428 | 2683 | 2908 | 3111 |
| 14450.00 | 1431 | 2068 | 2434 | 2689 | 2915 | 3119 |
| 14500.00 | 1434 | 2073 | 2440 | 2696 | 2922 | 3127 |
| 14550.00 | 1438 | 2078 | 2446 | 2703 | 2930 | 3135 |
| 14600.00 | 1442 | 2084 | 2452 | 2710 | 2937 | 3143 |
| 14650.00 | 1445 | 2089 | 2458 | 2716 | 2944 | 3151 |
| 14700.00 | 1449 | 2094 | 2464 | 2723 | 2952 | 3158 |
| 14750.00 | 1452 | 2099 | 2470 | 2730 | 2959 | 3166 |
| 14800.00 | 1456 | 2104 | 2476 | 2737 | 2966 | 3174 |
| 14850.00 | 1460 | 2110 | 2483 | 2743 | 2974 | 3182 |
| 14900.00 | 1463 | 2115 | 2489 | 2750 | 2981 | 3190 |
| 14950.00 | 1467 | 2120 | 2495 | 2757 | 2988 | 3198 |
| 15000.00 | 1471 | 2125 | 2501 | 2764 | 2996 | 3205 |
| 15050.00 | 1474 | 2130 | 2507 | 2770 | 3003 | 3213 |
| 15100.00 | 1478 | 2136 | 2513 | 2777 | 3010 | 3221 |
| 15150.00 | 1481 | 2141 | 2519 | 2784 | 3018 | 3229 |
| 15200.00 | 1485 | 2146 | 2525 | 2791 | 3025 | 3237 |
| 15250.00 | 1489 | 2151 | 2531 | 2797 | 3032 | 3245 |
| 15300.00 | 1492 | 2157 | 2538 | 2804 | 3040 | 3252 |
| 15350.00 | 1496 | 2162 | 2544 | 2811 | 3047 | 3260 |
| 15400.00 | 1500 | 2167 | 2550 | 2818 | 3054 | 3268 |
| 15450.00 | 1503 | 2172 | 2556 | 2824 | 3062 | 3276 |
| 15500.00 | 1507 | 2177 | 2562 | 2831 | 3069 | 3284 |
| 15550.00 | 1510 | 2183 | 2568 | 2838 | 3076 | 3292 |
| 15600.00 | 1514 | 2188 | 2574 | 2845 | 3083 | 3299 |
| 15650.00 | 1518 | 2193 | 2580 | 2851 | 3091 | 3307 |
| 15700.00 | 1521 | 2198 | 2586 | 2858 | 3098 | 3315 |
| 15750.00 | 1525 | 2203 | 2593 | 2865 | 3105 | 3323 |

| | | | | | | |
|---|---|---|---|---|---|---|
| 15800.00 | 1529 | 2209 | 2599 | 2872 | 3113 | 3331 |
| 15850.00 | 1532 | 2214 | 2605 | 2878 | 3120 | 3338 |
| 15900.00 | 1536 | 2219 | 2611 | 2885 | 3127 | 3346 |
| 15950.00 | 1539 | 2224 | 2617 | 2892 | 3135 | 3354 |
| 16000.00 | 1543 | 2230 | 2623 | 2899 | 3142 | 3362 |
| 16050.00 | 1547 | 2235 | 2629 | 2905 | 3149 | 3370 |
| 16100.00 | 1550 | 2240 | 2635 | 2912 | 3157 | 3378 |
| 16150.00 | 1554 | 2245 | 2641 | 2919 | 3164 | 3385 |
| 16200.00 | 1558 | 2250 | 2648 | 2926 | 3171 | 3393 |
| 16250.00 | 1561 | 2256 | 2654 | 2932 | 3179 | 3401 |
| 16300.00 | 1565 | 2261 | 2660 | 2939 | 3186 | 3409 |
| 16350.00 | 1568 | 2266 | 2666 | 2946 | 3193 | 3417 |
| 16400.00 | 1572 | 2271 | 2672 | 2953 | 3201 | 3425 |
| 16450.00 | 1576 | 2277 | 2678 | 2959 | 3208 | 3432 |
| 16500.00 | 1579 | 2282 | 2684 | 2966 | 3215 | 3440 |
| 16550.00 | 1583 | 2287 | 2690 | 2973 | 3223 | 3448 |
| 16600.00 | 1587 | 2292 | 2696 | 2980 | 3230 | 3456 |
| 16650.00 | 1590 | 2297 | 2703 | 2986 | 3237 | 3464 |
| 16700.00 | 1594 | 2303 | 2709 | 2993 | 3245 | 3472 |
| 16750.00 | 1597 | 2308 | 2715 | 3000 | 3252 | 3479 |
| 16800.00 | 1601 | 2313 | 2721 | 3007 | 3259 | 3487 |
| 16850.00 | 1605 | 2318 | 2727 | 3013 | 3266 | 3495 |
| 16900.00 | 1608 | 2323 | 2733 | 3020 | 3274 | 3503 |
| 16950.00 | 1612 | 2329 | 2739 | 3027 | 3281 | 3511 |
| 17000.00 | 1616 | 2334 | 2745 | 3034 | 3288 | 3519 |
| 17050.00 | 1619 | 2339 | 2751 | 3040 | 3296 | 3526 |
| 17100.00 | 1623 | 2344 | 2758 | 3047 | 3303 | 3534 |
| 17150.00 | 1626 | 2350 | 2764 | 3054 | 3310 | 3542 |
| 17200.00 | 1630 | 2355 | 2770 | 3061 | 3318 | 3550 |
| 17250.00 | 1634 | 2360 | 2776 | 3067 | 3325 | 3558 |
| 17300.00 | 1637 | 2365 | 2782 | 3074 | 3332 | 3566 |
| 17350.00 | 1641 | 2370 | 2788 | 3081 | 3340 | 3573 |
| 17400.00 | 1645 | 2376 | 2794 | 3088 | 3347 | 3581 |
| 17450.00 | 1648 | 2381 | 2800 | 3094 | 3354 | 3589 |
| 17500.00 | 1652 | 2386 | 2806 | 3101 | 3362 | 3597 |
| 17550.00 | 1655 | 2391 | 2813 | 3108 | 3369 | 3605 |
| 17600.00 | 1659 | 2396 | 2819 | 3115 | 3376 | 3613 |
| 17650.00 | 1663 | 2402 | 2825 | 3121 | 3384 | 3620 |
| 17700.00 | 1666 | 2407 | 2831 | 3128 | 3391 | 3628 |
| 17750.00 | 1670 | 2412 | 2837 | 3135 | 3398 | 3636 |
| 17800.00 | 1674 | 2417 | 2843 | 3142 | 3406 | 3644 |
| 17850.00 | 1677 | 2423 | 2849 | 3148 | 3413 | 3652 |
| 17900.00 | 1681 | 2428 | 2855 | 3155 | 3420 | 3660 |
| 17950.00 | 1684 | 2433 | 2861 | 3162 | 3427 | 3667 |
| 18000.00 | 1688 | 2438 | 2868 | 3169 | 3435 | 3675 |

| | | | | | | |
|---|---|---|---|---|---|---|
| 18050.00 | 1692 | 2443 | 2874 | 3175 | 3442 | 3683 |
| 18100.00 | 1695 | 2449 | 2880 | 3182 | 3449 | 3691 |
| 18150.00 | 1699 | 2454 | 2886 | 3189 | 3457 | 3699 |
| 18200.00 | 1703 | 2459 | 2892 | 3196 | 3464 | 3707 |
| 18250.00 | 1706 | 2464 | 2898 | 3202 | 3471 | 3714 |
| 18300.00 | 1710 | 2469 | 2904 | 3209 | 3479 | 3722 |
| 18350.00 | 1713 | 2475 | 2910 | 3216 | 3486 | 3730 |
| 18400.00 | 1717 | 2480 | 2916 | 3223 | 3493 | 3738 |
| 18450.00 | 1721 | 2485 | 2923 | 3229 | 3501 | 3746 |
| 18500.00 | 1724 | 2490 | 2929 | 3236 | 3508 | 3754 |
| 18550.00 | 1728 | 2496 | 2935 | 3243 | 3515 | 3761 |
| 18600.00 | 1732 | 2501 | 2941 | 3250 | 3523 | 3769 |
| 18650.00 | 1735 | 2506 | 2947 | 3256 | 3530 | 3777 |
| 18700.00 | 1739 | 2511 | 2953 | 3263 | 3537 | 3785 |
| 18750.00 | 1742 | 2516 | 2959 | 3270 | 3545 | 3793 |
| 18800.00 | 1746 | 2522 | 2965 | 3277 | 3552 | 3801 |
| 18850.00 | 1750 | 2527 | 2971 | 3283 | 3559 | 3808 |
| 18900.00 | 1753 | 2532 | 2978 | 3290 | 3567 | 3816 |
| 18950.00 | 1757 | 2537 | 2984 | 3297 | 3574 | 3824 |
| 19000.00 | 1761 | 2543 | 2990 | 3304 | 3581 | 3832 |
| 19050.00 | 1764 | 2548 | 2996 | 3310 | 3589 | 3840 |
| 19100.00 | 1768 | 2553 | 3002 | 3317 | 3596 | 3848 |
| 19150.00 | 1771 | 2558 | 3008 | 3324 | 3603 | 3855 |
| 19200.00 | 1775 | 2563 | 3014 | 3331 | 3610 | 3863 |
| 19250.00 | 1779 | 2569 | 3020 | 3337 | 3618 | 3871 |
| 19300.00 | 1782 | 2574 | 3026 | 3344 | 3625 | 3879 |
| 19350.00 | 1786 | 2579 | 3033 | 3351 | 3632 | 3887 |
| 19400.00 | 1790 | 2584 | 3039 | 3358 | 3640 | 3895 |
| 19450.00 | 1793 | 2589 | 3045 | 3364 | 3647 | 3902 |
| 19500.00 | 1797 | 2595 | 3051 | 3371 | 3654 | 3910 |
| 19550.00 | 1800 | 2600 | 3057 | 3378 | 3662 | 3918 |
| 19600.00 | 1804 | 2605 | 3063 | 3385 | 3669 | 3926 |
| 19650.00 | 1808 | 2610 | 3069 | 3391 | 3676 | 3934 |
| 19700.00 | 1811 | 2616 | 3075 | 3398 | 3684 | 3942 |
| 19750.00 | 1815 | 2621 | 3081 | 3405 | 3691 | 3949 |
| 19800.00 | 1819 | 2626 | 3088 | 3412 | 3698 | 3957 |
| 19850.00 | 1822 | 2631 | 3094 | 3418 | 3706 | 3965 |
| 19900.00 | 1826 | 2636 | 3100 | 3425 | 3713 | 3973 |
| 19950.00 | 1829 | 2642 | 3106 | 3432 | 3720 | 3981 |
| 20000.00 | 1833 | 2647 | 3112 | 3439 | 3728 | 3988 |

Obligation Worksheet A
(The worksheet for calculation of the total support obligation
under R.S. 9:315.8 and 315.10)

Court _____

Case Number _____

_____
Petitioner

Children          Date of Birth

_____

_____

_____

Parish _____ Louisiana

Div/CtRm _____

and _____

Respondent

Children          Date of Birth

_____

_____

_____

|  | A. Petitioner | B. Respondent | C. Combined |
|---|---|---|---|
| 1. MONTHLY GROSS INCOME (R.S. 9:315.2(A))<br>a. Preexisting child support payment.<br>b. Preexisting spousal support payment. | $<br>-<br>- | $<br>-<br>- |  |
| 2. MONTHLY ADJUSTED GROSS INCOME    (Line 1 minus 1a and 1b). | $ | $ |  |
| 3. COMBINED MONTHLY ADJUSTED GROSS INCOME (Line 2 Column A plus Line 2 Column B). (R.S. 9:315.2(C)) |  |  | $ |
| 4. PERCENTAGE SHARE OF INCOME (Line 2 divided by line 3). (R.S. 9:315.2(C)) | % | % |  |
| 5. BASIC CHILD SUPPORT OBLIGATION (Compare line 3 to Child Support Schedule). (R.S. 9:315.2(D)) |  |  | $ |

| | | | |
|---|---|---|---|
| a. Net Child Care Costs (Cost minus Federal Tax Credit). (R.S. 9:315.3) | | | + |
| b. Child's Health Insurance Premium Cost. (R.S. 9:315.4) | | | + |
| c. Extraordinary Medical Expenses (Uninsured Only). (Agreed to by parties or by order of the court). (R.S. 9:315.5) | | | + |
| d. Extraordinary Expenses (Agreed to by parties or by order of the court). (R.S. 9:315.6) | | | + |
| e. Optional. Minus extraordinary adjustments (Child's income if applicable). (R.S. 9:315.7) | | | - |
| 6. TOTAL CHILD SUPPORT OBLIGATION (Add lines 5, 5a, 5b, 5c, and 5d; Subtract line 5e). (R.S. 9:315.8) | | | $ |
| 7. EACH PARTY'S CHILD SUPPORT OBLIGATION (Multiply line 4 times line 6 for each parent). | $ | $ | |
| 8. DIRECT PAYMENTS made by the noncustodial parent on behalf of the child for work-related net child care costs, health insurance premiums, extraordinary medical expenses, or extraordinary expenses. | | - | |
| 9. RECOMMENDED CHILD SUPPORT ORDER (Subtract line 8 from line 7). | | $ | |

Comments, calculations, or rebuttals to schedule or adjustments if made under 8 above or if ordering a credit for a joint custodial arrangement:

Prepared by _____     Date _____

Obligation Worksheet B
(The worksheet for calculation of the total child support
obligation under R.S. 9:315.9)

Court _____          Parish _____ Louisiana

Case Number_____          Div/CtRm _____

_____          and _____
Petitioner                                         Respondent

Children            Date of Birth      Children                Date of Birth

_____          _____

_____          _____

_____          _____

| | A. Petitioner | B. Respondent | C. Combined |
|---|---|---|---|
| 1. MONTHLY GROSS INCOME (R.S. 9:315.2(A)) | $ | $ | |
| a. Preexisting child support payment. | - | - | |
| b. Preexisting spousal support payment. | - | - | |
| 2. MONTHLY ADJUSTED GROSS INCOME (Line 1 minus 1a and 1b). | $ | $ | |
| 3. COMBINED MONTHLY ADJUSTED GROSS INCOME (Line 2 Column A plus Line 2 Column B) (R.S. 9:315.2(C)) | | | $ |
| 4. PERCENTAGE SHARE OF INCOME (Line 2 divided by line 3) (R.S. 9:315.2(C)) | % | % | |
| 5. BASIC CHILD SUPPORT OBLIGATION (Compare line 3 to Child Support Schedule) (R.S. 9:315.2(D)) | | | $ |
| 6. SHARED CUSTODY BASIC OBLIGATION (Line 5 times 1.5) (R.S. 9:315.9(A)(2)) | | | $ |
| 7. EACH PARTY'S THEORETICAL CHILD SUPPORT OBLIGATION (Multiply line 4 times line 6 for each party)(R.S. 9:315.9(A)(2)) | $ | $ | |
| 8. PERCENTAGE with each party (Use actual percentage of time spent with each party, if percentage is not 50%) (R.S. 9:315.9(A)(3)) | % | % | |

| | | | |
|---|---|---|---|
| 9. BASIC CHILD SUPPORT OBLIGATION FOR TIME WITH OTHER PARTY (Cross Multiply line 7 for each party times line 8 for the other party) (R.S. 9:315.9(A)(3)) (For Line 9 Column A, multiply Line 7 Column A times Line 8 Column B) (For Line 9 Column B, multiply Line 7 Column B times Line 8 Column A) | $ | $ | |
| a. Net Child Care Costs (Costs minus Federal Tax Credit) (R.S. 9:315.3) | | | + |
| b. Child's Health Insurance Premium Cost (R.S. 9:315.4) | | | + |
| c. Extraordinary Medical Expenses (Uninsured only) (Agreed to by parties or by order of court (R.S. 9:315.5) | | | + |
| d. Extraordinary Expenses (Agreed to by parties or by order of the court) (R.S. 9:315.6) | | | + |
| e. Optional: Minus extraordinary adjustments (Child's income if applicable) (R.S. 9:315.7) | | | - |
| 10. TOTAL EXPENSES/ EXTRAORDINARY ADJUSTMENTS (Add lines 9a, 9b, 9c, and 9d; Subtract line 9e) | | | $ |
| 11. EACH PARTY'S PROPORTIONATE SHARE of Expenses/Extraordinary Adjustments (Line 4 times line 10) (R.S. 9:315.9(A)(4)) | $ | $ | |
| 12. DIRECT PAYMENTS made by either party on behalf of the child for work-related net child care costs, health insurance premiums, extraordinary medical expenses, or extraordinary expenses. Deduct each party's percentage share of the expense owed directly to a third party. (R.S. 9:315.9(A)(5)) | - | - | |
| 13. EACH PARTY'S CHILD SUPPORT OBLIGATION (Line 9 plus line 11 and minus line 12) (R.S. 9:315.9(A)(4) and (5)) | $ | $ | |

| | | | |
|---|---|---|---|
| 14. RECOMMENDED CHILD SUPPORT ORDER (Subtract lesser amount from greater amount in line 13 and place the difference in the appropriate column) (R.S. 9:315.9(A)(6)) | $ | $ | |

Comments, calculations, or rebuttals to schedule or adjustments:

Prepared by _____  Date _____

end of the year? Did your attorney know that the other parent made an arrangement with his boss to defer his earned compensation until after the court resolved the child-support issues?)

## 27. There Are 4.3 Weeks in Each Month

1. Use the "4.3 Factor" when calculating a parent's income. Mistakes are continually made in calculating a parent's income by the assumption that there are four weeks in a month. There are not. Each year contains fifty-two weeks in a twelve-month period. Fifty-two divided by twelve equals 4.3. Hence, if the other parent is claiming to earn $1,000 per week, he may be declaring only $4,000 in income per month. His actual monthly income may be $4,300.

2. Apply the "4.3 Factor" when calculating a child-support award, since similar mistakes can be made when doing so. An award of $100 per week does not equal $400 per month. If child support is ordered at $100 per week, the recipient of the child support would get $5,200 per year. If child support is ordered at $400 per month, the recipient gets only $4,800 that year.

The above example shows how easy it can be for a party to manipulate the child-support calculations using your state's guidelines.

### Quick Facts

In 1991, women custodial parents received an average of $3,011 in annual child-support payments. Male custodial parents received average annual child-support payments of $2,292 (U.S. Census Bureau).

Your state's child-support guidelines shall be presumed to be fair; however, most states allow for deviation from the standard guideline formulas based on the special circumstances of a parent or child.

## 28. Declared Income Can Be Manipulaetd

It is worth repeating in this chapter: in order to affect the numbers used in the calculation of child support and/or alimony, a spouse may attempt to manipulate the numbers.

Declared Income Can Be Manipulated by:

1. Changing standard of living
2. Postponing salary increases
3. Delaying bonuses
4. Encouraging the other spouse to get a job or change jobs

5. Reducing the number of hours worked
6. Reducing overtime hours worked
7. Increasing or decreasing child-care expenses
8. Failing to report actual income earned in tax returns
9. Putting assets/income in someone else's name (including new spouse)
10. Becoming "disabled"
11. Sheltering money in corporations, partnerships, or trusts
12. Having personal expenses paid through family business
13. Getting reimbursed by employer for personal expenses (i.e., auto expenses, meals, travel)
14. Making misrepresentations to the court on required financial affidavit

## 29. Looking at the Income of Your Ex's New Spouse

States view your ex's new spouse's income in various ways. Some states prohibit any consideration of this income in determining child support. Many states allow consideration of the income but do not provide guidelines to the court on how to consider it. And states such as Louisiana allow the courts to consider the income of the new spouse *only indirectly to the extent that your ex has shared living expenses with his or here new spouse and as such should have more disposable income available for child support.*

Generally, the new spouse's income will not be considered until or unless your attorney pushes for it (where allowed) and he or she has used discovery techniques to elicit the new spouse's income information.

## 30. Look at Financial Affidavits and In Forma Pauperis Application

Whether called a financial affidavit, financial declaration, or an income and expense declaration, representations made by a party on these pleadings often are the primary basis in the court's determination of a child-support award. Misrepresentation on these pleadings is rampant. If they go unchecked and/or without requests for supporting documentation, abuse can and likely will occur.

Additionally, many parties request the courts to waive the filing fees because of their reported inability to pay. These financial affidavits, often called In Forma Pauperis Applications, are sworn representations of the applying party's income and expenses. Once the form is filed, it is often forgotten. A sharp opponent will compare the representations made on this initial affidavit with the sworn representations made at the time of the child-support hearing. On occasion there are grave inconsistencies, which will aid in the impeachment of your spouse's credibility.

## 31. Deviations from Child-Support Guidelines

The court may allow a deviation from the child-support guidelines if the court finds that there are special needs of the child or extraordinary earnings of the parent. Generally, it is purely at the discretion of your judge as to whether he will permit a deviation from the guidelines.

Examples of grounds for deviation from the guidelines that might translate into a greater child support award are as follows:
- The domiciliary parent's use of the family home in lieu of partial payment of support
- The extraordinary medical expenses relating to the child, not covered by insurance
- The special educational needs and related expenses of the child
- The extraordinary expenses of the child
- The extraordinary length of time that a child spends with the parent receiving child support

Examples of grounds for deviation from the guidelines that might translate into a smaller child-support award are as follows:

- The income of a parent far exceeds the financial needs of a child
- The medical limitations and disabilities of a parent
- The wages earned and received by a child
- The extraordinary length of time that a child spends with the parent paying child support

The Federal Office of Child Support Enforcement compiled a list of the most common reasons that deviations from the guidelines were allowed.

- Agreement between the parents (21%)
- Needs of second households (14%)

- Extended or extraordinary visitation/custody expenses (13%)
- Noncustodial parent's low income (11%)
- An otherwise unjust result
- Extraordinary needs of the parent

Other common excuses heard in courts throughout the country for parents seeking to pay less child support include the following:

- Payer's physical or mental disabilities
- Payer's irregular or cyclical employment
- Custodial parent's interference with visitation rights
- Child-support payments not benefiting children
- Payer paid for other items for children
- Not payer's biological children
- Child is working
- Payer's incarceration

## 32. Watch Out for Cancellation of Insurance Policies

Occasionally, upon the filing of a divorce action, a spouse may cancel the health, life, and/or homeowner's insurance that covers the other spouse, the children, and the property property. Ask your lawyer to file an "ex parte" motion for a temporary restraining order/injunction prohibiting these actions.

If your spouse cancels the insurance, your attorney should ask the court to compel him to reinstate it and pay for any expenses that were incurred that would have been covered by the insurance had you or your child been covered at that time. Once again, ask your lawyer to file a motion for a temporary restraining order/injunction prohibiting the cancellation of the policy.

## 33. Watch Out for "Fifty-Fifty Split of Other Child-Related Expenses

Lawyers and judges often suggest a fifty-fifty split of expenses for medical insurance, extraordinary medical needs, day care, tuition, and the like. Whether such a proposal benefits you depends on what percentage of the two parents' combined gross income belongs to you.

## 34. Dependency Tax Credit

All tax consequences shall be discussed in chapter 14.

## 35. Temporary Award of Child Support Sets the Tone for Regular Child Support

A temporary award of child support and related child-care expenses often later becomes a permanent award. A child-support award is rarely reduced from the original temporary award. "Temporary" should not be equated to "not important" or "temporary" at all!

## 36. Modification of Child Support

As long as the court maintains jurisdiction of the case and the child is eligible to receive the benefits of child support, the judge has the discretion to modify the child-support award.

At the request of either party, the court can review the propriety of the child-support award in effect. A party may seek a change in child support based on a "substantial" and/or "material" change of circumstance (either increase or decrease) in a party's income, financial needs of the child, ineligibility of child due to age, or other factors, such as emancipation, or medical support not previously considered.

Many states, such as Louisiana, have no statutory criteria to determine what dollar change is required to be considered "substantial." Other states have provided standards to provide pecuniary measures as to whether a change is "substantial." Some states require a change in a party's average gross income, while others look to the proposed change in the actual child-support award. "Substantial" could be defined as, as little as $50 or a 10 percent change or as much of a minimum requirement of $100 or a 30 percent change. In many cases, the criteria established to allow a modification in child support are not rigidly followed.

As a recipient or payer of child support who has not sought a review in the award within the last several years, you should inquire as to whether an increase or decrease is in order. Your attorney's request for various income and expense documents may assist you in this evaluation. Child-support cases that involve AFDC, Title IV-E Foster Care, and/or Non-AFDC Medicaid should be reviewed every three years.

## 37. Timing of Child-Support Payments

Although a moral obligation to pay child support begins at the child's birth, in most states, a legal obligation to pay child support does not begin until it is requested by filing a pleading in court. In some states, such as Louisiana, the child-support obligation is only retroactive to the date of filing for child support. Hence, it is important for the custodial parent to file for child support as soon as possible after the child is born. Courts do not consider this a penalty, but rather a legal and moral obligation.

Once a legal obligation of child support is created by law and/or by a judgment of a court, then the timing of the payments must be established. Courts often require payments each month, each week, every two weeks, or on the payer's paycheck cycle.

A payer of child support may not get credit for payments made to the custodial parent prior to the custodial parent's formal request to the court for support. Likewise, a payer of child support may not get credit against his child-support obligation for the payment of child-related goods, such as diapers, food, and clothing.

Can the payer deduct for his expenses? Generally—no.

For the payer to receive full credit for each cent that is paid in child support, the payments should be made directly to the recipient custodial parent.

## 38. Get Proof of Payment

A payer should be able to prove payment of child support for a specified time period (i.e., month) by specifying in the memo of the check the following:

1. Payment of "child support"
2. Date (include period covered—i.e., "March of 2004")
Example: "Memo: Child Support for January of 2005"

The burden of proof that a child-support payment was made generally falls on the payer. Regardless of whether you are the recipient or payer of child support, you should keep records and copies of all child-support payments. This will assist you if a dispute occurs at a later date.

### Best Methods of Payment

1. Pay by personal check. (Keep canceled checks and check registry.) The payer should keep photocopies of checks in case the bank does not return canceled checks.
2. Pay by money orders or cashier's checks (keep copies).
3. Mail by "certified mail, return receipt requested."

4. Pay through the child-support-enforcement agency or clerk of the court.

5. Pay through an income assignment.

Never pay in cash. Cash is the worst method of payment of child support. Unless a receipt is made and signed by both parties, proof becomes a swearing match. Furthermore, receipts may become suspect in cases in which a spouse has threatened violence unless the custodial parent signed a fake receipt.

Payment should be made on or before the due date. Make sure that the payment is received by the recipient on or before the date ordered. If the payment is due on the first of each month, then it should be mailed before and not on the first day of the month.

Be careful of setting a precedent in child support. Many payers make the mistake of paying child support to the recipient parent in an amount much greater than the amount reasonably expected to be ordered to pay at the child-support hearing. Many times, these excessive payments are made out of guilt or other emotions. The payer should realize that the continual excessive payment of child support could set a precedent that the court feels is appropriate at the time of the hearing.

A more safe and accurate approach to paying the appropriate amount of child support is to do so with the help of your lawyer. Your attorney can use Louisiana's guidelines and suggest a figure that is fair.

It should be noted that any parent who has the ability and the desire to pay more child support than would be ordered should be commended.

Many parents who are ordered to pay child support complain that the other parent is not spending the child-support money on the children. Most courts will not entertain discussions in this area unless the payer can prove that the custodial parent is neglecting to pay for the necessities of the children.

## 39. Spousal Support vs. Child Support

Whether a payment is considered spousal support or child support has significant tax consequences. Please refer to chapter 14 for an in-depth discussion of these distinctions.

## 40. Watch for These Taxing Words: "Family Support"

Some states allow for the payment of a commingled combination of child support and alimony called "family support." Be cautious of any proposal regarding family support. Louisiana courts have not recognized this remedy. There will be tax consequences to such a transaction. Federal law allows alimony to be deductible to the payer and taxable to the recipient. Child support is neither deductible nor taxable to either party. Certain rules apply to the deductibility of family support. Before you entertain such a proposal, consult your attorney and tax advisor.

## 41. Bankruptcy and Child Support

The payer of child support cannot interrupt his legal obligation to pay child support by filing bankruptcy. Furthermore, past-due child support is not dischargeable in bankruptcy. See chapter 15.

Late payments may subject the payer to penalties and sanctions. A payer of child support may be subject to many court sanctions if he or she continually pays late. The penalties and sanctions are listed below.

## 42. Retroactivity of Child-Support Judgment

It is important for your attorney to file his or her pleadings requesting child support as soon as practicable, as Louisiana courts usually will grant a custodial parent with retroactive child support from the date of filing of the pleading requesting child support. It is also important that one remind the payer spouse that he or she may be responsible for the payment of the child support retroactively so that the prospective payer can start making payments, for which he or she will receive credit if the payments are made subsequent to the filing.

R.S. 9:315.21. Retroactivity of child support judgment

A. Except for good cause shown, a judgment awarding, modifying, or revoking an interim child support allowance shall be retroactive to the date of judicial demand, but in no case prior to the date of judicial demand.

B. (1) A judgment that initially awards or denies final child support is effective as of the date the judgment is signed and terminates an interim child support allowance as of that date.

(2) If an interim child support allowance award is not in effect on the date of the judgment awarding final child support, the judgment shall be retroactive to the date of judicial demand, except for good cause shown, but in no case prior to the date of judicial demand.

C. Except for good cause shown, a judgment modifying or revoking a final child support judgment shall be retroactive to the date of judicial demand, but in no case prior to the date of judicial demand.

D. Child support of any kind, except that paid pursuant to an interim child support allowance award, provided by the judgment debtor from the date of judicial demand to the date the support judgment is signed, to or on behalf of the child for whom support is ordered, shall be credited to the judgment debtor against the amount of the judgment.

E. In the event that the court finds good cause for not making the award retroactive to the date of judicial demand, the court may fix the date on which the award shall commence, but in no case shall this date be a date prior to the date of judicial demand.

## 43. When Child-Support Ends

Child support usually ends when a child reaches the "age of majority." Society deems the age of majority as the point in a child's life when he is able to be legally independent from his parents. To be declared legally and financially independent is referred to as being "emancipated." Emancipation is an event that generally terminates a child-support obligation.

The age of majority of a child, in reference to the termination of child support, varies from state to state. The following states generally terminate child's eighteenth birthday: Alaska, Arkansas, Arizona, Connecticut, Delaware, Florida, Georgia, Idaho, Iowa, Kansas, Kentucky, *Louisiana,* Massachusetts, Maine, Maryland, Michigan, Minnesota, Missouri, Nevada, New Mexico, North Carolina, North Dakota, Ohio, Oklahoma, Oregon, Pennsylvania,

Rhode Island, South Carolina, South Dakota, Tennessee, Texas, Utah, Vermont, Virginia, Washington, West Virginia, Wisconsin, and Wyoming.

Of the above-referenced states, most states, including Louisiana, have provisions for the continuation of child support beyond a specified age based on extraordinary medical or educational circumstances (generally until the age of nineteen).

States such as Hawaii and Massachusetts allow the extension of the obligation of child support through to the age of twenty-three, if the child is enrolled in full-time higher education.

Washington, DC; Mississippi; and New York consider the age of majority as being twenty-one.

As there are currently no uniform laws as to the definition of the age of majority throughout the United States, theoretically a custodial parent with a child could move from one state that defines the age of majority as eighteen to a state that has an age of majority as twenty-one, and extend the child-support obligation for another three years.

Events that may create a basis to terminate child support throughout the nation are

1. Obtaining the age of majority
2. Marriage of the child
3. Death of the child
4. Completion of the child's education
5. The child entering the military
6. The child's full-time employment
7. The incarceration of the child

## 44. Basis for Extending Child-Support Obligation beyond the Age of Majority

There are two basic reasons that a child-support obligation could extend beyond the child's age of majority:

1. The child has serious medical problems.
2. The child remains in secondary school.

Each state has laws that control extension of child-support payments beyond the child's age of majority. One thought is extremely prudent: If a parent wants an extension of child-support payments beyond the age of majority, then the parent should formally seek an extension from the court prior to the child reaching that age. When one or more children reach the age of majority, the entire child support obligation may be affected.

When parents have two or more minor children, a critical question arises as to what happens to the child-support obligation when one of the children reaches the age of majority (or the child-support obligation related to that child otherwise ends).

One of two circumstances can occur:

1. The amount of the child-support obligation continues unchanged.
2. The amount of the child-support obligation is reduced.

Prior to any of your children reaching the age of majority, consult your attorney and see how that event will affect you. A child-support agreement or order can have provisions for a change in the child-support award upon the occurrence of certain events (i.e., a child reaching the age of majority). Furthermore, a child-support award can be calculated in increments based on a per child basis.

File for modifications to, termination of, or extension on child support in advance of event. Although a change to or termination of a child-support obligation may be automatic by the occurrence of an event, such as the child's attainment of the age of majority, it is inadvisable to assume that a modification to, termination of, or extension on the obligation occurs without a formal request to the court. Speak with your lawyer to determine whether an action with the court is required. Failure to check with your lawyer prior to the event could be a costly mistake.

R.S. 9:315.22. Termination of child support upon majority or emancipation; exceptions

A. When there is a child support award in a specific amount per child, the award for each child shall terminate automatically without any action by the obligor upon each child's attaining the age of majority, or upon emancipation relieving the child of the disabilities attached to minority.

B. When there is a child support award in globo for two or more children, the award shall terminate automatically and without any action by the obligor when the youngest child for whose benefit the award was made attains the age of majority or is emancipated relieving the child of the disabilities attached to minority.

C. An award of child support continues with respect to any unmarried child who attains the age of majority, or to a child who is emancipated relieving the child of the disabilities attached to minority, as long as the child is a full-time student in good standing in a secondary school or its equivalent, has not attained the age of nineteen, and is dependent upon either parent. Either the primary domiciliary parent or the major or emancipated child is the proper party to enforce an award of child support pursuant to this Subsection.

D. An award of child support continues with respect to any child who has a developmental disability, as defined in *R.S. 28:381* (emphasis added), until he attains the age of twenty-two, as long as the child is a full-time student in a secondary school. The primary domiciliary parent or legal guardian is the proper party to enforce an award of child support pursuant to this Subsection.

## 45. Income Assignment/Garnishment

Louisiana courts should order that the child-support obligation is paid through an income assignment or garnishment, unless agreed in writing by the parties. The parties may wish to make other payment arrangements, as the government body that administers the income assignment usually charges the payer an additional fee, which generally ranges from 3 to 5 percent of the monthly child-support obligation.

R.S. 9:303. Income assignment; new orders; deviation

A. In all new child support orders after January 1, 1994, that are not being enforced by the Department of Social Services, the court shall include as part of the order an immediate income assignment unless there is a written agreement between the parties or the court finds good cause not to require an immediate income assignment.

B. For purposes of this Section:

(1) "Written agreement" means a written alternative arrangement signed by both parents, reviewed by the court, and entered into the record of the proceedings.

(2) "Good cause" exists upon a showing by the respondent that any of the following exist:

(a) There has been no delinquency in payment of child support for the six calendar months immediately preceding the filing of the motion for modification of an existing child support order.

(b) The respondent is agreeable to a consent judgment authorizing an automatic ex parte immediate income assignment if he becomes delinquent in child support payments for a period in excess of one calendar month.

(c) The respondent is not likely to become delinquent in the future.

(d) Any other sufficient evidence which, in the court's discretion, constitutes good cause.

C. An income assignment order issued pursuant to this Section shall be payable through the Louisiana state disbursement unit for collection and disbursement of child support payments as provided in *R.S. 46:236.11* (emphasis added) and shall be governed by the same provisions as immediate income assignment orders that are being enforced by the department, including *R.S. 46:236.3* (emphasis added) and 236.4. All clerks of court in the state shall provide information to the state disbursement unit on income assignment orders issued pursuant to this Section. The department shall promulgate rules and regulations to implement the provisions of this Section in accordance with the Administrative Procedure Act.

## 46. Reduction or Increase in Child Support

In order to receive a change from a prior support judgment,

the party seeking the change must prove a material change in circumstances as set forth in Louisiana Revised Statute 9:311.

R.S. 9:311. Reduction or increase in support; material change in circumstances; periodic review by DSS; medical support

A. An award for support shall not be reduced or increased unless the party seeking the reduction or increase shows a material change in circumstances of one of the parties between the time of the previous award and the time of the motion for modification of the award.

B. A judgment for past due support shall not of itself constitute a material change in circumstances of the obligor sufficient to reduce an existing award of support.

C. For purposes of this Section, in cases where the Department of Social Services is providing support enforcement services:

(1) A material change in circumstance exists when a strict application of the child support guidelines, Part I-A of this Chapter, would result in at least a twenty-five percent change in the existing child support award. A material change in circumstance does not exist under this Paragraph if the amount of the award was the result of the court's deviating from the guidelines pursuant to R.S. 9:315.1 (emphasis added) and there has not been a material change in the circumstances which warranted the deviation.

(2) Upon request of either party or on its own initiative and if the best interest of the child so requires, the department shall provide for judicial review and, if appropriate, the court may adjust the amount of the existing child support award every three years if the existing award differs from the amount which would otherwise be awarded under the application of the child support guidelines. The review provided hereby does not require a showing of a material change in circumstance nor preclude a party from seeking a reduction or increase under the other provisions of this Section.

D. A material change in circumstance need not be shown for purposes of modifying a child support award to include a court-ordered award for medical support.

E. If the court does not find good cause sufficient to justify an order to modify child support or the motion is dismissed prior to a hearing, it may order the mover to pay all court costs and reasonable attorney fees of the other party if the court determines the motion was frivolous.

F. The provisions of Subsection E of this Section shall not apply when the recipient of the support payments is a public entity acting on behalf of another party to whom support is due.

## 47. No Change of Circumstances Intended by Amendments

The Louisiana child-support laws were recently amended to create a schedule that encompassed combined, monthly, gross income of the parents up to $20,000 and for worksheets based on either shared or split custody. Any child-support order created before the change of these laws cannot be modified merely because of the amendments to the prior child-support laws.

R.S. 9:315.15. No change in circumstances intended
The enactment and subsequent amendment of this Part shall not for that reason alone be considered a material change in the circumstances of either party.

## 48. Accounting of Child Support

R.S. 9:312. Child support; accounting; requirements

A. On motion of the party ordered to make child support payments pursuant to court decree, by consent or otherwise, after a contradictory hearing and a showing of good cause based upon the expenditure of child support for the six months immediately prior to the filing of the motion, the court shall order the recipient of the support payments to render an accounting.

B. The accounting ordered by the court after the hearing shall be in the form of an expense and income affidavit for the child with supporting documentation and shall be provided quarterly to the moving party. The order requiring accounting in accordance with this Section shall continue in effect as long as support payments are made or in accordance with the court order.

C. The movant shall pay all court costs and attorney fees of the recipient of child support when the motion is dismissed prior to the hearing, and the court determines the motion was frivolous, or when, after the contradictory hearing, the court does not find good cause sufficient to justify an order requiring the recipient to render such accounting and the court determines the motion was frivolous.

D. The provisions of this Section shall not apply when the recipient of the support payments is a public entity acting on behalf of another party to whom support is due.

## 49. Child Support Orders May Include a Late-Payment-Fee Provision

If you are the recipient of child support, suggest that your attorney propose a provision in the agreement or order of child support that calls for a late-payment fee if the payer is delinquent in his child-support payment (the same principal can apply for spousal-support payments). You can argue that if the payer is sincere in his intent to pay timely, then he should not complain about a late-payment provision, as the event would never arise. The payer would only have an objection if he had concerns or an intent to not pay timely.

## 50. Don't Restrict Visitation because of a Refusal to Pay Child Support

It is commonly tempting to refuse or restrict visitation with the children if the payer is not providing child-support payments as ordered. Unless a refusal or restriction of visitation is pursuant a "linkage order" (discussed later in section 56), then the custodial parent is exposing himself or herself to contempt of court sanctions. Also remember that the custodial parent must be a "good parent" for the child's sake. Let the judge do his job in dealing with the non-paying parent. Let the wrath of the court come down only on the delinquent payer; otherwise, the wrath of the court may come down on both of you.

Another unintended result might occur. A few courts have ordered that child-support payments be suspended when a custodial parent has intentionally refused and/or interfered with visitation rights.

Always remember that the child suffers by a refusal or restriction of visitation rights (unless the visiting parent is neglectful or abusive). The payment of child support and visitation generally are separate issues.

Noncustodial parents who have joint custody and/or visitation rights are more likely to pay child support than those parents who do not have these rights. Of the 11.5 million custodial parents, 6.9 million have joint custody of their children (U.S. Census Bureau).

## 51. Collection of Child Support in Different States

According to the Federal Office of Child Support Enforcement, in excess of 30 percent of child-support claims involve parents who live in different states from their children.

## 52. The Uniform Reciprocal Enforcement of Support Act (URESA)

This federal act was created in 1950 to assist in the uniform enforcement of child-support orders across state lines. In 1968, the act was revised. States' use of URESA is decreasing, as it has only marginal desirability and effectiveness. Under URESA, a person seeking child support would request the attorney to file a petition in their "initiating" state. The pleadings would be sent to the "responding" state, where the noncustodial parent lives or owns property. It was the responsibility of the foreign, responding state to establish and/or enforce a child-support order. Under URESA, a noncustodial parent could argue before his or her home state (responding state) that a reduction in the amount is sought. The possibility of more than one child-support order could exist under URESA, thus creating a child-support discrepancy between the initiating and responding states' orders.

Many states have repealed their URESA legislation in favor of the Uniform Interstate Family Support Act (UIFSA).

## 53. The Uniform Interstate Family Support Act (UIFSA)

Under UIFSA, the establishment and enforcement of a child support obligation is assisted with one order. Unless an alternative is agreed upon by both parents, UIFSA provides that the state that originally makes the child-support decree continues to have jurisdiction ("continuing exclusive jurisdiction") as long as one parent continues to reside in the state. This ensures that only one child-support order is in effect. Courts evaluate whether jurisdiction exists on a case-by-case basis. The court will consider the following factors in deciding whether jurisdiction exists:

1. Whether the noncustodial parent is personally served in the state
2. Whether the noncustodial parent consents to the jurisdiction of the state
3. Whether the noncustodial parent had resided with the child within the state
4. Whether the noncustodial parent had sexual intercourse in the state that lead to the conception of the child
5. Whether the child resides in the state as a result of any action of the noncustodial parent
6. Whether the noncustodial parent acknowledged the child in the state
7. Any other facts that the court deems relevant

UIFSA legislation allows one state's income-withholding order to be directly sent to an employer of the noncustodial parent in another state.

Each state has a central registry for the collection of interstate child-support orders.

Your lawyer can give you more information on how these federal acts affect one's ability to collect child support.

## 54. Twenty Ways to Collect Child Support in America

1. Income withholding/wage assignment/garnishment/payroll deduction
2. Contempt of court
3. Collect attorney fees, court costs, and related expenses
4. Intercept of federal and state income-tax refund

5. Property seizure and sale/restraining notices and orders to prohibit transfer of property
6. Suspension/revocation of Louisiana licenses
7. Arrest warrants and jail
8. "Most Wanted" lists
9. New-hire reporting
10. Intercept of unemployment benefits, worker's copensatio benefits, social-security and disability benefits, state lottery winnings, and pensions/benefits of state employees
11. Appointment of receiver
12. Require a bond/security
13. Judicial and administrative liens
14. Report to credit bureaus
15. File a creditor's suit
16. Private collection agencies
17. Linkage order
18. Collect from the military
19. Private attorney
20. Child-support enforcement office

## 1. Income Withholding/Wage Assignment/Garnishment/ Payroll Deduction

Two-thirds of all child-support dollars collected by state child-support agencies come from income withholding.

Courts can order that the noncustodial parent pay child-support through an income assignment. This forces payment of part or all of the support obligation, with the assistance of the obligor's employer. In many states, failure of an employer to withhold to the extent ordered and/or allowed by law could result in the employer becoming liable for the amount of child support that should have been properly withheld.

If an employer fails to withhold earnings pursuant to a garnishment order, the failure of the employer to garnish does not excuse or relinquish the payer's obligation to pay the support.

Pursuant to the Family Support Act of 1988 (Title IV, Part D of the Social Security Act), states should impose automatic income assignments to all new or modified child-support decrees. Although mandated by the federal government, many courts are lax in the application of this law.

When Congress first enacted legislation to garnish the wages of federal employees for child support in the late 1970s, fewer than

1,000 federal employees were affected annually. Now the federal government garnishes over 3,500 federal-employee checks per month (Defense Finance and Accounting Service).

## 2. Contempt of Court

The court will consider several factors in determining whether a party is in contempt of court:

1. The existence of a valid written order
2. The payer's knowledge of the order
3. The payer's ability to comply with the order
4. The payer's willful disobedience of the order

R.S. 13:4611. Punishment for contempt of court

Except as otherwise provided for by law:

(1) The supreme court, the courts of appeal, the district courts, family courts, juvenile courts, and the city courts may punish a person adjudged guilty of a contempt of court therein, as follows:

(a) For a direct contempt of court committed by an attorney at law, by a fine of not more than one hundred dollars, or by imprisonment for not more than twenty-four hours, or both; and, for any subsequent contempt of the same court by the same offender, by a fine of not more than two hundred dollars, or by imprisonment for not more than ten days, or both;

(b) For disobeying or resisting a lawful restraining order, or preliminary or permanent injunction, by a fine of not more than one thousand dollars, or by imprisonment for not more than twelve months, or both, except in juvenile courts and city courts, in which punishment may be a fine of not more than one thousand dollars or imprisonment for not more than six months, or both.

(c) For a deliberate refusal to perform an act which is yet within the power of the offender to perform, by imprisonment until he performs the act; and

(d) For any other contempt of court, including disobeying an order for the payment of child support or spousal support or an order for the right of custody or visitation, by a fine of not more than five hundred dollars, or imprisonment for not more than three months, or both.

(e) In addition to or in lieu of the above penalties, when a parent has violated a visitation order, the court may order any or all of the following:

(i) Require one or both parents to allow additional visitation days to replace those denied the noncustodial parent.

(ii) Require one or both parents to attend a parent education course.

(iii) Require one or both parents to attend counseling or mediation.

(2) Justices of the peace may punish a person adjudged guilty of a direct contempt of court by a fine of not more than fifty dollars, or imprisonment in the parish jail for not more than twenty-four hours, or both.

(3) The court or justice of the peace, when applicable, may suspend the imposition or the execution of the whole or any part of the sentence imposed and place the defendant on unsupervised probation or probation supervised by a probation office, agency, or officer designated by the court or justice of the peace, other than the division of probation and parole of the Department of Public Safety and Corrections. When the court or justice of the peace places a defendant on probation, the court or the justice of the peace may impose any specific conditions reasonably related to the defendant's rehabilitation, including but not limited to the conditions of probation as set forth in *Code of Criminal Procedure Article 895* (emphasis added). A term of probation shall not exceed the length of time a defendant may be imprisoned for the contempt, except in the case of contempt for disobeying an order for the payment of child support or spousal support or an order for the right of custody or visitation, when the term of probation may extend for a period of up to two years.

C.C.P. Art. 225. Same; procedure for punishing

A. Except as otherwise provided by law, a person charged with committing a constructive contempt of court may be found guilty thereof and punished therefor only after the trial by the judge of a rule against him to show cause why he should not be adjudged guilty of contempt and punished accordingly. The rule to show cause may issue on the court's own motion or on motion of a party to the action or proceeding and shall state the facts alleged to constitute the contempt. A person charged with committing a constructive contempt of a court of appeal may be found guilty thereof and punished therefore after receiving a notice to show cause, by brief, to be filed not less than forty-eight hours from the date the person receives such notice why he should not be found guilty of contempt and punished accordingly. The person so charged shall be granted an oral hearing on the charge if he submits a written request to the clerk of the appellate court within forty-eight hours after receiving notice of the charge. Such notice from the court of appeal may be sent by registered or certified mail or may be served by the sheriff. In all other cases, a certified copy of the motion, and of the rule to show cause, shall be served upon the person charged with contempt in the same manner as a subpoena at least forty-eight hours before the time assigned for the trial of the rule.

B. If the person charged with contempt is found guilty the court shall render an order reciting the facts constituting the contempt, adjudging the person charged with contempt guilty thereof, and specifying the punishment imposed.

Each state has different penalties for being held in contempt of court, some of which are mentioned in this chapter. Speak to your lawyer to find what penalties apply in your state.

### 3. Collect Attorney Fees, Court Costs, and Related Expenses
In Louisiana, when a parent owes past-due child support, most courts will permit the parent seeking child support to collect money for attorneys fees, court costs, and related expenses actually incurred in the custodial parent's attempt to collect the past-due obligation. Often judges do not award the full amount of attorney fees incurred by the parent seeking the past-due child support.

Furthermore, it is imperative that when a parent seeks child support, he or she formally request reimbursement for attorney fees and court costs incurred in that legal pursuit.

### 4. Intercept of Federal and State Income-Tax Refunds

Your state can intercept the noncustodial parent's state income-tax return for past-due child support. Often the noncustodial parent will be more willing to allow the entire tax refund to be intercepted as payment for past-due support, as the noncustodial parent has never seen the money; therefore, it seems to hurt less.

### Quick Facts

Every year the state child-support enforcement agencies contact the Internal Revenue Service with the names of parents who owe past-due child support.

For the 1995 tax year, the federal government collected over 1 billion dollars in past-due child-support payments through intercepts of income tax-refunds. Since 1982, over 6 billion dollars have been collected from approximately 10 million intercepted, federal, tax refunds.

Contact your state's child-support enforcement agency as soon as possible in order to begin the process of seeking a federal tax-refund offset, as tax returns are filed only once a year. You want to make sure that your state agency has enough time to properly submit your claim to the IRS before the refund is sent to the delinquent parent.

### 5. Property Seizure and Sale/Restraining Notices and Orders to Prohibit Transfer of Property

Courts have procedures that allow a recipient of child support to seize property of a nonsupporter to collect a support debt. A variety of assets—ranging from real estate, automobiles, boats, jewelry, money in checking and savings accounts, and cash—can be seized.

### 6. Suspension/Revocation of Louisiana Licenses

Many states, such as Louisiana, allow the suspension and/or revocation of driver's licenses, hunting licenses, fishing licenses, and professional licenses (such as a license to practice law, medicine, and the like) for those delinquent with child-support payments.

### Suspension of Licenses for Nonpayment of Child Support

R.S. 9:315.30. Family financial responsibility; purpose

The legislature finds and declares that child support is a basic legal right of the state's parents and children, that mothers and fathers have a legal obligation to provide financial support for their children, and that child support payments can have a substantial impact on child poverty and state welfare expenditures. It is therefore the legislature's intent to facilitate the establishment of paternity and child support orders and encourage payment of child support to decrease overall costs to the state's taxpayers while increasing the amount of financial support collected for the state's children. To this end, the courts of this state are authorized to suspend certain licenses of individuals who are found to be in contempt of court for failure to comply with a subpoena or warrant in a child support or paternity proceeding or who are not in compliance with a court order of child support.

R.S. 9:315.31. Definitions

As used in this Subpart:

(1) "Board" means any agency, board, commission, or office, public or private, that issues any license for activity specified in Paragraph (6) of this Section.

(2) "Compliance with an order of support" means that the support obligor is no more than ninety days in arrears in making payments in full for current support or in making periodic payments as set forth in a court order of support, and has obtained or maintained health insurance coverage if required by an order of support.

(3) "Contempt of court" means that a person has been found guilty of a direct contempt of court for a contumacious failure to comply with a subpoena, pursuant to Code of *Civil Procedure Article 222(5)* (emphasis added), or a constructive contempt of court for willful disobedience of a lawful order of the court, pursuant to *Code of Civil Procedure Article 224(2)* (emphasis added), in or ancillary to a child support or paternity proceeding.

(4) "Court" means any court exercising jurisdiction over the

determination of child support, paternity, or criminal neglect of family proceedings.

(5) "Department" means the Department of Social Services when rendering child support enforcement services in TANF or non-TANF cases.

(6) "License" means any license, certification, registration, permit, approval, or other similar document evidencing admission to or granting authority for any of the following:

(a) To engage in a profession, occupation, business, or industry.

(b) To operate a motor vehicle.

(c) To participate in any sporting activity, including fishing and hunting.

(7) "Licensee" means any individual holding a license, certification, registration, permit, approval, or other similar document evidencing admission to or granting authority to engage in any activity specified in Paragraph (6) hereof. The term "licensee" may be used interchangeably with "obligor".

(8) "Obligee" means any person to whom an award of child support is owed and may include the department.

(9) "Obligor" means any individual legally obligated to support a child or children pursuant to an order of support. The term "obligor" may be used interchangeably with "licensee".

(10) "Order of support" means any judgment or order for the support of dependent children issued by any court of this state or another state, including any judgment or order issued in accordance with an administrative procedure established by state law that affords substantial due process and is subject to judicial review.

(11) "Suspension" means a temporary revocation of a license for an indefinite period of time or the denial of an application for issuance or renewal of a license.

R.S. 9:315.32. Order of suspension of license; noncompliance with support order; contempt of court

A. (1) (a) In or ancillary to any action to make past-due child support executory, for contempt of court for failure to comply with an order of support, or a criminal neglect of family proceeding, the court on its own motion or upon motion of an obligee or the department shall, unless the court determines good cause exists, issue an order of suspension of a license or licenses of any obligor who is not in compliance with an order of child support. The court shall give specific written and oral reasons supporting its determination of good cause including a finding as to the particular facts and circumstances that warrant a determination not to suspend a license or licenses of an obligor who is not in compliance with an order of child support. The reasons shall become part of the record of the proceeding.

(b) An order suspending a license to operate a motor vehicle may provide specific time periods for the suspension at the court's discretion.

(2) In or ancillary to any child support or paternity proceeding, the court on its own motion or upon motion of any party or the department may issue an order of suspension of a license of any person who is guilty of contempt of court for failure to comply with a subpoena or warrant. Provided that before the issuance of an order for a suspension of a license of any person in, or ancillary to, any paternity proceeding where paternity has not yet been established, the court shall notify such person by personal service.

B. The order of suspension shall contain the name, address, and social security number of the obligor, if known, and shall indicate whether the suspension is for a particular, specified license, or all licenses which the obligor may possess, or any combination thereof at the discretion of the court.

C. An order of suspension may include a provision whereby the obligor is required to disclose to the court information concerning the types of licenses which the obligor possesses, which written disclosure when attached to the order of suspension becomes a part thereof.

R.S. 9:315.33. Suspension of license; notice of suspension from licensing board; temporary license

A. Within thirty days of receipt of a certified order of suspension of license for noncompliance with an order of support or contempt of court, sent by first class mail from either the court or the attorney representing the obligee, the board shall suspend all licenses which it issued to the obligor, or other person in contempt, or a particular license as specified in the order.

B. The board shall specify an exact date and hour of suspension, which date shall be within thirty days from the board's receipt of the order of suspension, and shall promptly issue a notice of suspension informing the licensee of all of the following:

(1) His license has been suspended by order of the court, including the suit name, docket number, and court as indicated on the order.

(2) The effective date of the suspension.

(3) To apply for reinstatement, the obligor must obtain an order of compliance from the court.

(4) Any other information prescribed by the board.

C. Upon being presented with a court order of partial compliance and at the request of an obligor whose motor vehicle operator's license, permit, or privilege has been suspended under this Subpart, the office of motor vehicles may issue the obligor a temporary license valid for a period not to exceed one hundred twenty days.

R.S. 9:315.34. Subsequent compliance; order of compliance; order of partial compliance

A. (1) An obligor is in subsequent compliance with an order of support when all of the following occur:

(a) The obligor is up to date with current child support payments.

(b) All past-due support has been paid or, if periodic payment for past-due support has been ordered by the court, the obligor is making such payments in accordance with the court order.

(c) The obligor has fulfilled the required health insurance provisions, if any, in the order of support.

(2) A person is in subsequent compliance with a subpoena or court order when the court rescinds the order of contempt.

B. (1) Upon motion of an obligor who is in subsequent compliance with an order of support and after a contradictory hearing or upon rescission of an order of contempt, the court shall issue an order of compliance indicating that the obligor is eligible to have all licenses reissued. In cases where the department is providing support enforcement services, the court shall issue an ex parte order of compliance upon filing of written certification by the department that the obligor is in compliance.

(2) At the request of an obligor or other individual for whom an undue financial hardship will occur or has occurred as a result of the loss of his driver's license and upon a showing of good faith, the court may issue an order of partial compliance authorizing the issuance of a temporary license in accordance with *R.S. 9:315.33*(C) (emphasis added).

**Reissuance of License after Payment of Child Support**

R.S. 9:315.35. Reissuance of license

A. A board shall issue, reissue, renew, or otherwise extend an obligor's or other individual's license in accordance with the board's rules upon receipt of a certified copy of an order of compliance from the court.

B. After receipt of an order of compliance, the board may

waive any of its applicable requirements for issuance, reissuance, renewal, or extension if it determines that the imposition of that requirement places an undue burden on the person and that waiver of the requirement is consistent with the public interest.

### 7. Arrest Warrants and Jail

Many states have criminal sweeps called roundup days. In these cases, an arrest warrant has been issued and the deadbeat is a fugitive from justice.

### When All Else Fails, Consider Relief Pursuant to the Child Support Recovery Act of 1992

The Child Support Recovery Act of 1992 makes it a federal crime to willfully fail to pay arrearages in a child support award if the child lives in a state different from the payer. For the law to apply, the past-due child support must remain unpaid in excess of one year or the past-due child support must be greater than $5,000. The United States Attorney's Office will look at various factors in deciding whether to prosecute a case under the act. Factors include whether the nonpaying parent is moving from state to state to avoid paying the child support, whether the parent is using deceit to avoid payment (such as using a fictitious name or social-security number), whether the parent has refused to pay child support after being held in contempt of court by a state court, and whether the failure or refusal to pay is related to another federal crime, such as bankruptcy or mail fraud.

Penalties for violation of this federal law include the following: first offense—six months in prison and/or a fine— subsequent offense—two years in prison and/or a fine.

### 8. "Most Wanted" Lists

The United States Post Office displays "Most Wanted" lists of persons who owe child support. States are encouraged to create and maintain a similar program. Private organizations have also considered using "wanted lists"; however, much of the private participation in this program has been stifled by concerns regarding defamation lawsuits.

Many states have most wanted lists that provide the picture, name, and other information on the deadbeat parent. Louisiana has used these "wanted lists" on a very limited scale. Unless the parent owes a very substantial sum, it is highly unlikely that this method of collection will be available to you.

### 9. New-Hire Reporting

Under the Personal Responsibility and Work Opportunity Act of 1996 (HR 3734), all states must establish a directory of new hires. States have implemented a "New Hire Reporting" policy, which requires employers to provide data to the state on the employment and/or reemployment of individuals. The data is sent to the state's Office of Child Support Enforcement. All states must have complied with this federal law by October 1, 1998.

This federal New Hire Reporting law requires that all employers report the hiring/rehiring of all new/rehired workers within twenty days of the hire. The employer's report must include the following information:

1. The full name of the employee
2. The employee's social security number
3. The employee's home address
4. Date of employee's first day at work
5. The employer's name, address, and Federal Employer Identification Number (FEIN)
6. The employer's staFte identification number

Reports can be submitted by using the employee's W-4 form. After the information is registered in the state and federal system, the information is processed to see if there is a match to a person who owes past-due child support. If a match is found, an order is sent to the employer that compels the employer to withhold wages for the payment of child support.

### Quick Facts

According to the United States Department of Health and Human Services, within the next ten years, the New Hire Reporting Program is expected to increase child support collections by 6.4 billion dollars.

## 10. Intercept of Unemployment Benefits, Worker's Compensation Benefits, Social-Security and Disability Benefits, State Lottery Winnings, and Pensions/Benefits of State Employees

Federal law mandates that all states have procedures for withholding unemployment compensation benefits for payment of past-due child-support obligations.

States are particularly strict on their own employees.

### 11. Appointment of Receiver

When a debtor of child support has a company or other means of receiving funds, a court may appoint an individual, often called a receiver, to manage the company and collect the funds from the business to pay the child-support obligation.

### 12. Require a Bond/Security

Courts may require the delinquent payer to provide a cash bond and/or other security to ensure that the child-support obligation is paid.

A few courts have directed property of a payer to be placed in a trust. States that allow such a trust include the following: Indiana, Iowa, Kansas, Michigan, New Mexico, North Carolina, Oklahoma, Oregon, Vermont, Washington, Wisconsin, and Wyoming. Louisiana judges have the discretion after a trial on the merits to be placed in a trust to insure payment of the child-support obligation.

### 13. Judicial and Administrative Liens

A Louisiana court may order that a lien be placed on an asset, so when it is sold, payment toward the child-support obligation can be made.

### 14. Report to Credit Bureaus

The noncustodial parent will not want to have a poor credit rating on his report.

### 15. File a Creditor's Suit

If you become aware of property that belongs to the delinquent payer of child support but is in the hands of third parties, your attorney may be able to file a creditor's suit against the other party with the intent to retrieve the asset(s) as partial or full payment of the past-due child-support debt.

## 16. Private Collection Agencies

Many national and local collection companies offer their services to collect past-due child support. Caution should be taken when considering the use of a private collection agency, as the actual cost incurred in the use of such a service may be significant in comparison to the cost of hiring a family-law attorney or seeking relief from your parish, district attorney's office.

## 17. Linkage Order

Although not uniformly favored throughout the country, some courts have made "linkage orders," linking a parent's ability to have visitation rights with his or her compliance with the payment of child support. Linkage orders are not used in Louisiana; however, you should be aware of such orders, in the event that a parent relocates to a state that permits them.

## 18. Collect from the Military

The United States Armed Forces makes a concerted effort to have their soldiers pay child-support obligations. If the noncustodial parent is in the military, contact the appropriate branch offices. A listing can be found at the end this chapter.

## 19. Private Attorney

Whether you seek to collect child support through a private attorney or the state office of child-support enforcement, the information requested in appendix A will be of significant value to your attorney. Be sure to answer the questions, keep the information in a safe place, and provide your attorney with a copy.

## 20. Office of Child Support Enforcement

Report problems to the Office of Child Support Enforcement.

If you find that a certain agency or court is failing to pursue the enforcement of your order awarding child support, you may seek assistance by reporting the problems, via certified mail, to the following federal office:

Federal Parent Locator Service
Department of Health and Human Services
Family Support Administration
Office of Child Support Enforcement

4th Floor
370 L'Enfant Promenade S.W.
Washington, DC 20447
(202) 252-5443 (Federal Parent Locator Service)
(202) 252-5343 (Family Support Administration)
(202) 475-0257 (Department of Health and Human Resources)

The Office of Child Support Enforcement (OCSE) is an agency of the United Stated Department of Health and Human Services that works in conjunction with state agencies. The OCSE also may assist in the collection of alimony if the past-due alimony is due pursuant to a prior order establishing both alimony and child support.

The OCSE will not assist a party in obtaining a divorce, property settlement, and/or the pursuit of a new order for alimony.

### Quick Facts

In a recent year, state child-support-enforcement agencies established over a million new child-support orders, enforced and/or modified over 5 million child-support orders, and collected $10.8 billion dollars in child-support payments. In the same period, the state agencies also established paternity for 903,400 children.

State offices of child-support enforcement assist in the following:
1. Locating noncustodial parents
2. Establishing paternity
3. Establishing child-support orders
4. Enforcing child-support orders/collecting child support

Louisiana's Office of Support Enforcement Services is as follows:
Louisiana Enforcement Services
Department of Health and Human Services
P.O. Box 44276
Baton Rouge, LA 70804
(504) 342-4780
www.dss.state.la.us/departments/of/Support_Enforcement_Services.htm

## Louisiana Department of Social Services Child-Support-Enforcement Services Regional Offices

Alexandria
900 Murray Street
P.O. Box 832
Alexandria, LA 71309-0832
(318) 487-5202
Covered parishes: Avoyelles, Catahoula, Concordia, Grant, La Salle, Rapides, Vernon, and Winn

Amite
407 N.W. Central Avenue
P.O. Box 338
Amite, LA 70422-0338
(504) 748-2006
Covered parishes: Livingston, St. Helena, St. Tammany, Tangipahoa, and Washington

Baton Rouge
333 Laurel Street, Second Floor
P.O. Box 829
Baton Rouge, LA 70821
(225) 342-5760
Covered parishes: Ascension, Assumption, East Baton Rouge, East Feliciana, Iberville, Pointe Coupee, St. James, West Baton Rouge, and West Feliciana

Gretna
802 Second Street
Gretna, LA 70053
Covered parish: Jefferson

Lafayette
825 Kaliste Saloom Road, Suite 200
P.O. Box 3867
Lafayette, LA 70508-3867
(337) 262-5813
Covered parishes: Acadia, Iberia, Lafayette, St. Martin, St. Mary, and Vermilion

Lake Charles
1417 Gadwell Street
Lake Charles, LA 70615
(337) 491-2111
Covered parishes: Beauregard, Calcasieu, Cameron, and Jefferson Davis

Monroe
2006 Tower Drive
P.O. Box 3144
Monroe, LA 71210-3144
(318) 362-5271
Covered parishes: Bienville, Caldwell, Claiborne, Franklin, Jackson, Lincoln, Morehouse, Ouachita, Richland, Union, and West Monroe

Natchitoches
1774 Texas Street
P.O. Box 1317
Natchitoches, LA 71458
(318) 357-3109

Covered parishes: De Soto, Natchitoches, Red River, and Sabine

New Orleans
2235 Poydras Street
P. O. Box 53446
New Orleans, LA 70153-3446
(504) 826-2222
Covered parishes: Orleans, Plaquemines, and St. Bernard

Shreveport
9310 Normandie Drive
P.O. Box 18590
Shreveport, LA 71138
(318) 676-7010
Covered parishes: Bossier, Caddo, and Webster

Tallulah
1614 Felicia Drive

P.O. Box 431
Tallulah, LA 71282-0431
(318) 574-0486
Covered parishes: East Carroll, Madison, and Tensas

Thibodaux
1000-A Plantation Road
P.O. Box 1427
Thibodaux, LA 70302-1427
(985) 447-0952
Covered parishes: Lafourche, St. Charles, St. John the Baptist, and Terrebonne

Ville Platte
318 Nita Drive
P.O. Box 119
Ville Platte, LA 70586
(337) 363-6638
Covered parishes: Allen, Evangeline, and St. Landry

## State and Other Child-Support-Enforcement Offices in America

Alabama
Division of Child Support
Activities
Bureau of Public Assistance
State Department of Pensions
and Security
64 N. Union Street
Montgomery, AL 36130
(205) 242-9300
http://www.state.al.us/

Alaska
Child Support

Enforcement Agency
Department of Revenue
201 E. 9th Avenue, Room 302
Anchorage, AK 99501
(907) 276-3441
http://www.revenue.state.ak.us

Guam
Child Support
Enforcement Unit
Department of Public Health
and Social Services
Government of Guam

P.O. Box 2816
Agana, GU 96910
(671) 734-2947

Hawaii
Child Support Enforcement
Agency
770 Dapiolani Boulevard, Suite
606
Honolulu, HI 96813
(808) 548-5779
www.hawaii.gov/csea/csea.htm

Idaho
Bureau of Child Support
Enforcement
Department of Health and
Welfare
Statehouse Mail
Boise, ID 83720
(208) 334-4422
http://www.state.id.us/

Illinois
Bureau of Child Support
Department of Public Aid
316 South Second Street
Springfield, IL 62762
(217) 782-1366
www.state.il.us/dpa/cse.htm

Indiana
Child Support Enforcement
Division
State Department of Public
Welfare
4th Floor
141 South Merridian Street

Indianapolis, IN 46224
(317) 232-4894
http://www.ai.org/fssa/cse/

Iowa
Child Support Recovery Unit
Iowa Department of Social
Services
1st Floor
Hoover Building
Des Moines, IA 50319
(515) 281-5580
http://www2.legis.state.ia.us/ga-
/76ga/legislation/sf/02300/sf0-
2344/current.htl

Kansas
Child Support Enforcement
Program
Department of Social and
Rehabilitation Services
Perry Building, 1st Floor
2700 West Sixth
Topeka, KS 66606
(913) 296-3237
http://www.ink.org/public/srs-
/srswanted.html

Kentucky
Human Resources Cabinet
Family Services Division
275 East Main Street
Frankfort, KY 40621
(502) 564-6852
www.state.ky.us/oag/childs.htm

**Louisiana**
**Louisiana Enforcement Services**
**Department of Health and**

**Human Services**
**P.O. Box 44276**
**Baton Rouge, LA 70804**
**(504) 342-4780**
**www.dss.state.la.us/main-**
**fram.htm**

Maine
Support Enforcement and
Location Unit
Department of Human Services
State House Station II
Augusta, ME 04333
(207) 289-2886
http://www.state.me.us/

Maryland
Child Support Enforcement
Administration
Department of Human
Resources
5th Floor
300 West Preston Street
Baltimore, MD 21201
(301) 383-4773
www.state.md.us/srv_csea.htm

Massachusetts
Child Support Enforcement
Unit
Massachusetts Department of
Revenue
213 First Street
Cambridge, MA 02142
(617) 621-4759
www.mst,oa.net:8002/macse.html

Michigan
Office of Child Support

Enforcement
Department of Social Services
P.O. Box 30037
Landsing, MI 48909
(517) 373-7570
http://www.mfia.state.mi.us

Minnesota
Department of Human Services
Space Center Building
444 Lafayette Road
St. Paul, MN 55101
(612) 296-2499
http://www.co.hennnepin.mnu-
s/weapsupp.html

Mississippi
Child Support Division
State Department of Public
Welfare
P.O. Box 352
515 East Amite Street
Jackson, MS 39205
(601) 354-0341
www.mdhs.state.ms.us/cse.html

Missouri
Child Support Enforcement
Unit
Division of Family Services
Department of Social Services
P.O. Box 88
Jefferson City, MO 65103
(314) 751-4301
http://services.state.mo.us/dss-
/cse/cse.htm

Montana
Child Support Enforcement
Bureau

P.O. Box 5955
Helena, MT 59604
(406) 444-3347
http://www.dphhs.mt.gov/who-
what/csed.htm

Nebraska
Office of Child Support
Enforcement
Department of Social Services
P.O. Box 95026
Lincoln, NE 68509
(402) 471-3121
http://www.unl.edu/ccfl/cse.htm

Nevada
Child Support Enforcement
Program
Welfare Division
2527 North Carson Street
Carson City, NV 89710
(702) 885-4474
http://state.mv.us/

New Hampshire
Office of Child Support
Enforcement
Division of Welfare
Health and Welfare Building
Hazen Drive
Concord, NH 03301
(603) 271-4426
http://little.nhlink.net/nhlink/-
governme/county/dhs/chld_su-
p.htm

New Jersey
Child Support and Paternity
Unit

Department of Human Services
CN 716
Trenton, NJ 08625
(609) 633-6268
http://www.state.nj.us/judici-
ary/prob01.htm

New Mexico
Child Support Enforcement
Bureau
Department of Human Services
P.O. Box 2348 —PERA Building
Santa Fe, NM 85793
(505) 827-4230
http://www.mostwanted.com/n-
h/support.htm

New York
Office of Child Support
Enforcement
Albany, NY 12260
(518) 474-9081
http://www.state.ny.us/dss/

North Carolina
Child Support Enforcement
Section
Division of Social Services
Department of Human
Resources
433 North Harrington Street
Raleigh, NC 27603
(919) 733-4120
http://www.state.nc.us/cse/

North Dakota
Child Support Enforcement
Agency
North Dakota Department of

Human Services
State Capitol
Bismarck, ND 58505
(701) 224-3582
http://www.state.nd.us/hms/

Ohio
Bureau of Child Support
Ohio Department of Human
Services
State Office Tower
31st Floor
30 East Broad Street
Columbus, OH 43215
(614) 466-3233
http://www.ohiogov/odhs/

Oklahoma
Division of Child Support
Department of Human Services
P.O. Box 25352
Oklahoma City, OK 73125
(405) 424-5871
http://www.acf.dhhs.gov/acf-
programs/cse/fct/sp_ok.html

Oregon
Child Support Program
Department of Human
Resources
Adult and Family Services
Division
P.O. Box 14506
Salem, OR 97309
(503) 378-6093
http://170.104.17.50/rss/rogue-
s.html

Pennsylvania
Child Support Enforcement
Program
Department of Public Welfare
P.O. Box 8018
Harrisburg, PA 17105
(717) 783-1779
http://www.state.pa.us/pa_exec-
/public_welfare/overview.html

Puerto Rico
Child Support Enforcement
Department of Social Services
Fernandez Juncos Station
P.O. Box 11398
Santurce, PR 00910
(809) 722-4731

Rhode Island
Bureau of Family Support
Department of Social and
Rehabilitative Services
77 Dorance Street
Providence, RI 02903
(401) 277-2409
http://www.state.ri.us/

South Carolina
Division of Child Support
Public Assistance Division
Bureau of Public Assistance and
Field Operations
Department of Social Services
P.O. Box 1520
Columbia, SC 29202
(803) 758-8860
http://www.state.sc.us/

South Dakota
Office of Child Support
Enforcement
Department of Social Services
700 Illinois Street
Pierre, SD 57501
(605) 773-3641
http://www.state.sd.us/state/exec-
utive/social/social.html

Tennessee
Child Support Services
Department of Human Services
5th floor
111-19 Seventh Avenue
Nashville, TN 37203
(615) 741-1820
http://www.state.tn.us/humanserv/

Texas
Child Support Enforcement
Branch
Texas Department of Human
Resources
P.O. Box 2960
Austin, TX 78769
(512) 463-2005
http://www.oag.state.tx.us/web-
site/childsup.htm

Utah
Office of Recovery Services
P.O. Box 15400
3195 South Main Street
Salt Lake City, UT 84115
(801) 486-1812
http://www.state.ut.us/

Vermont
Child Support Division
Department of Social Welfare
103 South Main Street
Waterbury, VT 05676
(802) 241-2868
www.dsw.state.vt.us/ahs/ahs.htm

Virgin Islands
Paternity and Child Support
Program
Department of Law
P.O. Box 1074
Christiansted
St. Croix, VI 00820
(809) 773-8240

Virginia
Division of Support
Enforcement Program
Department of Social Services
8004 Franklin Farm Drive
Richmond, VA 23288
(804) 662-9108
http://www.state.va.us/-
dss/childspt.html

Washington
Office of Child Support
Enforcement
Department of Social and
Health Services
P.O. Box 9162-MS PI-11
Olympia, WA 98504
(206) 459-6481
www.wa.gov/dshs/csrc.html

West Virginia
Office of Child Support
Enforcement
Department of Human Services
1900 Washington Street, East
Charleston, WV 25305
(304) 348-3780
http://www.state.wv.us/

Wisconsin
Department of Health and
Human Services
Division of Community
Services
1 West Wilson Street
P.O. Box 7851
Madison, WI 53707

(608) 266-9909
http://dhss.state.wi.us/dhss/
pubs/html/childsp.html

Wyoming
Child Support Enforcement
Section
Division of
Public Assistance and Social
Services
State Department of Health and
Social Services
Hathaway Building
Cheyenne, WY 82002
(307) 777-6083
http://www.dfsweb.state.wy.us/c-
sehome/wybody1.htm

## 55. Information and Documents to Bring to Your Office of Child-Support Enforcement

1. Name of noncustodial parent
2. Last-known address of noncustodial parent
3. Child's birth certificate
4. Any child-support order
5. Any divorce decree (if applicable)
6. Last-known name and address of noncustodial parent's employer
7. Any other information regarding the whereabouts and/or income/assets of the noncustodial parent

## 56. Locate "Deadbeats"

The Parent Locator Service is one of the most effective methods of tracking down noncustodial parents who live in or out of your state. The computerized system locates parents by the use of driver's license numbers, social-security numbers, and other means of identification.

States differ in the extent of their ability to trace a person through their state agencies. States typically contact the following sources:

- Credit-bureau contacts
- Department of Corrections
- Department of Human Services (food stamps and other programs)
- Department of Labor/Employment Security (food stamps and unemployment benefits)
- Department of Public Safety/Motor Vehicles/Transportation
- Department of Revenue/Taxation
- Department of Social Services
- Department of Vital Statistics (birth certificates)
- Department of Wildlife and Fisheries (fish and game licenses)
- IV-A/Medicaid Database
- New Hire Reporting System
- Registrar of Voters/Department of Elections (voter registration)
- Secretary of State

## 57. Suspension of or Modification to Child-Support Obligation When Secreting a Child

R.S. 9:315.23. Suspension or modification of child support-obligation; secreting of child

If one joint custodial parent or his agent is intentionally secreting a child with the intent to preclude the other joint custodial parent from knowing the whereabouts of the child sufficiently to allow him to exercise his rights or duties as joint custodial parent, the latter may obtain from the court an order suspending or modifying his obligation under an order or judgment of child support. However, such circumstances shall not constitute a defense to an action for failure to pay court- ordered child support or an action to enforce past due child support.

## 58. Award of Attorney Fees

R.S. 9:375. Award of attorney's fees.

A. When the court renders judgment in an action to make executory past-due payments under a spousal or child support award, or to make executory past-due installments under an award for contributions made by a spouse to the other spouse's education or training, it shall, except for good cause shown, award attorney's fees and costs to the prevailing party.

B. When the court renders judgment in an action to enforce child visitation rights it shall, except for good cause shown, award attorney's fees and costs to the prevailing party.

## 59. Costs; Action to Make Child Support Executory

R.S. 9:304.1. Court costs; action to make child support executory

A. An action to make past due child support executory may be filed by any plaintiff, who is unable to utilize the provisions of Chapter 5 of Title I of Book IX of the Code of Civil Procedure, without paying the costs of court in advance or as they accrue or furnishing security therefor, if the court is satisfied that the plaintiff because of poverty or lack of means cannot afford to make payment.

B. When the action has been filed without the payment of costs as provided in Subsection A and the plaintiff is not the prevailing party, except for good cause, the court shall order the plaintiff to pay all costs of court.

## 60. Disavowal of Paternity Relating to Child-Support Obligation

R.S. 9:305. Disavowal of paternity; ancillary to child support proceeding

A. Notwithstanding the provisions of *Civil Code Art. 189* (emphasis added) and for the sole purpose of determining the proper payor in child support cases, if the husband, or legal father who is presumed to be the father of the child, erroneously believed, because of misrepresentation, fraud, or deception by the mother, that he was the father of the child, then the time for filing suit for disavowal of paternity shall be suspended during the period of such erroneous belief or for ten years, whichever ends first.

B. No provision of this Section shall affect any child support payment or arrears paid, due, or owing prior to the filing of a disavowal action if an order of disavowal is subsequently obtained in such action.

## 61. Criminal Neglect of Family

R.S. 14:74. Criminal neglect of family

A. (1) Criminal neglect of family is the desertion or intentional nonsupport:

(a) By a spouse of his or her spouse who is in destitute or necessitous circumstances; or

(b) By either parent of his minor child who is in necessitous circumstances, there being a duty established by this Section for either parent to support his child.

(2) Each parent shall have this duty without regard to the reasons and irrespective of the causes of his living separate from the other parent. The duty established by this Section shall apply retrospectively to all children born prior to the effective date of this Section.

(3) For purposes of this Subsection, the factors considered in determining whether "necessitous circumstances" exist are food, shelter, clothing, health, and with regard to minor children only, adequate education, including but not limited to public, private, or home schooling, and comfort.

B. (1) Whenever a husband has left his wife or a wife has left her husband in destitute or necessitous circumstances and has not provided means of support within thirty days thereafter, his or her failure to so provide shall be only presumptive evidence for the purpose of determining the substantive elements of this offense that at the time of leaving he or she intended desertion and nonsupport. The receipt of assistance from the Family Independence Temporary Assistance Program (FITAP) shall constitute only presumptive evidence of necessitous circumstances for purposes of proving the substantive elements of this offense. Physical incapacity which prevents a person from seeking any type of employment constitutes a defense to the charge of criminal neglect of family.

(2) Whenever a parent has left his minor child in necessitous circumstances and has not provided means of support within thirty days thereafter, his failure to so provide shall be only presumptive evidence for the purpose of determining the substantive elements of this offense that at the time of leaving the parent intended desertion and nonsupport. The receipt of assistance from the Family Independence Temporary Assistance Program (FITAP) shall constitute only presumptive evidence of necessitous circumstances for the purpose of proving the substantive elements of this offense. Physical incapacity which prevents a person from seeking any type of employment constitutes a defense to the charge of criminal neglect of family.

C. Laws attaching a privilege against the disclosure of communications between husband and wife are inapplicable to proceedings under this Section. Husband and wife are competent witnesses to testify to any relevant matter.

D. (1) Whoever commits the offense of criminal neglect of family shall be fined not more than five hundred dollars or be imprisoned for not more than six months, or both, and may be placed on probation pursuant to *R.S. 15:305* (emphasis added).

(2) If a fine is imposed, the court shall direct it to be paid in whole or in part to the spouse or to the tutor or custodian of the child, to the court approved fiduciary of the spouse or child, or to the Louisiana Department of Social Services in a FITAP or Family Independence Temporary Assistance Program case or in a non-FITAP or Family Independence Temporary Assistance Program case in which the said department is rendering services, whichever is applicable; hereinafter, said payee shall be referred to as the "applicable

payee." In addition, the court may issue a support order, after considering the circumstances and financial ability of the defendant, directing the defendant to pay a certain sum at such periods as the court may direct. This support shall be ordered payable to the applicable payee. The amount of support as set by the court may be increased or decreased by the court as the circumstances may require.

(3) The court may also require the defendant to enter into a recognizance, with or without surety, in order that the defendant shall make his or her personal appearance in court whenever required to do so and shall further comply with the terms of the order or of any subsequent modification thereof.

E. For the purposes of this Section, "spouse" shall mean a husband or wife.

Ch.C. Art. 1353. Support provisions; contempt; penalties

A. If the defendant violates the terms of the court order, the court, upon motion, may issue an order directing the defendant to show cause why he or she should not be found in contempt of court for failure to pay the court ordered support or maintain health care insurance, which rule shall be tried in a summary manner.

B. If on the hearing of such rule the court finds the accused guilty of contempt for failure to comply with the judgment of the court in paying the support assessed, the court may punish for such contempt as follows, either:

(1) The court may sentence the defendant to be imprisoned for not more than six months. The court in its discretion may suspend this term of imprisonment in whole or in part on condition that the defendant pay the total amount of unpaid support and obtain health care insurance in a manner to be determined by the court and on such other conditions as set by the court. If the court suspends the sentence in whole or in part, the court may place the defendant on probation

under *R.S. 15:305* (emphasis added) with conditions of probation to be set by the court. In addition, the court may fine the defendant an amount not to exceed one hundred dollars to be paid to the applicable payee.

(2) The court may order the defendant to pay the total amount of unpaid support to the applicable payee and obtain health care insurance within a period of time fixed by the court. During this period of time, the defendant may be released upon giving bond for his appearance in court if he fails to comply with the order of the court within the period of time fixed. Should the defendant not pay the total amount of unpaid support which the court has ordered, the defendant shall be imprisoned for not more than six months.

C. Upon a second or subsequent finding of contempt, the court shall sentence the defendant to imprisonment for not more than six months. At the discretion of the judge, the sentence may be suspended by the court upon the occurrence of all of the following:

(1) Payment of the amount of unpaid support.

(2) Payment of the amount of unpaid support accrued since the date of the said order.

(3) Payment of the amount of all attendant court costs.

(4) Proof of health care insurance.

D. Upon recommendation of the state attorney or the support enforcement officer, or both, the remainder of the sentence may be suspended upon payment of a lesser amount, plus attendant court costs. Such payment shall apply toward but not extinguish the total amount due.

E. If the court finds the accused guilty of contempt, the court shall also render judgment directing the defendant to obtain health care insurance and to pay the total amount of unpaid support to the applicable payee, and attendant court costs. Such judgment for the payment of unpaid support and court costs shall have the same force and effect as a final judgment for money damages against the defendant. This judgment may be made executory by any Louisiana court of competent jurisdiction on petition of the department or the district attorney.

F. If the defendant has entered into a recognizance in the amount fixed by the court to insure the payment of the support and maintenance of health care insurance, the court may order the forfeiture of the recognizance and enforcement thereof by execution. The sum recovered shall be paid in whole or in part to the applicable payee. However, should the court order both the forfeiture of the recognizance and at the same time order the defendant to pay all unpaid support under the sentence for contempt, the amount of unpaid support plus attendant court costs and fines shall be the maximum payable.

## 62. Watch Out for "Child-Support Blackmail"

It is all too common for a spouse to threaten a custody battle unless the other spouse concedes to a lower child support, alimony, and/or property settlement. This blackmail should not be tolerated. Report these threats to your attorney. Any evidence of these threats should also be given to your attorney.

## 63. Negotiating Child Support

Child support blackmail is despicable and should not be tolerated. On the other hand, a negotiation regarding the payment of past-due child support is a common practice throughout the United States. Many proposals are accepted for a percentage of what is legally owed. It may be mutually beneficial to come to a compromise rather than endure a lengthy and expensive court battle. Weigh your options and make an informed decision.

## 64. Statute of Limitations

There is a statute of limitations regarding the time period in which one can seek enforcement of a former child-support award. In many states, including Louisiana, if a parent avoids payment of past-due child support for a period of time longer than the state's statute of limitations, then that part of the child-support obligation extending beyond the enforceable time period would be legally forgiven (there are exceptions, which your attorney can discuss with you in greater detail).

For example, state "A" has a statute of limitations of five years. If the payer owes six years of past-due child support, then only the last five years would be legally collectible.

Some states other than Louisiana have taken the enlightened view that a child-support obligation is never excused by the mere passage of time.

## 65. For Further Support, Contact a Parents without Partners Group

If you would like a support group to help you through these trying times, contact a local Parents Without Partners support group by calling their toll-free telephone number at (800) 638-8078.

### Father's Rights Support Group

Louisiana Dads
P.O. Box 216
Milton, LA 70558
www.homestead.com/ladads.html

## 66. How to Enforce Child Support Abroad

Although the United States does not have a treaty with any country regarding the enforcement of child-support orders, many states have reciprocal arrangements with the following foreign countries. Contact the Louisiana Attorney General's Office to see if the country in question is under an agreement with Louisiana.

Australia
Austria
Bermuda
Canada
Czech Republic
Fiji
Finland
France
Germany
Hungary
Ireland
Jamaica
Mexico
New Zealand
Norway
Poland
Slovak Republic

South Africa
Sweden
United Kingdom (England, Scotland, Northern Ireland,
and Wales)

Your first step in an attempt to get foreign enforcement of your child-support award is to contact your state's office of child-support enforcement.

If the parent who owes the child support lives and/or works abroad yet works for a company based in the United States or for the United States government, then you likely will be able to enforce your support order through your state's office of child-support enforcement or a private attorney in order to garnish wages.

## 67. If No Reciprocal Agreement Exists with Your State and the Foreign Country, Retain a Foreign Attorney

You may be able to retain a foreign attorney on a contingency basis. The United States Department Office of American Citizens Services can provide you with a listing of English-speaking foreign attorneys. Furthermore, many countries have legal aid services. Call and/or write for the address and telephone number of the applicable foreign embassy in Washington, DC. Additionally, the International Social Service (ISS) may be able to lend you assistance. The ISS can be contacted at the following:

International Social Service
10 W. 40th Street
New York, NY 10018
(212) 532-6350

## 68. Contact the Foreign-Based Employer

Additional pressure can be levied by sending a certified, translated copy of outstanding child-support orders to the deadbeat's employer. A list of company presidents and other individuals in the corporate hierarchy may be found by consulting with a branch of the company and by using business directories such as *Standard & Poor's* (http://www.stockinfo.standardpoor.com/) and *Dunn & Bradstreet* (http://dbisna.com/dbis/dbishome.htm).

## 69. Collect Support from a Parent Who Is Serving Aboard in the United States Military of Who Is a U.S. Military Retiree Residing Abroad

Your state child-support-enforcement office or private attorney can contact the United States Armed Forces.

For garnishment, contact the Pentagon at (703) 545-6700, and you will be directed to the appropriate judge advocate general's office. Please refer to http://www.jagc.army.mil/jagc2.htm.

For Service of Process on Military Personnel, contact the judge advocate general's office for the appropriate branch of the armed forces.

Air Force Judge Advocate General's Office:
http://www.ja.hq.af.mil
Army Judge Advocate General's Office:
http://21taacom.army.mil/aerja/
Navy Judge Advocate General's Office:
http://www.jag.navy.mil

**Locate Military Personnel**

To locate a person in the United States Armed Forces, contact the following:

Air Force
Headquarters
AFMPC/DPMD003
Attn: Worldwide Locator
Randolph Air Force Base, TX 78150-6001
(210) 652-5774

Army
Commander
U.S. Army EREC
Army Worldwide Locator Service
Fort Benjamin Harrison, Indiana 46249-5301
(317) 542-4211

Coast Guard
Commandant
United States Coast Guard
Coast Guard Locator Service
GPE 3-45 (Enlisted Personnel)
GPE-42 (Officers)
2100 2nd Street, S.W.
Washington, DC 20593
(202) 267-1615 (Enlisted Personnel)
(202) 267-1667 (Officers)

Marine Corps
Commander of the Marine Corps
Code MMRB-10
Attn: Locator Service
Washington, DC 20380-0001
(202) 694-1610

Navy
Naval Military Personnel Command
Navy Annex
Washington, DC 20370
(202) 694-3155

Chapter 9

# Spousal Support

"My husband supported me since we married. Will he have
to pay me spousal support so that I have the same standard
of living?"

—Zelda P.
age 51, divorcing, no children, substitute teacher
Natchitoches, Louisiana

## 1. Spousal Support

Spousal support, also known as alimony or maintenance, is a payment from one spouse, the breadwinner, to the other spouse who
earns less income. Permanent alimony may last the extent of the
recipient's life. The underlying rationale for alimony is to assist the
spouse of less fortune, opportunities, and/or abilities with living
expenses and other needs. It may be classified by the time period in
which it is to be paid.

Rehabilitative, or restitution, alimony lasts for a definitive period
of time, with the goal of helping the other spouse to become self-
sufficient. The reason for the need of rehabilitation may result from
the recipient spouse's previous forgoing of educational and/or
employment opportunities during the marriage that he or she
would have reasonably expected to otherwise have experienced.
Unlike child support, alimony is not calculated by using state guidelines, but rather, the figure is derived from the agreement of the
parties or at the discretion of the judge.

## 2. Spousal Support Is an Endangered Species

"My lawyer tells me that I may not get alimony because

I have a steady job, but my husband has always made so much more than me."

—Sarah S.
age 36, divorcing, two children, restaurant manager
New Orleans, Louisiana

Throughout the country, we are seeing a shift in the view of courts toward permanent alimony. With an increasing number of women entering the work force, and the decreasing focus on gender, many states are moving away from the term "alimony" to the term "maintenance." The seemingly subtle shift in the use of terms is an example of the growing paradigmatic shift of today's courts. As a public policy, Texas has had no provisions for alimony (although it may in the near future). Other state courts are becoming more resistant to awarding spousal support, except in cases in which a spouse has been and remains financially dependent on the other spouse for a lengthy period of time.

Louisiana classifies spousal support into two categories: interim periodic support and final periodic support.

C.C. Art. 111. Spousal support; authority of court

In a proceeding for divorce or thereafter, the court may award interim periodic support to a party or may award final periodic support to a party free from fault prior to the filing of a proceeding to terminate the marriage, based on the needs of that party and the ability of the other party to pay, in accordance with the following Articles.

## 3. Interim Spousal Support (Temporary Alimony)

C. C. Art. 113. Interim spousal support allowance pending final spousal support award

Upon motion of a party or when a demand for final spousal support is pending, the court may award a party an interim spousal support allowance based on the needs of that party, the ability of the other party to pay, and the standard of living of the parties during the marriage, which award of interim spousal support allowance shall terminate upon the rendition of a judgment of divorce. If a claim for final spousal support is pending at the time of the rendition of the judgment of divorce, the interim spousal support award shall thereafter terminate upon rendition of a judgment awarding or denying final spousal support or one hundred eighty days from the rendition of judgment of divorce, whichever occurs first. The obligation to pay interim spousal support may extend beyond one hundred eighty days from the rendition of judgment of divorce, but only for good cause shown.

Predivorce alimony, commonly called interim spousal support, is alimony established for the period of time from the date of filing a pleading asking for such relief until the date of the divorce. Some states provide exceptions that permit the obligation of "temporary" alimony to extend beyond the date of the divorce. This is most common in cases in which permanent spousal support is also requested by a spouse, and the court has not been able to have the trial regarding the issue of permanent spousal support.

Although states vary in the application of factors used to determine whether or not and to what extent temporary alimony should be paid, generally, the courts will look at both parties' prior standard of living. Fault for the breakup of the marriage, as well as each spouse's assets, are either not considered or given less consideration during the evaluation for and calculation of temporary spousal maintenance.

## 4. Final Periodic Spousal Support

C.C. Art. 112. Determination of final periodic support

A. The court must consider all relevant factors in determining the entitlement, amount, and duration of final support. Those factors may include:

(1) The needs of the parties.

(2) The income and means of the parties, including the liquidity of such means.

(3) The financial obligations of the parties.

(4) The earning capacity of the parties.

(5) The effect of custody of children upon a party's earning capacity.

(6) The time necessary for the claimant to acquire appropriate education, training, or employment.

(7) The health and age of the parties.

(8) The duration of the marriage.

(9) The tax consequences to either or both parties.

B. The sum awarded under this Article shall not exceed one-third of the obligor's net income.

Final periodic spousal support is financial support of a spouse after the termination of the marriage. Like in the case of temporary spousal support, states vary on the factors used in addressing such support. In order to determine whether permanent spousal support is appropriate, and to what degree and for what duration, if any, it should be paid, the court weighs the relative positions of each party.

## 5. When Can Final Periodic Spousal Support Be Modified or Terminated?

C.C. Art. 114. Modification or termination of award of periodic support

An award of periodic support may be modified if the circumstances of either party materially change and shall be terminated if it has become unnecessary. The subsequent remarriage of the obligor spouse shall not constitute a change of circumstance.

## 6. Look at Your Insurance Needs before Your Divorce Is Final

"I'm covered on my wife's HMO."

—John V.
age 39, married, two children, carpenter
Norco, Louisiana

Upon the filing of a divorce decree, your medical-insurance coverage may be affected.

Prior to the divorce, make arrangements to ensure that you and your children will remain covered. Generally, dependent children can remain on a policy after a divorce decree. Yet the nonemployee former spouse will most likely be dropped from the policy unless other provisions are made.

Pursuant to federal law, a nonemployee former spouse may

remain on the employee spouse's medical insurance through the payment of additional premiums through COBRA. COBRA allows the nonemployee former spouse to be maintained on the health-insurance policy for up to three years after the divorce decree. Ask your attorney how to take advantage of the benefits provided by COBRA.

Additionally, a vindictive spouse may attempt to cancel the other spouse's medical- and dental-insurance coverage prior to the judgment of divorce. Ask your attorney to verify your spouse's medical- and dental-insurance coverage and request the filing of a restraining order that the insurance be maintained until the divorce is finalized.

Likewise, a spouse may attempt to change the life-insurance beneficiaries prior to a divorce decree. Your attorney should request that the existing life insurance be maintained and the designated beneficiaries remain unchanged at the same coverage amount. Your attorney may request notification of any beneficiary change or failure to pay the premium.

## 7. Consolidated Omnibus Budget Reconciliation Act of 1985 (COBRA)

A divorce usually terminates an ex's right to be covered under the former spouse's employer's medical-insurance plan (unless each spouse works for the same employer and is covered under the same insurance plan). Under the Consolidated Omnibus Budget Reconciliation Act of 1985 (COBRA), upon request, a nonemployee former spouse can receive continued insurance coverage with the same insurance carrier for up to three years. This helps to eliminate the immediate postdivorce concern over a potential lapse in medical-insurance coverage. The insurance company (insurance agent) should be immediately notified of your desire to exercise your COBRA rights.

## 8. Watch Out for Manipulation of Income and Expenses for Purposes of Affecting Spousal-Support Award

> "He will hide his income as he gets paid in cash."
> —Stephanie K.
> age 39, divorcing, one child, gift-shop salesperson
> Baton Rouge, Louisiana

A manipulation of events can occur that directly affects the alimony award. A spouse may attempt the following:

1. Control, possess, and/or hide assets
2. Decrease income/earning capacity while seeking to increase spouse's income/earning capacity
3. Increase expenses (allowing less disposable funds to be available to spouse) while decreasing spouse's expenses (thereby decreasing her "need" for alimony)
4. Attempt to withhold funds from spouse to the point that the spouse is under financial duress and is more likely to concede to a less-favorable alimony award

In order to affect the numbers used in the calculation of alimony, a spouse may attempt the following:

1. Change standard of living
2. Postpone salary increases
3. Delay bonuses
4. Encourage the other spouse to get a job or change jobs
5. Reduce the number of hours worked
6. Reduce overtime hours worked
7. Increase or decrease expenses
8. Fail to report actual income earned in tax returns
9. Put assets/income in someone else's name
10. Become "disabled"
11. Shelter money in corporations, partnerships, or trusts
12. Have personal expenses paid through family business
13. Get reimbursed for expenses on the side by employer (i.e., auto expense, meals, travel, etc.)
14. Make misrepresentations to the court about his income or expenses

(The same acts can occur in an attempt to manipulate a child-support award.)

Prior to or during the divorce process, a breadwinning spouse may encourage the other spouse to do the following:

1. Seek employment and/or training
2. Increase hours worked
3. Seek higher pay
4. Seek a second job
5. Decrease expenses
6. Sign a consent agreement to waive alimony or to accept a less-favorable spousal-support award

## 9. Know the Tax Consequences and Requirements of Spousal Support

Alimony creates a tax deduction, for the Internal Revenue Service considers alimony completely different from its treatment of child support. The payment of child support is neither deductible nor treated as income to either the payer or the recipient. For an extensive discussion of the tax consequences and requirements of alimony, refer to chapter 14.

## 10. Be Wary of Reconciliation

As previously noted, reconciliation may defeat prior grounds of fault. Be wary of your spouse's attempt(s) to reconcile, as it may be solely for the purpose of eliminating a crucial consideration used in the determination of spousal support.

## 11. Watch Out for "Spousal-Support Blackmail"

Unfortunately, and frequently, a spouse will threaten a custody battle unless the other spouse concedes to waiving alimony or receiving a lower alimony and/or child-support award. Report any such threats to your attorney. Any evidence of these threats should be tendered to your lawyer.

## 12. Get or Encourage Educational and Vocational Rehabilitation

Although often used to lessen an alimony award, educational and/or vocational training and rehabilitationcan have a long-term benefit to both spouses. The spouse paying alimony may receive the benefit of having the payment period shortened or terminated, and the spouse receiving alimony will achieve a point of rehabilitation to allow him or her to become financially independent.

Vocational experts can assist in the evaluation and placement of training and/or employment in the job market.

## 13. Seek Reimbursement for Other Spouse's Education, Training, and/or Increased Earning Capacity

Many states allow a financial award, generally considered separate and apart from an award of alimony or of a property division, permitting a spouse to receive money for his or her contribution to the other spouse's education, training, and/or increased earning capacity that was not realized and benefited from during the marriage. See your attorney for more details. This award is found in cases such as one involving one spouse putting the other through medical or law school and being divorced soon after the degree was earned.

C.C. Art. 121. Claim for contributions to education or training; authority of court

In a proceeding for divorce or thereafter, the court may award a party a sum for his financial contributions made during the marriage to education or training of his spouse that increased the spouse's earning power, to the extent that the claimant did not benefit during the marriage from the increased earning power.

The sum awarded may be in addition to a sum for support and to property received in the partition of community property.

## 14. Get All Retirement-Plan Information

"My husband and I have retired. That's our sole source of income. How can I ensure that I get my fair share of the retirement plan?"

—Lindsay F.
age 64, married, two adult children, retired
Ruston, Louisiana

In order to handle a property settlement or decree properly, your lawyer and the court need information about each spouse's retirement plans. According to the Employee Retirement Income Security Act (ERISA), information regarding pension plans and trusts should be made available to the plan participants and designated beneficiaries.

Various ERISA plans include defined benefit plans, defined contribution plans, profit-sharing plans, stock-bonus plans, stock-option plans, Tax Reform Act stock plans, savings plans, incentive plans, thrift plans, and others. With this information, your attorney may negotiate a property settlement favorable to your needs.

Most plans have administrators who manage the retirement funds. The retirement plans of either spouse may have certain requirements necessary to alter the scheduled payments and/or recipients of the retirement funds. Your lawyer should seek an order from the court, known as a Qualified Domestic Relations Order (QDRO), instructing the retirement-plan administrator to handle the plan in a particular manner. The QDRO should have the necessary language required by the retirement-plan administrator.

# Chapter 10

# PREVENT ABUSE AND HARASSMENT

## 1. National Statistics on Domestic Violence

According to the Federal Bureau of Investigation, 85 percent of domestic-violence victims are women. Battered persons come from all socioeconomic classes. It is also estimated that approximately 85 percent of children who live in violent homes personally witness domestic violence.

Experts estimate that each year approximately 3 to 10 million children are impacted by domestic violence. Law-enforcement officers spend approximately one-third of their time responding to domestic-violence complaints. Annually, over 1 million women seek medical assistance as a result of injuries caused by domestic battery. Of the 3.5 million cases of alleged child abuse reported to child-protection agencies annually, investigators verify that 1,250,000 children had been neglected and/or abused. Approximately 16 out of every 1,000 children are verified victims of abuse. Of these abused children, 26 percent were physically abused, 15 percent were sexually abused, 45 percent were neglected, and 3 percent endured emotional abuse. The remaining 11 percent of the abused children encountered other abuse or abandonment. Most abuse occurs at home.

Child Protection Services agencies have confirmed approximately 2,000 annual fatalities related to child abuse and neglect. It seems almost inconceivable that nearly five or six children perish each day from abuse or neglect.

## 2. Louisiana Statistics on Domestic Violence

According to the Governor's Office of Women's Services, Louisiana's domestic-violence shelters and related programs served over 19,219 women and served 13,318 in twelve months.

### 3. Forms of Domestic Abuse

Abuse can take three basic forms.

1. Harassment—takes the form of verbal and nonverbal acts that are intended to emotionally hurt, demean, and ridicule the other person.
2. Physical Abuse—involves acts of physical contact intended to create fear, pain, and/or injury to the other person.
3. Sexual Abuse—involves acts of nonconsensual sexual behavior often accompanied by the threat of force or greater emotional pain. Sexual abuse also can take the form of sexual demands, violence, and fetishes.

The most common trait of someone who is being abused is that he or she mistakenly believes that the abuser will change and ultimately cease the abuse. Unfortunately, this is rarely the case without significant legal and mental-health intervention. The abuser's primary goal is to control, manipulate, and have power over the victim.

Abuse is behavior used to control or dominate the other person by means of threats, manipulation, physical, and/or sexual assaults. The abuser creates hurtful feelings of fear, insecurity, helplessness, guilt, paranoia, rejection, isolation, humiliation, ridicule, shame, denial, and/or depression. The abuse is often accompanied by chemical and/or financial dependency. A major hurdle to be overcome is the fear of the abuser's retaliation.

According to the United States Department of Justice, although victims of abuse can be either men or women, approximately 85 percent of reported abuse victims are women. The pervasiveness of abuse in our society is appalling, with most cases remaining unreported.

### 4. Immediately Protect Your Children and Yourself!

The first rule to follow, and the safest way to protect your children and yourself, is to flee to a safe location. If that is not possible, immediately call the police and/or your lawyer.

The Safest Action
1. Flee with your children.
2. Call the police.
3. Call your attorney.

To flee is not an act of cowardice; it is usually the most prudent thing for you to do. Be sure to keep your location a secret from your abusive spouse. Leave the house or get a lawyer to keep spouse out of house.

State laws have been created that legally force an abuser out of the house or apartment in which you live. You should contact your lawyer about the details necessary to accomplish these goals.

## 5. Ask the Following Questions as You Develop a "Safety Plan"

- Am I knowledgeable about the shelter, legal, and welfare options in my community?
- Do I have reliable transportation?
- Do I have the number to a hot line for abused victims?
- Do I know about restraining orders?
- Do I have a friend that I can "safely" call if things get really bad? Can I identify myself to my friend? Is there some sort of code that the two of us could devise?
- Can I predict what will happen to me if I do leave? What should I anticipate and plan for now
- Does he know the whereabouts of all of my friends or relatives?
- Whose home might be considered for a safe refuge?
- Whose whereabouts does he know? Would they set up a communication linkage with me in the event that he looks for me there?
- What can I do to avoid being found?
- In the event that I need to go to another state, do I have national shelter phone numbers?
- In the event that I need to leave hurriedly, do I have an extra set of keys for the house or car?
- Do I have access to money? Credit cards? Do I have blank checks?
- Do I have quick access to all important documents, like birth certificates, social-security cards, car registration, etc.?
- Do I know what toy or blanket will make my child feel secure? (Metropolitan Battered Women's Program)

## 6. Where to Go

A significant problem of most people being abused by a spouse is that they have no planned destination in the event that abuse or a threat of abuse occurs.

## Contact the Louisiana Family Violence Program in Your Area

Faith House
Lafayette, LA
337-232-8954

Family Counseling
Agency/ Turning Point
Center
Alexandria, LA
318-448-0284; 318-442-
7196; 800-960-9436

The Haven
Houma, LA
985-853-0045;
985-872-0450

Jeff Davis Communities
Against Domestic Abuse
Jennings, LA
337-616-8419

June N Jenkins Women's
Shelter
De Ridder, LA
337-462-1452

LCADV
Baton Rouge, LA
225-752-1296

Metropolitan Battered
Women's Program
Jefferson, LA
504-837-5455
(Crisis) 504-837-8900

New Start Center

St. Martinville, LA
337-394-8559

Safe Harbor
Slidell, LA
985-781-4852;
985-781-4856

Safety Net for Abused
Persons/S.N.A.P.
New Iberia, LA
337-367-7627

Southeast Spouse Abuse
Program
Hammond, LA
985-542-8384

St. Bernard Battered
Women's Program
Chalmette, LA
504-277-3178

Taylor House/Project
Celebration
Many, LA
318-256-2064

Y.W.C.A. of Northeast
Monroe, LA
318-651-9314

Y.W.C.A. of Greater New
Orleans B.W.P.
New Orleans, LA
504-486-0377

For assistance in areas not listed, contact the Governor's Office of Women's Policy at (225) 922-0959.

Consider temporary housing with the following:

1. Hotels
2 New apartment
3. Other family members
4. Friends
5. Shelters for battered women (or men)
6. Hospital
7. YMCA or YWCA
8. Community centers
9. Churches
10. Other shelters
11. Your own house or apartment after it is secured and/or restrain
    ing orders or peace bonds have been placed against the abuser

## 7. Go to a Battered-Women's Shelter or a Rape-Crisis Center

Use the local yellow pages to find the hospitals, clinics, and treatment programs that are available in your community. There are over one thousand battered-women's shelters across the country. The yellow pages usually lists these services under the following categories: "social services," "shelters," "crisis intervention services," "support groups," "counseling," and "women's services."

Should you be unsuccessful in finding a battered-women's shelter or rape-crisis center through the telephone directory or directory assistance, call the National Domestic Violence Hot line at (800) 799-SAFE.

This hot line is answered twenty-four hours a day, seven days a week, including holidays. They can refer you to shelters in your community. For additional information regarding protecting yourself and your family from abuse, call the National Coalition Against Domestic Violence at (303) 839-1852.

Many of these shelters will allow you to stay for up to one or two months.

If your child is being abused, telephone the National Child Abuse Hot line at (800) 422-4453.

### Domestic-Abuse and Violence Hot Lines

National Domestic
Violence Hot line
(National Coalition
Against Domestic
Violence)
(800) 333-SAFE (7233)

For Hearing Impaired:

(800) 873-3636
National Child-Abuse
Hot line
(800) 422-4453

National Rape Crisis
Center Hot line
(202) 333-7273

### Missing Children Hot Lines

For Assistance to Runaway or
Abducted Children:
(800) I AM LOST (426-5678)
(Child Find, Inc.)

Covenant House
(800) 999-9999
For Assistance for Parental
Abductors:
(800) A WAY OUT
(292-9688)

National Center
for Missing
and Exploited Children
(800) 843-5678
(800) THE LOST
(843-5678)

National Runaway
Switchboard Hot Line
(800) 231-6946

## 8. Spousal Rape

The primeval notion that a husband, while married, cannot rape his own wife is coming to an end. Many states have implemented criminal laws that make it a crime for one spouse to force the other into nonconsensual sexual acts. Should this occur, contact the police or a rape-crisis center.

## 9. Love and Respect Yourself

A common trait of persons subjected to a long history of abuse is learning to become helpless against the abuse. Continual degradation by the abuser creates learned helplessness and insecurity in the victim. The victim believes that he or she cannot predict the behavior of the abuser, and the victim feels a huge sense of having no control. You must understand that all violence is unacceptable. You are not to blame for the abuse; you are valuable and deserve to love and respect yourself.

## 10. Change Locks and Alarm Codes

Should you get the sole possession of your residence, change the locks and alarm codes. If you don't have an alarm, consider getting one. Many alarm companies offer personal alarm devices that you can wear around your neck. Once you press the button, you can immediately summon the police.

Also consider adding deadbolts, garage-door locks, as well as locks to your fuse box.

## 11. Get Extra Keys to Your House and Car

As a measure of additional control, an abuser may take all of the keys to your house or car. In order to prevent the abuser's desired result, have additional copies of your keys made and put them in a secure location outside of the abuser's reach. Also consider keeping another set of keys in your wallet or purse.

## 12. Call the Police and Get a Police Report

In many states, if you call the police as a result of your spouse striking you, the police officers have no alternative but to take your spouse to jail. However, this is handled according to local law-enforcement policies or city or parish ordinances. Call 911 or your local police telephone number.

## 13. Get Evidence of Your Abuse

1. Get a police report or incident number. Don't forget to ask the police officer to write a police report. With the incident number from the police officer, later, you or your attorney can get the police report. This can be a valuable tool in your divorce case.
2. Take photographs of any bruises, scratches, and cuts.
3. Go to a doctor and/or hospital.
4. Ask for your medical, psychological, and/or psychiatric records.
5. Get audio- or videotapes.
6. Collect all pieces of physical evidence of the abuse including broken dishes, torn articles of clothing, weapons, and the like.
7. Get witnesses' names, addresses, and telephone numbers.

## 14. Request Terminated or Supervised Visitation of Your Spouse

Louisiana courts must suspend visitation upon a judicial finding of domestic abuse affecting the children.

## 15. Save Money for Emergency Fund

Experts recommend that a person who fears the other spouse should seek immediate assistance. Should a victim or potential victim leave her or his residence, funds that are secure from the grasp of the abuser may be very important during a safe transitional period.

## 16. Talk with Your Children

Children can be affected by the abuse of a parent from the fetal state until old age. If abuse occurs, tell the children that they are not to blame themselves for the abuse. Tell them that you will protect them and encourage them to talk about their concerns. The generation cycle of abuse must stop through your courage to end the abuse and seek appropriate counseling.

### 17. Prevent Excessive Corporeal Punishment by Your Spouse

Many parents take disciplining of a child to an extreme that borders on and/or crosses the line of abuse. Should your spouse use excessive force or extremely unorthodox measures to discipline the children, consider getting a court order against this excessive punishment. If the extreme corporeal punishment continues, immediately contact your local law enforcement and a family-law attorney.

### 18. List Emergency Telephone Numbers and Addresses

In a near and secure place, keep a list of telephone numbers to use in the case of an emergency.

### 19. Stop the Stalker

Stalking is an obsessive pattern of behavior, primarily motivated by passion, anger, and/or rejection and intended to get the attention of and/or frighten the victim. Most states, including Louisiana, have implemented antistalking laws that provide potentially harsh criminal penalties against the stalker.

Unfortunately, laws, police, and courts cannot guarantee protection against a stalker. Avoiding contact with the stalker is your safest plan of action. You also may take self-defense classes and/or learn to use defensive weapons, such as mace, pepper spray, and/or a whistle.

### 20. Take Valuables and Important Records

Should you have the time to accumulate your valuable and sentimental items, do so. Once you leave or otherwise seek help, the abuser may hide, sell, or destroy these items out of revenge and anger.

If you leave the abuser, take all the important records that you can find. A list of the types of documents to look for can be found in section 37 of chapter 5.

### 21. Do Not Take the Law into Your Own Hands

Do not shoot the abuser unless it is clearly in self-defense and you are in legitimate and reasonable fear of severe bodily harm or death. The abuser is not worth going to prison. Get the police involved and walk away.

## 22. Alert Work, Schools, and Day-Care Centers

Your spouse may attempt to harass you at work. Alert your boss, the receptionist, and the building security of any potential problems.

Your spouse also may attempt to take your children out of their school or day-care facility. Have your lawyer get an order prohibiting your spouse from contacting your children at school and from taking the children away from the school or day-care center. Once you have this order, provide the principal, pertinent teachers, and day-care providers with a certified copy of the order, instructing them to call you and the police should your spouse attempt to violate the order.

## 23. Get Ex Parte Orders and/or a Peace Bond

Temporary court orders can assist you in most abusive situations. These orders can address the victim's safety at home, work, school, and/or any other location where the victim may be. Such orders may also prohibit telephone threats of intimidation.

A peace bond is a court order that requires the abuser to put up money that will be forfeited to the court if the abuser violates the order.

Although your spouse may not have harassed you during your marriage, it is remarkable the acts of harassment and abuse that occur after one files for a divorce. Like Dr. Jekyll and Mr. Hyde, your once-passive spouse may become a dangerous monster when issues regarding custody and money are raised. When in doubt, get a protective order against such potential harassment, stalking, violence, and/or abuse.

## 24. Injunctions/Peace Bonds/Temporary Restraining Orders/Ex Parte Relief

Acting swiftly to protect your rights is one of the most effective maneuvers in your divorce case. Insist that your lawyer file pleadings asking for ex parte relief. Ex parte relief is simply a request for a judge to grant orders without a hearing or prior notice to your spouse. This is beneficial, because your lawyer can ask for certain orders without your spouse or his or her lawyer being present in court to argue against your requests.

These ex parte requests seek temporary relief until a full hearing can occur. Ex parte orders usually protect people and property.

1. Ask for an order of temporary physical custody of your children.
2. If you suspect abuse or neglect, ask for an order temporarily determinating the other parent's visitation rights until an investigation into the allegations can be made.
3. Ask for an order preventing the other parent from taking the children out of your parish, state, or the jurisdiction of the court.
4. Ask for an order preventing the other parent from having someone of the opposite sex spend the night when he or she has physical custody of the children or are exercising his or her visitation rights.
5. Ask for an order requiring your spouse to stay a specified minimum distance from
    a. you
    b. your children
    c. your residence
    d. your place of employment
    e. other family members who live with you
    f. your children's school
    g. your children's day-care facility
    h. any other place that your children may be found
6. Protect your children and yourself by asking for an order prohibiting your spouse from
    a. any form of abuse
    b. harassment
    c. alienation of your children's affection

## 25. The Louisiana Protective Order Registry

In 1997 the Louisiana legislature passed Louisiana Revised Statute 46.2136.2 (the Louisiana Protective Order Registry). The registry is the statewide repository for court orders issued for the purpose of preventing harassing, threatening, or violent acts against a spouse, intimate cohabitant, dating partner, family, or household member. The registry is available to judges, prosecutors, probation officers, law-enforcement personnel, victim-assistance providers, and attorneys with specific information regarding specific orders and allegations. As of October 31, 2002, the registry contained

60,934 orders providing protection (www.LPOR.org). For more information about the registry, contact the registry director:

LPOR Director
Judicial Administrator's Office
Louisiana Supreme Court
1555 Poydras Street, Suite 1540
New Orleans, LA 70112

R.S. 46:2136.2. Louisiana Protective Order Registry

A. In order to provide a statewide registry for abuse prevention orders to prevent domestic violence and to aid law enforcement, prosecutors and the courts in handling such matters, there shall be created a Louisiana Protective Order Registry administered by the Judicial Administrator's Office, Louisiana Supreme Court. The Judicial Administrator's Office shall collect the data transmitted to it from the courts of the state and enter it into the Louisiana Protective Order Registry.

B. The Louisiana Protective Order Registry encompasses peace bonds, temporary restraining orders, protective orders, preliminary injunctions, permanent injunctions, and court-approved consent agreements resulting from actions brought pursuant to R.S. 46:2131 et seq., R.S. 9:361 et seq., R.S. 9:372, Children's Code Article 1564 et seq., Code of Civil Procedure Article 3604, or as part of the disposition, sentence, or bail condition of a criminal matter pursuant to Code of Criminal Procedure Article 327.1 or Article 871.1 (emphasis added) as long as such order is issued for the purpose of preventing violent or threatening acts or harassment against, contact or communication with, or physical proximity to, another person.

C. The courts of this state shall use a uniform form for the issuance of any protective or restraining order, which form shall be developed, approved, and distributed by the Judicial Administrator's Office, shall be titled the "Uniform Abuse Prevention Order".

D. The clerk of the issuing court shall send a copy of the order or any modification thereof to the Louisiana Protective Order Registry as expeditiously as possible but no later than by the end of the next business day after the order is filed with the clerk of court. Transmittal of the Uniform Abuse Prevention Order may be made by facsimile transsmission, mail, or direct electronic input, where available, as expeditiously as possible, but no later than the end of the next business day after the order is filed with the clerk of court.

E. Upon formation, the registry shall immediately implement a daily process of expungement of records and names of the parties in all cases where either a temporary restraining order expires without conversion to an injunction or, after an evidentiary hearing, it is determined that a protective order is not warranted.

F. The judicial administrator's office shall make the Louisiana Protective Order Registry available to state and local law enforcement agencies, district attorney offices, the Department of Social Services, office of family support, support enforcement services, and the courts.

## 26. Use Your Telephone as a Shield and a Sword

Should your spouse start harassing you with repeated telephone calls and/or vulgar, threatening or emotional messages, consider the following:

1. Screen your telephone calls by getting an answering machine or using a voice-mail system provided by your local telephone company. If your spouse leaves an inappropriate message, save the recorded message and give it to your attorney so that he or she can present it to the judge.
2. Change your telephone number to an unpublished listing.
3. Keep a written log of the dates, times, and content of each and every harassing telephone call.
4. Use Caller ID, which is provided by your local telephone company.
5. Use Call Blocking, which is provided by your local telephone company. This service allows you to block out or otherwise prevent your spouse from calling from specific telephone numbers.
6. Use Call Forwarding, provided by your local telephone company. Should your spouse continue to call you late at night with harassing messages, simply "call forward" your calls to your attorney's office or to a voice-mail service.
7. Use Call Tracing, provided by your local telephone company. The telephone company can provide documents that can prove calls were made from a certain location. You may need an appropriate person from the telephone company to come testify as to the accuracy and authenticity of these documents.

8. It's extremely wise to ask for an order preventing your spouse from alienating, hiding, or disposing of property without a court order or without your written permission (exceptions are usually made for necessary and ordinary living expenses and regular business expenditures).

9. Likewise, you can ask for an order prohibiting your spouse from incurring greater debt, which you might be responsible for, without a court order or your written permission (again, exceptions are usually made for necessary and ordinary living expenses and regular business expenditures).

10. If you own a business with your spouse, you can ask for an order that will
    a. prohibit your spouse from firing or hiring certain critical employees;
    b. limit business expenditures over a certain sum of money without your written approval or a court order; and/or
    c. compel a full accounting of all business operations.

Chapter 11

# PREVENT PARENTAL KIDNAPPING

## 1. Background and Statistics

In 1995, the FBI reported that 969,264 persons were reported missing and entered into the National Crime Information Computer. The FBI estimates that 85 to 90 percent of these missing persons are children (823,000 to 872,000) (Child Find of America). The number of parents who wrongfully take a child out of the state or country has been steadily growing. An estimated 354,100 children have been abducted by family members. Parents also are refusing to return children after scheduled visitation. The majority of these abducted children are less than ten years old. Approximately 90 percent of the parental abductors are emotionally unstable and/or are substance abusers.

Family abductions occur in two basic ways (each occurs approximately 50 percent of the time): either the child is taken in violation of a custody order or agreement or the parent refuses to return the child according to a custody order or agreement.

Eighty one percent of family abductions are committed by parents during a divorce proceeding or custody battle. Statistics indicate that parental-abduction cases involve a relatively equal number of men and women parents (The National Incidence Studies of Missing, Abducted, Runaway, and Throwaway Children in America, 1988; The American Bar Association; Child Find of America).

If serious threats are made, take the following steps to lessen the chances of a parental kidnapping:
1. Inform your attorney of these threats and instruct him to file restraining orders against the other parent.
2. Without scaring your children, tell them your concerns and inform them what to do if the other parent tries to take them away.

     a. Speak with your children to set up a daily schedule.

     b. Teach your children a "Mayday" password or phrase to be used if they are unable to normally communicate with you, their teachers, baby-sitters, etc.

     c. Teach your children to notice their whereabouts.

     d. Teach your children to memorize your address and telephone numbers.

3. Speak with your children's teachers, school principals, supervisors at day-care facilities, and baby-sitters about the threats of abduction. Provide each of these individuals with a certified copy of the restraining and/or custody order obtained by your attorney.

4. Take a color photograph of your child every six months.

5. Ask the court to require supervised visitation with specific instructions to the person supervising, in the event that the parent attempts to remove the child.

6. Ask the court to require the other parent to post a hefty bond that would be forfeited if there were any attempt to abduct.

## 2. Custody/Visitation Order

A prerequisite to any claim that the other parent wrongfully has your child is to obtain a certified copy of the custody/visitation order. Make sure you have several certified copies.

## 3. Keep File on Spouse and Children

By answering all of the information sought in the data sheets found in appendix A, you will have collected valuable information that can be used to help identify and locate the abducting parent.

Additional Information and Documents That Will
Assist Your Search

1. Photographs of spouse and children
2. Addresses of relatives, friends, employers, and business associates
3. Spouse's driver's license and social-security numbers
4. Information on spouse's vehicle, including license-plate number
5. Spouse's credit-card numbers
6. List of all spouse's magazine subscriptions and club memberships
7. Your children's identification cards, including pictures, fingerprints, and notices of birth marks and/or scars
8. Child's passport (know passport number, date, and place of issuance)
9. Possible airlines or public transportation that spouse would likely use

## 4. Child Identification Sheet

(Use and safeguard each child's identification record. Complete one form for each child.)

Update the photograph and signature every few years.

Child's full name:_____
Child's current address: _____
Child's current telephone number:_____
Child's date of birth: _____
Child's place of birth: _____
Child's social-security number:_____
Child's blood type and other special medical needs:_____
_____
All identifying marks, scars, birthmarks, or other identifying characteristics:_____
_____
_____

Child's passport number (if applicable):_____
Child's signature:_____
Date of signature:_____

***Please attach recent color photograph of child!***

Fingerprint each hand (all fingers and thumb).
LEFT HAND:
Fingers on Left Hand                                    Thumb


RIGHT HAND:
Thumb                                    Fingers on Right Hand


(Keep all of this information in a secure location.)

## 5. Understand the Basics of the Uniform Child Custody Jurisdiction Act (UCCJA)

The Uniform Child Custody Jurisdiction Act (UCCJA) states that a state lacks jurisdiction over a custody dispute if a child has been wrongfully transported into the state. Under the act, a state has jurisdiction for a custody dispute if the child lives in the state or has lived in the state for at least six months before one files a pleading regarding custody. Additionally, a state may have jurisdiction for a custody dispute if the child and one or more parents have a "significant connection" with the state. The UCCJA has been adopted throughout the country. This legislation establishes jurisdiction across state lines.

A powerful tool of the UCCJA is that it allows "emergency" jurisdiction for child custody if the child is physically present in the state and an emergency order is required to protect the child from abuse or neglect. The "emergency" provision of the UCCJA can be a valuable shield to help protect a child from harm, yet it also provides an avenue to abuse the system in order to find a more favorable forum for a custody dispute in another state.

Federal law also provides that every state shall enforce and not modify any child-support determination by a court of another state. The Parental Kidnapping Prevention Act (28 U.S.C. 1738A) applies to all judgments, decrees, or other orders of a court providing for the custody or visitation of a child, including permanent and temporary orders.

R.S. 13:1700 Purposes of Part; construction of provisions

A. The general purposes of this part are to:

(1) Avoid jurisdictional competition and conflict with courts of other states in matters of child custody which have in the past resulted in the shifting of children from state to state with harmful effects on their well-being.

(2) Promote cooperation with the courts of other states to the end that a custody decree is rendered in that state which can best decide the case in the interest of the child.

(3) Assure that litigation concerning the custody of a child takes place ordinarily in the state with which the child and his family have the closest connection and where significant evidence concerning his care, protection, training, and personal relationships is most

readily available, and to assure that the courts of this state decline the exercise of jurisdiction when the child and his family have a closer connection with another state.(4) Discourage continuing controversies over child custody in the interest of greater stability of home environment and of secure family relationships for the child.

(5) Deter abductions and other unilateral removals of children undertaken to obtain custody awards.

(6) Avoid relitigation of custody decisions of other states in this state insofar as feasible.

(7) Facilitate the enforcement of custody decrees of other states.

(8) Promote and expand the exchange of information and other forms of mutual assistance between the courts of this state and those of other states concerned with the same child, and

(9) Make uniform the law of those states which enact it.

B. This Part shall be construed to promote the general purposes stated in this Section.

R.S. 13:1702 Jurisdiction

A. A court of this state which is competent to decide child custody matters has jurisdiction to make a child custody determination by initial or modification decree if:

(1) This state (i) is the home state of the child at the time of commencement of the proceeding, or (ii) had been the child's home state within six months before commencement of the proceeding and the child is absent from this state because of his removal or retention by a person claiming his custody or for other reasons, and a parent or person acting as parent continues to live in this state; or

(2) It is in the best interest of the child that a court of this state assume jurisdiction because (i) the child and his parents, or the child and at least one contestant, have a significant connection with this state, and (ii) there is available in this state substantial evidence concerning the child's present or future care, protection, training, and personal relationships; or

(3) The child is physically present in this state and (i) the child has been abandoned or (ii) it is necessary in an emergency to protect the child because he has been subjected to or threatened

with mistreatment or abuse or is otherwise neglected or dependent; or

(4) (i) It appears that no other state would have jurisdiction under prerequisites substantially in accordance with Paragraphs (1), (2), or (3), or another state has declined to exercise jurisdiction on the ground that this state is the more appropriate forum to determine the custody of the child, and (ii) it is in the best interest of the child that this court assume jurisdiction.

B. Except under Paragraphs (3) and (4) of Subsection A, physical presence in this state of the child, or of the child and one of the contestants, is not alone sufficient to confer jurisdiction on a court of this state to make a child custody determination.

C. Physical presence of the child, while desirable, is not a prerequisite for jurisdiction to determine his custody.

R.S. 13:1703 Notice and opportunity to be heard

Before making a decree under this Part, reasonable notice and opportunity to be heard shall be given to the contestants, any parent whose parental rights have not been previously terminated, and any person who has physical custody of the child. If any of these persons is outside this state, notice and opportunity to be heard shall be given pursuant to Section 1704.

R.S. 13:1704 Notice to persons outside this state; submission to jurisdiction

A. Notice required for the exercise of jurisdiction over a person outside this state shall be given in a manner reasonably calculated to give actual notice, and may be:

(1) By personal delivery outside of this state in the manner prescribed for service of process within this state; or

(2) By registered or certified mail; or

(3)(a) If the party is a nonresident or absentee who cannot be served by the methods provided in Paragraphs (1) and (2) of this Subsection, either personally or through an agent for service of process, and who has not waived objection to jurisdiction, the court shall appoint an attorney at law to represent him.

(b) If the court appoints an attorney at law to represent the party, all proceedings against the party shall be conducted contradictorily against the attorney at law appointed by the court to represent him. The qualifications and duties of such attorney and his compensation shall be governed by the provisions of Articles 5092 through 5096 of the Code of Civil Procedure.

B. Notice under this Section shall be served, mailed and delivered, or last published at least ten days before any hearing in this state.

C. Proof of service outside this state may be made by affidavit of the individual who made the service, or in the manner prescribed by the law of this state, the order pursuant to which the service is made, or the law of the place in which the service is made. If service is made by mail, proof may be a receipt signed by the addressee or other evidence of delivery to the addressee.

D. Notice is not required if a person submits to the jurisdiction of the court.

R.S. 13:1705 Simultaneous proceedings in other states

A. A court of this state shall not exercise its jurisdiction under this Act if at the time of filing the petition a proceeding concerning the custody of the child was pending in a court of another state exercising jurisdiction substantially in conformity with this Part, unless the proceeding is stayed by the court of the other state because this state is a more appropriate forum or for other reasons.

B. Before hearing the petition in a custody proceeding the court shall examine the pleadings and other information supplied by the parties under Section 1708 and shall consult the child custody registry established under Section 1715 concerning the pendency of proceedings with respect to the child in other states. If the court has reason to believe that proceedings may be pending in another state it shall direct an inquiry to the state court administrator or other appropriate official of the other state.

C. If the court is informed during the course of the proceeding that a proceeding concerning the custody of the child was pending in another state before the court assumed jurisdiction it shall stay the proceeding and communicate with the court in which the other proceeding is pending to the end that the issue may be litigated in the more appropriate forum and that information be exchanged in accordance with Sections 1718 through 1721. If a court of this state has made a custody decree before being informed of a pending proceeding in a court of another state it shall immediately inform that court of the fact. If the court is informed that a proceeding was commenced in another state after it assumed jurisdiction it shall likewise inform the other court to the end that the issues may be litigated in the more appropriate forum.

R.S. 13:1706 Inconvenient forum

A. A court which has jurisdiction under this Part to make an initial or modification decree may decline to exercise its jurisdiction any time before making a decree if it finds that it is an inconvenient forum to make a custody determination under the circumstances of the case and that a court of another state is a more appropriate forum.

B. A finding of inconvenient forum may be made upon the court's own motion or upon motion of a party or a curator ad hoc or other representative of the child.

C. In determining if it is an inconvenient forum, the court shall consider if it is in the interest of the child that another state assume jurisdiction. For this purpose it may take into account the following factors, among others:

(1) If another state is or recently was the child's home state.

(2) If another state has a closer connection with the child and his family or with the child and one or more of the contestants.

(3) If substantial evidence concerning the child's present or future care, protection, training, and personal relationships is more readily available in another state.

(4) If the parties have agreed on another forum which is no less appropriate, and

(5) If the exercise of jurisdiction by a court of this state would contravene any of the purposes stated in Section 1700.

D. Before determining whether to decline or retain jurisdiction the court may communicate with a court of another state and exchange information pertinent to the assumption of jurisdiction by either court with a view to assuring that jurisdiction will be exercised by the more appropriate court and that a forum will be available to the parties.

E. If the court finds that it is an inconvenient forum and that a court of another state is a more appropriate forum, it may dismiss the proceedings, or it may stay the proceedings upon condition that a custody proceeding be promptly commenced in another named state or upon any other conditions which may be just and proper, including the condition that a moving party stipulate his consent and submission to the jurisdiction of the other forum.

F. The court may decline to exercise its jurisdiction under this Part if a custody determination is incidental to an action for divorce or another proceeding while retaining jurisdiction over the divorce or other proceeding.

G. If it appears to the court that it is clearly an inappropriate forum it may require the party who commenced the proceedings to pay, in addition to the costs of the proceedings in this state, necessary travel and other expenses, including attorneys' fees, incurred by other parties or their witnesses. Payment is to be made to the clerk of the court for remittance to the proper party.

H. Upon dismissal or stay of proceedings under this Section the court shall inform the court found to be the more appropriate forum of this fact, or if the court which would have jurisdiction in the other state is not certainly known, shall transmit the information to the court administrator or other appropriate official for forwarding to the appropriate court.

I. Any communication received from another state informing this state of a finding of inconvenient forum because a court of this state is the more appropriate forum shall be filed in the custody registry of the appropriate court. Upon assuming jurisdiction the court of this state shall inform the original court of this fact.

R.S. 13:1707 Jurisdiction declined by reason of conduct

A. If the petitioner for an initial decree has wrongfully taken the child from another state or has engaged in similar reprehensible conduct the court may decline to exercise jurisdiction if this is just and proper under the circumstances.

B. Unless required in the interest of the child, the court shall not exercise its jurisdiction to modify a custody decree of another state if the petitioner, without consent of the person entitled to custody, has improperly removed the child from the physical custody of the person entitled to custody or has improperly retained the child after a visit or other temporary relinquishment of physical custody. If the petitioner has violated any other provision of a custody decree of another state the court may decline to exercise its jurisdiction if this is just and proper under the circumstances.

C. In appropriate cases a court dismissing a petition under this

Section may charge the petitioner with necessary travel and other expenses, including attorneys' fees, incurred by other parties or their witnesses.

R.S. 13:1712 Recognition of out-of-state custody decrees

The courts of this state shall recognize and enforce an initial or modification decree of a court of another state which had assumed jurisdiction under statutory provisions substantially in accordance with this Part or which was made under factual circumstances meeting the jurisdictional standards of the Part, so long as this decree has not been modified in accordance with jurisdictional standards substantially similar to those of this Act.

R.S. 13:1713 Modification of custody decree of another state

A. If a court of another state has made a custody decree, a court of this state shall not modify that decree unless it appears to the court of this state that the court which rendered the decree does not now have jurisdiction under jurisdictional prerequisites substantially in accordance with this Part or has declined to assume jurisdiction to modify the decree and the court of this state has jurisdiction.

B. If a court of this state is authorized under Subsection A of this Section and Section 1707 to modify a custody decree of another state it shall give due consideration to the transcript of the record and other documents of all previous proceedings submitted to it in accordance with Section 1721.

## 6. If Your Child Is Missing

If your child is missing, immediately contact your attorney, the police, the National Center for Missing and Exploited Children, your local prosecutor's office, and the FBI (when applicable). In each case, provide your contact with a certified copy of your custody or visitation order that currently is in effect.

### The Police

When you call the police, file a missing-person report. Additionally, give them your spouse's car description and license-plate number so that they can enter the information in the National Crime Information Center (NCIC) computer. Likewise, request the law-enforcement agency to contact the Federal Parent Locator Service.

**The National Center for Missing and Exploited Children**

The National Center for Missing and Exploited Children
2101 Wilson Boulevard
Suite 550
Arlington, VA 22201
Toll free: (800) 843-5678

**FBI**

If the child is wrongfully taken across state lines, the FBI can be of assistance. The FBI will get involved if you have an order showing custody, a local felony warrant has been issued, and the local district attorney's office has sent a letter to the FBI requesting assistance. Speak to your local district-attorney's office to expedite the process.

**Relatives and Friends of Abducting Parent**

See if child is at the residence of the abductor's friends or family. Ask them to contact you if the abductor of child arrives.

**State Department**

Since the late 1970s, the United States Department of State has been contacted with over 11,000 inquiries for assistance in recovering children who were wrongfully taken outside the country by a parent.

There are forty-three foreign countries that are participants in the Hague Convention, honoring other countries' custody orders:

| | | |
|---|---|---|
| Argentina | Republic of | Luxembourg |
| Australia | Macedonia | Mauritius |
| Austria | Denmark | Mexico |
| Bahamas | Ecuador | Monaco |
| Belize | Finland | Netherlands |
| Bosnia and | France | New Zealand |
| Herzegovina | Germany | Norway |
| Burkina Faso | Greece | Panama |
| Canada | Honduras | Poland |
| Chile | Hong Kong | Portugal |
| Colombia | Hungary | Romania |
| Croatia | Iceland | Slovenia |
| Cyprus | Israel | South Africa |
| Former Yugoslav | Italy | Spain |

St. Kitts-Nevis          United          Zimbabwe
Sweden                   Kingdom
Switzerland              Venezuela

The State Department will work with one of the above countries in an attempt to have your child returned. You may contact the State Department at the following address and telephone number:

Office of Children's Issues
U.S. Department of State
Room 4811
Washington, DC 20520-4818
(202) 736-7000
Fax: (202) 647-2835

### Keep and Flag Child's Passport

If your child previously has been issued a passport, keep it. If your child has not been issued a passport, contact the Office of Passport Policy and Advisory Services and request that it flag your child's name. The office has a name-check service. Give the office a certified copy of your custody/visitation order that shows that you have sole custody or that the other parent is prohibited from taking the child out of the country. Note that the State Department will not revoke a passport once it has been issued to a child.

If you have reason to be alarmed that the other parent might attempt to take your child to another country, ask the court to order the other parent to surrender his passport.

Office of Passport Policy and Advisory Services
Passport Services
Suite 260
1111 19th Street, NW
Washington, DC
(202) 955-0377
Fax: (202) 955-0230

## 7. Stop the Other Parent from Taking Children Out of the State or Country

"I love living in Lafayette and my ex-husband won custody at the hearing. After years of relative cooperation in scheduling visitation, he now wants to move to Houston and take the kids with him. Can I fight this move?"

—A. G.
age 43, divorced, three children
college professor
Lafayette, Louisiana

Until a court has issued a ruling regarding temporary or permanent custody of the acknowledged children, either parent is free to take the child out of the state and/or even the country. Hence, you see the importance in rushing to the courthouse and request temporary custody and a temporary restraining order prohibiting the other parent from removing the child from the state and country, as well as from secreting the child in any manner.

When a custody-and-visitation plan is being created by the judge or the parties, insist that the order reads that neither parent shall be able to remove the child outside of the United States without an order of the court and/or without the written, notarized authorization of both parties.

Chapter 12

# PROPERTY DIVISION

## 1. Recap on Chapter 5

You have already taken advantage of the tips provided in the chapter encouraging you to "Get Possession of Children and Property."

1. Get possession of
   a) children
   b) property and sentimental items
   c) pets
   d) money
   e) the house/apartment/furnishings
2. Inventory everything
   a) financial records
   b) information from computers
3. Videotape and/or photograph your residence
4. File ex parte motions

## 2. Before You Get Divorced, Speak with Your Attorney about Dividing the Community Assets and Debts

Quite often individuals postpone resolving the division of marital property until after the divorce. Many people who get divorced feel a huge burden off of their backs after the final divorce judgment is rendered. For many reasons, some financial and some emotional, litigants frequently stop the litigation between their now former spouse without formally dividing up community-property assets and debts. Consult your attorney as to the pros and cons of pursuing a partition of the community property. A failure to divide the assets and debts may cause problems in the future regarding valuations, potential reimbursements for use, loss or destruction of items, commingled separate and community debts, subsequent marriage property rights, and inheritance rights.

### 3. Ways to Divide Property in America

Each state has a slightly different way to divide property of a divorcing couple. The three basic ways that states divide assets are as follows:

1. Equitable distribution
2. Common-law division
3. Community-property division (used in Louisiana)

### 4. Equitable Distribution

Equitable distribution is the most common means of property division. Under the equitable-distribution basis, property is divided and/or distributed based on concepts of fairness and equity. In such cases, many lawyers casually refer to spouses as if they were partners in a business endeavor.

### 5. Common-Law Prfoperty Division

Mississippi is the sole state that distributes property on the basis of whose name is on the title or registration of an asset (common law). The state does not formally recognize the property value associated with homemaking and contributions to increased earning capacity associated with the obtainment of professional degrees. Only that property that is jointly owned by both spouses can be divided by the court.

### 6. Community-Property Division

Community-property distribution states, such as Louisiana, acknowledge a general joint interest in property acquired during the marriage. Community-property laws provide exceptions for property that was acquired with proceeds of separate property as well as with property excluded by valid prenuptial or postnuptial agreements.

In general, separate property is defined as any property owned prior to the marriage or acquired by inheritance or marital contract.

In evaluating which spouse gets certain marital property, courts may review the following:

1. The duration of the marriage
2. The respective age, health, skills, and abilities of each spouse
3. The standard of living of each party
4. The financial needs of each spouse
5. The financial resources of each spouse
6. The separate and postmarital property of each spouse
7. Each spouse's contribution to the acquisition and/or improvement of the marital or separate property
8. Each spouse's contribution to the education and/or increased
earning capacity of the other spouse
9. Tax consequences for each party
10. The need of the custodial parent to remain in the family home with minor children
11. Any award of alimony and/or child support
12. The liquidity of property
13 The ability of a spouse to operate a family business
14. The anticipated wasteful dissipation of property by a party
15. The potential loss or gain of inheritance and pension rights of a spouse upon divorce
16 Individual gifts/donations to a party
17. Other considerations deemed relevant by the court

## 7. Don't Get Hung up on Definitions of Property

Many books go into lengthy discussions of how you should legally define an asset or debt. These books often fail to emphasize the importance of data-gathering and categorization as set forth above. *Yes, you are dealing with Louisiana community-property laws, but don't get caught up in the trap of trying to define whether certain property is "separate" or "community."* After you have divided the property into categories, then you should have a discussion with your attorney as to the legal interpretation of each asset and debt. Ultimately, this is a job for your attorney; that's what you pay him or her for. Although there is a natural tendency for you to try to define each asset and debt, you have not been trained to interpret the legal description of assets. Let your lawyer do his or her job. Ask to be provided with your lawyer's interpretation of how each asset and debt likely will be categorized by the court, as well as the ramifications of such interpretations.

## 8. Separate Property in Louisiana

C.C. Art. 2341. Separate property.

The separate property of a spouse is his exclusively. It comprises: property acquired by a spouse prior to the establishment of a community property regime; property acquired by a spouse with separate things or with separate and community things when the value of the community things is inconsequential in comparison with the value of the separate things used; property acquired by a spouse by inheritance or donation to him individually; damages awarded to a spouse in an action for breach of contract against the other spouse or for the loss sustained as a result of fraud or bad faith in the management of community property by the other spouse; damages or other indemnity awarded to a spouse in connection with the management of his separate property; and things acquired by a spouse as a result of a voluntary partition of the community during the existence of a community property regime.

## 9. Community Property in Louisiana

C.C. Art. 2338. Community property.

The community property comprises: property acquired during the existence of the legal regime through the effort, skill, or industry of either spouse; property acquired with community things or with community and separate things, unless classified as separate property under Article 2341; property donated to the spouses jointly; natural and civil fruits of community property; damages awarded for loss or injury to a thing belonging to the community; and all other property not classified by law as separate property.

## 10. Presumption of Community

C.C. Art. 2340. Presumption of community.

Things in the possession of a spouse during the existence of a regime of community of acquets and gains are presumed to be community, but either spouse may prove that they are separate property.

## 11. Termination of Community

C.C. Art. 3526. Termination of community; movables and

Louisiana immovables acquired by a spouse while domiciled in another state

Upon termination of the community, or dissolution by death or by divorce of the marriage of spouses either of whom is domiciled in this state, their respective rights and obligations with regard to immovables situated in this state and movables, wherever situated, that were acquired during the marriage by either spouse while domiciled in another state shall be determined as follows:

(1) Property that is classified as community property under the law of this state shall be treated as community property under that law; and

(2) Property that is not classified as community property under the law of this state shall be treated as the separate property of the acquiring spouse. However, the other spouse shall be entitled, in value only, to the same rights with regard to this property as would be granted by the law of the state in which the acquiring spouse was domiciled at the time of acquisition.

## 12. Management of Community Property

C.C. Art. 2346. Management of community property.

Each spouse acting alone may manage, control, or dispose of community property unless otherwise provided by law.

## 13. Duty to Preserve Community Property

C.C. Art. 2369.3. Duty to preserve; standard of care

A spouse has a duty to preserve and to manage prudently former community property under his control, including a former community enterprise, in a manner consistent with the mode of use of that property immediately prior to termination of the community regime. He is answerable for any damage caused by his fault, default, or neglect.

A community enterprise is a business that is not a legal entity.

## 14. Possession and Use of Family Residence or Community Movables or Immovables

R.S. 9:374 Possession and use of family residence or community movables or immovables

A. When the family residence is the separate property of either spouse, after the filing of a petition for divorce or in conjunction therewith, the spouse who has physical custody or has been awarded temporary custody of the minor children of the marriage may petition for, and a court may award to that spouse, after a contradictory hearing, the use and occupancy of the family residence pending the partition of the community property or one hundred eighty days after termination of the marriage, whichever occurs first. In these cases, the court shall inquire into the relative economic status of the spouses, including both community and separate property, and the needs of the children, and shall award the use and occupancy of the family residence to the spouse in accordance with the best interest of the family. The court shall consider the granting of the occupancy of the family home in awarding spousal support.

B. When the family residence is community property or the spouses own community movables or immovables, after or in conjunction with the filing of a petition for divorce or for separation of property in accordance with *Civil Code Article 2374* (emphasis added), either spouse may petition for, and a court may award to one of the spouses, after a contradictory hearing, the use and occupancy of the family residence and use of community movables or immovables to either of the spouses pending further order of the court. In these cases, the court shall inquire into the relative economic status of the spouses, including both community and separate property, and the needs of the children, if any, and shall award the use and occupancy of the family residence and the use of any community movables or immovables to the spouse in accordance with the best interest of the family. If applicable, the court shall consider the granting of the occupancy of the family home and the use of community movables or immovables in awarding spousal support.

C. A spouse who uses and occupies or is awarded by the court the use and occupancy of the family residence pending either the termination of the marriage or the partition of the community property in accordance with the provisions of R.S. 9:374(A) or (B) shall not be liable to the other spouse for rental for the use and occupancy, unless otherwise agreed by the spouses or ordered by the court.

D. The court may determine whether the family home is separate or community property in the contradictory hearing authorized under the provisions of this Section.

E.(1) In a proceeding for divorce or thereafter, upon request of either party, where a community property regime existed, a summary proceeding may be undertaken by the trial court within sixty days of filing, allocating the use of community property, including monetary assets, bank accounts, savings plans, and other divisible movable property pending formal partition proceeding, pursuant to *R.S. 9:2801* (emphasis added).

(2) Upon court order, each spouse shall provide the other a complete accounting of all community assets subsequent to said allocation and in compliance with *Civil Code Article 2369.3* (emphasis added), providing the duty to preserve and prudently manage community property.

(3) The court shall determine allocation of community assets after considering:

(a) The custody of the children and exclusive possession of the house.

(b) The total community assets.

(c) The need of one spouse for funds to maintain a household prior to formal partition.

(d) The need of a spouse to receive legal representation during the course of the divorce proceeding.

## 15. Locate and Preserve Important Documents

- Adoption papers
- Appraisals
- Articles of incorporation for family business
- Bank documents
- Baptism certificates
- Birth certificates
- Citizenship documents
- Computer data
- Contracts
- Copies of all expenses
- Credit-card statements
- Diplomas
- Driver's license
- Education records
- Employment benefit documents
- Employment income-related documents
- Evidence for any purpose

- Expense records
- Financial records
- Insurance policies
- Immigration documents
- Income records
- Inventories
- Investments
- Loans
- Marriage certificate/license
- Medical records
- Passports
- Paycheck stubs/records
- Photographs and videotapes
- Power-of-attorney records
- Prenuptial agreement
- Real estate-act of sale and mortgages
- Receipts for expenses
- Receipts for improvements to property
- Receipts for missing assets
- Retirement documents
- Sentimental items
- Social-security cards
- Tax returns
- Wills
- Vaccination records
- Vehicle titles

## 16. Protect Your Property

After you locate, inventory, and possess all documents, assets, and debts, you must continue to protect these items.

1. After speaking with your attorney, consider changing the locks to your dwelling.
2. Get restraining orders against your spouse's use, disposal, or alienation of your marital property, separate and/or personal.
3. Having inventoried, photographed, and/or videotaped your belongings, if your furniture, tools, jewelry, or other items "mysteriously" disappear, then you have record and evidence of their existence.
4. Give your attorney any documents that you fear will be lost or taken.
5. Put all valuables in a secure location that your spouse cannot get to.

## 17. Give a List of Missing Items to Your Attorney

It is quite common for items that were acquired before or during your marriage to become missing when you are attempting to resolve property-division issues. The cause of the property's absence may or may not be intentional. By providing a list of missing items to your attorney, you arm your lawyer with the appropriate documents to seek accountability for your former spouse for these pieces of property. Some courts have gone so far as to make the spouse last possessing the property adequately account for its whereabouts or have a value imputed for that lost item to the detriment of the one who last possessed it.

## 18. Locate Hidden Assets

"I married a man substantially older than me. He's very shrewd. He and his partner have done quite well. Before we got married, he treated me like a princess. Now he treats me like a possession. I've had enough. I hope he doesn't try to screw me like another one of his business deals."

—Betty P.
age 33, married, adult children, unemployed
Bunky, Louisiana

Quite often, a spouse attempts to hide assets or income. Your attorney should know how to discover these deceptive practices. For example, a spouse may have more expenses than the income he is claiming. A review of these expenses may reveal to the court that your spouse has not been honest. You should assist your lawyer by suggesting the following:

1. Look for assets in the names of others or in fictitious names.
2. Tell your lawyer of your spouse's prior and present attempts to hide property and/or cheat others.
3. Suggest using proper-discovery practices, such as issuing subpoenas and taking depositions, through which your attorney may find these hidden assets or income.
4. Have a discussion with your attorney about your concerns that your spouse has hidden assets or income.

## 19. Divide All Property and Debts into Categories

Your lawyer will be able to assist in protecting and maximizing your property interests after you provide him or her with a comprehensive list that is divided into meaningful categories. When you list assets into categories, *do not concern yourself with whether you think that the item is "separate," "community," or any other legal description.* Leave that task to your competent attorney. At this time, do not concern yourself with whether or not your spouse is claiming property as being "separate," "marital," or "community." The most important task for you to accomplish is to divide the assets into the following categories:

1. Property owned by you prior to the marriage
2. Property owned by your spouse prior to the marriage
3. Property solely held in your name that was acquired after the marriage (but before the filing of the divorce petition/complaint)
4. Property solely held in your spouse's name that was acquired after the marriage (but before the filing of the divorce petition/complaint)
5. Property items held jointly by you and your spouse that were purchased after marriage (but before the filing of the divorce petition/complaint)
6. Property acquired by you after the filing of the divorce petition/complaint
7. Property acquired by your spouse after the filing of the divorce petition/complaint
8. Property acquired jointly by you and your spouse after the filing of the divorce petition/complaint
9. Contributions that you made to the acquisition or improvement of property owned in the name of your spouse
10. Contributions that you made to the acquisition or improvement of property owned in the name of both you and your spouse
11. Debt created by you prior to the marriage
12. Debt created by your spouse prior to the marriage
13. Debt that was incurred in your name alone that was created after the marriage
14. Debt that was incurred in your spouse's name alone that was created after the marriage
15 Debt created in your name as well as the name of your spouse that was created after the marriage
16. Debt created by you after the filing of the divorce petition
17. Debt created by your spouse after the filing of the divorce petition
18. Debt created by both you and your spouse after the filing of the divorce petition/complaint

Dividing assets and liabilities into the above categories is a painstaking and tedious task, yet your efforts will provide very helpful information for your attorney's use. Your efforts will be rewarded in many ways during the litigation, including but not limited to, lowering your attorney fees.

Don't forget to list anticipated tax refunds and previously paid utility deposits.

## 20. Provide Values for Each Piece of Property

For each asset that you listed and categorized, provide your attorney the known cost of each, along with the date (approximately) of purchase/acquisition. If you do not know the cost or value when acquired, simply indicate your lack of knowledge regarding that asset.

Additionally, provide your attorney with the fair-market value of each item at the time of your marriage and/or at the present.

## 21. Provide/Seek Appraisals and Financial Statements

Provide your attorney with a copy of all written valuations and/or appraisals of any asset. Your attorney may request further valuations/appraisals of certain items. Typical appraisals value the following:

1. real estate
2. jewelry
3. furniture
4. artwork
5. vehicles

For automobile valuations, refer to the *Kelley Blue Book Used Car Guide*.

Also, acquire statements from financial institutions. These documents are valuable sources of information regarding the value of a stock and/or account at a particular point in time.

Naturally, each spouse will attempt to associate as little value as possible with each asset that he or she wishes to keep and will associate the highest value possible with each asset that might be retained or attributed to the other spouse. The benefit of valuation lies in the art of finding the most favorable and persuasive appraiser(s). Speak to your attorney about his contacts and experiences with various appraisers.

When an appraisal is required and funds are tight, it may be beneficial to recommend that the parties split or pay a proportionate share of the cost for a single unbiased appraiser.

Have all decreed assets placed in your name. Have your attorney file all necessary documents (certificates of title, etc.) into the proper parish registry.

## 22. Provide Values for Each Debt

"I have a shoebox full of unpaid bills."

—Amy M.
age 21, married, no children, student
Baton Rouge, Louisiana

Provide a list of all debt and include the following:
1. the date the debt was created
2. the original amount of the debt
3. the amount/value of each debt at the date of marriage
4. the amount/value of each debt on the date of the filing of the divorce petition/complaint

## 23. Information You Should Give Regardless of Where You Live or Where the Property Is Located

1. Identify the asset/property.
2. State the date acquired.
3. State how it was acquired (e.g., gift, inheritance, purchase, etc.).
4. State who acquired it.
5. State its value at the following times:
    a. on the date acquired
    b. on the date of your marriage
    c. on the date sold
    d. on the date of the divorce
    e. on the date of trial
6. State whether there have been any enhancements or damage to item since acquisition,
7. State the names of persons if the asset is registered, titled, or otherwise associated with a particular person.
8. State whether the property is described as separate or otherwise based on a prenuptial or postnuptial agreement.

## 24. Know the Tax Consequences of Any Transaction

There are many tax consequences associated with the transfer of property. Please refer to chapter 14 regarding taxes and consult a tax advisor regarding the ramifications of your divorce proceedings.

One notable, present, tax consequence is as follows:

If both spouses own a house titled in both of their names and one spouse transfers his interest in the house to the other spouse as part of a property settlement, then the spouse who receives the full title and later sells the house, that recipient spouse will have taxable capital gains equal to the difference of the original purchase price and the ultimate sale price of the house. You may wish to have the potential capital-gains tax taken into consideration in your negotiations associated with any property settlement.

## 25. Watch Out for Blackmail for Gain of Property Rights

"She won't drop the bogus sexual-abuse charges unless I give her the house free and clear."

—Thomas C.
age 37, married, one child, professional photographer
Harahan, Louisiana

As with issues of child support and alimony, refrain from giving into a spouse's threats to challenge custody or other issues unless you concede your property rights. Report any such threats to your attorney. Any evidence of these threats should be tendered to your lawyer.

## 26. Don't Fight Over the "Crab Traps"

"I have no idea what property is considered community and what is separate."

—Vicki T.
age 28, married, one child, retail sales associate
Metairie, Louisiana

"Evelyn insists on keeping our lawn furniture. There's no way I'm going to let her have it!"

—Howard N.
age 55, married, two adult children, mechanic
Amite, Louisiana

Do not pay your lawyer more than what he or she is worth! It is remarkable how many people spend hundreds or thousands of dollars in legal fees to fight over items that have nominal or no financial value at all. Although it may be worth it to fight over sentimental property, generally a cost-benefit analysis should be made. Don't fight over a toaster or crab traps!

Chapter 13

# PRENUPTIAL AND POSTNUPTIAL AGREEMENTS

## 1. What Is a Prenuptial Agreement?

> "My husband is a doctor. He said he wouldn't marry me unless I signed a prenuptial agreement. At first, I resisted, but I finally gave in. Although I understand why he asked me to sign one, somewhere deep in my psyche I feel cheated."
>
> —Lauren F.
> age 43, married, no children, office manager
> Hammond, Louisiana

A prenuptial agreement is a contract entered into by the future bride and groom prior to the marriage attempting to bind various aspects regarding money and property in the event of a divorce. Remember that between 43 and 50 percent of all people who enter into a marriage get a divorce.

A major criticism of the prenuptial agreement is that it sets up the marriage for failure and creates an expectation of divorce.

## 2. Blaming Your Lawyer

> "My fiancé gave me a prenuptial agreement to review and sign. I'm not going to sign it, but I made an appointment with an attorney so that I can tell my boyfriend that the lawyer recommended that I not sign it."
>
> —Cynthia W.
> age 36, single, contemplating marriage, no children, nurse
> Covington, Louisiana

In order to defeat your significant other's complaints about entering into a prenuptial agreement, be honest, or blame it on your lawyer.

### 3. Are Prenuptial Agreements Enforceable?

"When I married my current husband, I signed a prenuptial agreement. Things aren't working out. He wants to control my every move. If I leave, I leave with nothing. Things would be different if I could challenge the prenuptial."

—Tiffany J.
age 52, married, one child from prior marriage, housewife
Lafayette, Louisiana

Whether a prenuptial agreement is enforceable is the most common question asked about these contracts. The answer is It depends!

1. Does the agreement violate the state law or public policy?
2. Did the parties, in good faith, enter into a fair agreement being fully informed and of their own free will?

### Increase Your Chances of Having an Enforceable Prenuptial Agreement

In order to increase your chances of a court of law enforcing your prenuptial agreement, follow these steps:

1. The future bride and groom should have their own separate attorneys.
2. The prenuptial agreement should not be signed immediately prior to the wedding. A party might later claim that he or she signed under duress and coercion. Hence, both parties should sign the agreement as early as possible.
3. Fully disclose your wealth, including all assets and debts. It's best to list and specifically identify as many assets and liabilities as possible. When in doubt, overestimate your worth when disclosing your wealth.
4. The prenuptial agreement should contain written language stating that the legal rights have been explained to both parties.
5. Videotape the ceremony of signing the prenuptial agreement. This helps show that the other party entered the agreement without coercion or duress.

### 4. Prenuptial Clauses That Are Frowned Upon

"Should I disclose the full extent of my wealth to my fiancé?"
—Manny D.
age 49, divorced, two children, stockbroker
Jennings, Louisiana

Here are some additional tips to keep in mind when creating a prenuptial agreement:

1. Don't add clauses that would clearly be unenforceable, such as strict agreements on custody and/or child support. Judges are hesitant to enforce agreements that restrict children's rights.
2. Don't add clauses that would restrict the other spouse's right to defend himself or herself. This might be construed as a clause that would encourage or facilitate divorce.
3. Be careful about adding clauses that would provide for a gross inequity in the distribution of property.
4. Additionally, ask your attorney if any of the prenuptial-agreement clauses may be construed as being against the state's public policy.

## 5. Ways to Defeat a Prenuptial Agreement

In order to successfully persuade a judge to render the prenuptial agreement unenforceable, attack the following potential flaws in the contract:

1. state laws that the agreement violates
2. public policy that the agreement violates (i.e., encouraging divorce)
3. the unfair nature of the agreement
4. the other party's lack of good faith
5. any duress or coercion that you experienced before or at the time of signing
6. any influences of alcohol or drugs that you may have been under the influence of at the time of signing
7. any physical or mental illnesses at the time of signing
8. your tender age at the time of signing
9. the fact that the agreement was signed immediately prior to the wedding ceremony
10 the lack of witnesses to the signing of the contract
11. the lack of the full disclosure of assets, liabilities, and wealth at the time of signing
12. the fact that you did not create the document
13. oral promises and/or comments made before or at the time of signing that are not reflected in the agreement

Consult your attorney for other defects in the creation or execution of the agreement that might make it, or a part thereof, unenforceable.

## 6. What Are Postnuptial Agreements?

Postnuptial agreements are similar to prenuptial agreements; however, they are executed some time after the marriage ceremony. In most states, including Louisiana, in order to enter into a postnuptial agreement, a court must formally approve the agreement.

The enforceability and impeachability of the agreement are dependent upon similar inquiries as those referred to for prenuptial agreements.

Before entering into any prenuptial or postnuptial agreement, consult a lawyer who has extensive experience in drafting and/or litigating the validity of these agreements.

Chapter 14

# TAXES

## 1. Be Aware of the Tax Consequences of Each Transaction between You and Your Spouse/Former Spouse

"I consider myself a good businesswomn; however, I have to admit that I'm not sure how this divorce is going to affect my taxes."

—Roxanne L.
age 61, married, two adult children, teacher
Ruston, Louisiana

Divorced and separated individuals should be aware of the tax consequences of their changing marital status. The following discussions regarding taxes are general principles that may be subject to modifications, exceptions, and/or other requirements. To get a precise evaluation regarding your particular situation, you should always consult a tax advisor and/or the Internal Revenue Service. The following tax tips will provide you with necessary information to plan a strategy maximizing your tax benefits and eliminating tax pitfalls: the bottom line—saving you money.

## 2. Inform the IRS and the Louisiana Department of Revenue of Any Change of Address

If you have moved, contact the IRS and ask for Form 8822, Change of Address. Properly filing this form will prevent your spouse from withholding your future forms and other vital communication from the IRS. Also remember to inform the Louisiana Department of Revenue of any changes.

**LOUISIANA DEPARTMENT OF REVENUE**

Personal Income-Tax Assistance
(225) 219-0101

Request for Louisiana Tax Forms
(225) 219-2113
Louisiana Department of Revenue Web Site:
www.rev.state.la.us

## 3. Federal Tax Publications Frequently Used during a Divorce

- 503 Child and Dependent Care Expenses
- 504 Divorced or Separated Individuals
- 508 Tax Benefits for Work-Related Education
- 521 Moving Expenses
- 523 Selling Your Home
- 525 Taxable and Nontaxable Income
- 551 Basis of Assets
- 552 Recordkeeping for Individuals (and a list of tax publications)
- 561 Determining the Value of Donated Property
- 929 Tax Rules for Children and Dependents
- 8822 Change of Address

Toll-Free Telephone Number for IRS Publications
1-800-424-3676
IRS Web Site
www.irs.gov/formspubs/

## 4. Know Your Filing Status

"I got divorced on November 23. What is my filing status for this past year?"

—Cassandra I.
age 29, divorced, one child
Gretna, Louisiana

Your tax status establishes your tax-filing requirements and determines your eligibility to claim various deductions and credits. The primary factor in proving your filing status is to determine your marital status on December 31 of the taxable year. Filing status is divided into the following categories: unmarried/single and married.

## 5. Does the IRS Consider You Single?

You may have an unmarried filing status for the entire tax year if one of the following events occurs:

A. You have obtained a divorce or separation decree by the last day of your tax year. (However, you must file under a married status if you get a divorce decree in one year in order to obtain an unmarried tax status and intend to remarry the following year.)
B. You have obtained a decree of annulment.

## 6. The IRS May Consider You Married after Your Divorce

Even if you get divorced on January 1, you will have a "married" filing status for the entire tax year. The IRS considers you married until the year after you obtain a divorce or separation decree. (However, if you live apart from your spouse, under certain exceptions, you may be able to file as the "Head of Household"—see section 11.)

## 7. Know the Facts about Filing a Joint Tax Return

"During our marriage, I was the only one who worked. We were divorced in May. Do I file a joint return this year?"

—Donald J.
age 34, divorced, no children, landscape architect
West Monroe, Louisiana

You may file a joint return under the requirements noted in the anecdote above. If you qualify under those circumstances, you may file a joint return, including the income, exemptions, deductions, and credits applicable for both spouses. A joint return may be filed in cases in which both spouses receive income or where only one spouse has income or deductions.

To file a joint return, at least one spouse must be a United States citizen or legal resident during the tax year. In order for a tax return to be considered as "joint," both spouses must sign it.

## 8. You Are Liable for Taxes, Interest, and Penalties Associated with a Joint Return

"My ex-husband always had our joint returns prepared. He simply gave the papers to me for my signature. The IRS has contacted me indicating that he did not pay his share of the taxes for our last year of marriage. Now, they want me to pay."

—Regan F.
age 46, divorced, one adult child, nurse
Jefferson, Louisiana

Regardless of whether or not only one spouse earned all of the income, both spouses are legally responsible for all taxes, interest, and penalties due pursuant to the joint tax return. This means the IRS can come after either spouse it desires. Think twice before signing a joint return if you have concerns about your spouse's desire, intent, and/or ability to contribute to paying the joint tax debt. If you believe that these concerns are legitimate, consult a tax expert.

Even if you are divorced during a tax year, you remain jointly liable for the taxes, interest, and penalties of a joint return, regardless of if you have entered into an agreement or divorce decree that attempts to allocate the tax debt to a particular spouse.

### The "Innocent Spouse" Exception

If you are an "innocent spouse," under noncommunity property rules, you may not be responsible for the further tax debt associated with an understatement of more than $500 on the joint return if your spouse either omitted income or claimed an improper deduction and/or credit. To be an innocent spouse, you must prove that you were not aware of the tax understatement and that it would be unfair for you to be levied with the additional tax debt.

## 9. Know the Facts about Filing Separate Returns

> "I've consulted with my CPA, who indicates that I should file a separate tax return."
>
> —Arthur C.
> age 61, divorced, three adult children, mechanical engineer
> Lake Charles, Louisiana

If you are eligible to file a separate return, you should only report your income, exemptions, deductions, and credits.

If both you and your spouse file separate returns, you will only be responsible for the tax debt associated with your return.

## 10. Figure Your Taxes under Joint and Separate Returns

The IRS suggests that if both you and your spouse earned income, you should calculate your taxes under both a joint return as well as separate returns in order to determine which means of filing gives you the lowest tax (Internal Revenue Service, Publication 504, 1997).

After considering the above facts, it is important to know that generally the combined federal-tax debt of both spouses will be higher if you file separate returns instead of filing a joint return because the tax rate is higher for people filing married-and-separate returns.

## 11. Who Is the Head of Household for Tax Purposes?

The IRS may consider you the head of household if you are unmarried at the end of the tax year and have paid for more than half of the household upkeep costs for more than half of the year. Household upkeep costs include mortgage payments (including interest, taxes, and home insurance), rent, utilities, repairs and maintenance, and food consumed at the home.

If you qualify as the head of household, you can claim the following tax benefits:

1. standard deduction (regardless of whether your spouse itemizes deductions on a married-filing-separate return)
2. a higher, standard deduction than would be otherwise allowed by fiing a separate single or married return
3. additional credits
4. tax rate may be lower than would be otherwise allowed by filing a separate single or married return

## 12. Know Your Federal Exemptions

"Now that I'm divorced, how many exemptions can I claim?"
—Roger R.
age 30, divorced, one child, florist
Metairie, Louisiana

Under current tax law, you are permitted an exemption that you are entitled to claim (special phase-out rules apply for individuals who make higher incomes). Consult your tax advisor.

You are entitled to your own exemption unless someone else is claiming you as a dependent. If you are filing a joint return, you and your spouse may claim an exemption for each person. If you filed a separate return, you may claim your spouse only if your spouse makes no income and is not a claimed dependent of someone else. Furthermore, in the year that you paid alimony to your spouse, you cannot take an exemption for that spouse. For the tax year that you obtained a divorce decree, you are not able to take an exemption for that former spouse.

### Take Exemptions for Dependents

You may take an exemption for each person who qualifies as a dependent. To be a dependent, the person must satisfy the following requirements:

1. The dependent must be related to you or have lived in your household for an entire year (exceptions apply).
2. The dependent cannot file a joint tax return for the taxable year.
3. The dependent must be a United States citizen or resident or a resident of either Canada or Mexico during some part of the year.
4. The dependent cannot receive more income than a specified amount under the tax code.
5. The dependent must receive at least 50 percent of his support for the year from you.

## 13. Who Is the Primary Custodial Parent for Tax Purposes?

"Randy and I have shared custody of our children on a roughly fifty-fifty basis. We never got an order regarding custody because we have very strong beliefs that both of us should be integrally involved in our children's lives."

—Julie M.
age 28, divorced, two children, attorney
Covington, Louisiana

Generally, the primary custodial parent, who has custody of a child for the greater portion of the year, is entitled to claim the dependency exemption as long as the other dependency requirements have been met. The IRS will look at the most recent applicable custody decree (or custody agreement in the absence of a custody decree).

In cases where no custody decree or agreement exists, or where a split-custody decree or agreement is implemented, the parent who had physical custody for the majority of the year will be entitled to claim the dependency exemption.

### The Noncustodial Parent May Get the Dependency Exemption

A noncustodial parent, who does not have physical custody of a child for the majority of the year, may be able to claim the child as a dependent if the other parent signs IRS Form 8332, Release of Claim to Exemption for Child of Divorced or Separated Parents. This form states that the custodial parent agrees not to take the dependency exemption. The noncustodial parent must attach the signed form to his federal tax return.

Additionally, a noncustodial parent may use the dependency exemption if a pre-1985 decree or custody agreement expresses that the noncustodial parent provides at least $600 of support for the child during the tax year and is entitled to the dependency exemption.

If, after 1984, a modification is made that states that the provision does not apply, then the regular dependency rules apply.

## 14. Medical-Expense Deduction

"My daughter has battled asthma for years. Can I claim a deduction for my out-of-pocket medical expenses?"

—Terri T.
age 29, divorced, one child
Destrehan, Louisiana

The divorced or separated parent who incurs medical expenses for his or her dependent child may deduct these expenses regardless of which parent claims the child as a dependent for exemption purposes.

## 15. Know the Tax Consequences and Requirements of Spousal Support

"Can I deduct my alimony payments to my ex-wife?"

—Wade N.
age 47, divorced, one child, physician
Baton Rouge, Louisiana

Alimony creates a tax deduction for the payer in the year paid and is taxable as income to the recipient in the year received. The IRS treats alimony completely different from its treatment of child support. The payment of child support is neither deductible nor treated as income to either the payer or the recipient.

For spousal support to meet the requirements to be considered deductible alimony for tax purposes (for divorce/separation agreements executed after 1985), all of the following requirements must be met:

**1. Cash.** The spousal-support payments must be paid in

cash, which includes checks and money orders (Internal Revenue Code 71 [b][1]). The cash can be paid directly to the other spouse or indirectly on the spouse's behalf under the terms of an agreement or decree to pay for expenses such as rent, mortgage payments, spouse's tuition, health insurance, medical and/or dental payments (I.R.C. 71[b][1][A]).

The payment of spousal support with property or services does not satisfy the requirements of the IRS. Property settlements, whether lump sums or installments, are not considered as alimony for tax purposes.

**2. Order or Agreement.** A court order (decree) or written agreement in which the payments are designated as alimony and are not designated for another purpose is required. Any payment to a spouse made without a decree or written agreement shall not be considered alimony for tax purposes (I.R.C. 71 [b][2]).

**3. Not Members of Same Household.** After the divorce or during the separation, both spouses cannot live in the same household when the payment is made (I.R.C. 71[b][1][C]).

**4. Spousal Support Has No Life after Death.** The obligation to pay alimony must not exist beyond the death of the recipient spouse (I.R.C. 71[b][1][D]). The decree or written agreement must have provisions that the alimony ends upon the death of the spouse, if not before. Alimony does not have to continue until one's death in order to be deductible; however, it cannot outlive its recipient.

**5. Alimony Is Not Intended as Child Support or a Property Division.** The alimony payment cannot be treated as child support (I.R.C. 71[1][c], as well as 71[1][f]). If there is a decree of both alimony and child support, and the payer pays less than the total required by both alimony and child-support orders, then the first payments made shall be treated by the IRS as child-support payments until such time that the entire current child support obligation is satisfied. The surplus payments, above and beyond the child-support obligation, may be considered as alimony.

*Caution:* In order for the alimony payment to be deductible, it cannot be linked to any consideration regarding your children.

Although the written agreement may call a payment "alimony," if the payment is connected to a contingent event related to your child, then it will not be considered deductible alimony by the IRS (e.g., a provision in a written agreement or decree that provides for payments called "alimony" and calls for a change in the amount of the payments upon the child's eighteenth birthday or upon the child's graduation from high school will not be considered deductible alimony).

Also note that it is unwise to have an agreement with provisions of alimony and child support that does not distinguish between the specific amount to be paid for each.

### An Agreement to Take or Receive Spousal Support Instead of Child Support Can Have Tax Benefits or Consequences That Should Be Weighed Thoroughly

Speak to your attorney and/or tax advisor before entering into any agreement regarding alimony and/or child support.

*Caution:* As an additional consideration, no one can claim the tax benefits of alimony in any year that the spouses file a joint tax return.

### Be Aware of the "Recapture" Rules

Congress enacted laws that discourage attempts to characterize property distributions as alimony. The recapture rules apply to "alimony" that is "front-loaded" (having excessive payments in the first three years of the alimony agreement). If the alimony payments decrease or cease during the first three years, then the payer spouse must "recapture" the funds and include them in his or her taxable gross income. Whether an alimony payment is excessive depends on the calculation of front-loading rules followed by the federal government. Consult your attorney and tax advisor as to whether these rules may apply to you.

## 16. Know How a Qualified Domestic Relations Order (QDRO) Affects Your Taxes

A Qualified Domestic Relations Order, known as a QDRO, is a court's decree that may relate to allocation of benefits to the spouses in a qualified retirement plan and/or a tax-sheltered annuity; the payment of child support and alimony; and the division of marital property.

Under a QDRO, benefits paid to the child or dependent or the retirement plan's participant are treated for tax purposes as though they were paid directly to the plan's participant. Yet, benefits allocated to a spouse or former spouse made pursuant to a QDRO are included in the recipient spouse's income for tax purposes.

Generally, retirement-plan benefits allocated to the spouse of a retirement-plan participant can be "rolled over" tax free into the recipient spouse's new or existing individual retirement arrangement (IRA) or other qualified retirement plan as long as the transfer occurs within sixty days. Special rules apply, so contact your tax specialist or the IRS for more details.

## 17. Individual Retirement Arrangements (IRA)

As stated above, a transfer to a spouse of all or a portion of funds in an IRA can be accomplished tax free as long as the transfer is made pursuant to a court order or written agreement formally associated with the court order. From the date of the official transfer of funds, the interest accruing on the transferred IRA funds will be considered as the interest of the recipient spouse.

## 18. Property Settlements

The IRS does not consider a transfer of property between spouses as a taxable gain or loss. However, for a transfer of property to a former spouse to have no taxable gain or loss, then the transfer must occur incident to the divorce.

If the marital property is sold to a third party while it is still owned by both spouses, then each spouse must report the proceeds or loss attributed to them by virtue of property settlement.

### Watch Out for Transfer of Property to Third Parties

Although a transfer between spouses is generally considered a tax-free event, a subsequent transfer to a third party is a taxable event to the spouse who became the recipient owner of the property. Pursuant to I.R.C. 1041, the owner/former spouse shall be subject to tax consideration based on any capital gain or loss, which the IRS has special methods to calculate. Consult your tax advisor for the precise tax ramifications that may affect you.

**Remember to Consult Your Tax Advisor Prior to Entering into Any Property Agreement or Transfer**

The most important message you should take from this section is to use a tax expert to advise you on any agreement or property transfer. The cost of the advisor's services should be worth the advice, as the tax ramifications of an agreement or transfer can be significant.

# Chapter 15

# CREDIT CONCERNS AND BANKRUPTCY

## 1. Background

> "I worked my whole life to live the American dream. It's now become a nightmare. I have to pay my subcontractors and other bills, but the money is not coming in. I'm also several months behind in my child-support payments. Bankruptcy is now a real option."
>
> —Chris P.
> age 42, divorced, three children, building contractor
> Kentwood, Louisiana

American families have an average credit-card debt balance of $4,000. In the late 1990s, national credit-card debt reached approximately $400 billion (nearly 40 percent of the $1 trillion national consumer debt).

Personal bankruptcies have steadily increased throughout the past decade. In the late 1990s, personal bankruptcies reached an all-time high of over 1 million filings.

"Financial problems" is one of the most cited reasons why people file for divorce. When the stress of financial concerns is compounded by the seemingly insurmountable anxiety associated with a divorce, many people feel overwhelmed, throw up their hands, give up, and file for bankruptcy protection.

Even when you have no intent to file bankruptcy, you may continue to have legitimate concerns about how a bankruptcy could affect you if your spouse files or threatens to file for bankruptcy protection.

## 2. Gain Control by Knowing the Ramifications of Bankruptcy Applicable to You

Many people file for bankruptcy protection in order to gain control of their finances and the associated stress. Before you take this leap, which could affect you for at least ten years, first consider the potential negative stigma and other ramifications of filing for potential bankruptcy.

The most common type of bankruptcy is Chapter 7 bankruptcy. Chapter 7 allows for a liquidation and complete discharge on nonexempt debts. Individuals, partnerships, and corporations may file Chapter 7 bankruptcy. Others bankruptcies are available under Chapters 11, 12, and 13 and allow for rehabilitation through an extended time to pay the debts. Then a bankruptcy trustee is appointed to supervise the assets and devise a plan to ultimately pay off creditors. Consult a qualified bankruptcy attorney to see what type of bankruptcy, if any, would be appropriate for you.

Additionally, you should examine how bankruptcy affects your rights associated with the following issues (among others):

1. Child support
2. Alimony/spousal maintenance
3. Property division

### 3. Child Support Is Not Dischargeable in Bankruptcy

"My ex has threatened to file bankruptcy if I take him to court to get the child support arrearages."

—Diana V.
age 34, divorced, two children
cellular/digital-telephone sales associate
Harahan, Louisiana

When a debt is considered discharged in a bankruptcy proceeding, the creditor cannot collect the debt from the debtor. The discharged debt is forgiven for the person who filed for federal bankruptcy protection.

The obligation of child support is not dischargeable in bankruptcy. The person who has past-due and/or present child-support obligations will continue to have the same child-support debt regardless of the bankruptcy proceeding.

Once a spouse owing child support files for bankruptcy, the family court will be able to enforce child-support orders during the pendency of the bankruptcy proceeding; however, the family court cannot rule on a modification of child support until the bankruptcy proceeding is over. Under Chapter 13 bankruptcy, a payment plan may be approved by the bankruptcy court to allow past-due child support to be paid in full within three to five years.

## 4. Spousal Support Is Not Dischargeable in Bankruptcy

> "I owe my ex-wife around twenty thousand dollars in spousal support. She has hired a high-powered lawyer to get it. I'll file bankruptcy before I'll pay."
>
> —Robert C.
> age 64, divorced, three adult children
> office administrator
> New Orleans, Louisiana

Similar to child-support payments in this aspect, alimony is not dischargeable in a bankruptcy proceeding.

Under a Chapter 13 bankruptcy, a payment plan may be approved by the bankruptcy court to allow past-due alimony to be paid in full within three to five years.

## 5. Some Attorney Fees Are Not Dischargeable

A bankruptcy will not relieve a debtor spouse from being required to pay court-ordered attorney's fees to the other spouse's attorney.

## 6. Other Debts That Are Not Dischargeable in Bankruptcy

1. Certain tax debts
2. Debts created by fraudulent or unlawful acts
3. Some student loans
4. Certain fines, restitution, or penalties ordered by criminal courts
5. Other specific debts associated with federal depository institutions
6. Other items to be identified by your bankruptcy attorney

## 7. A Property Debt May Be Dischargeable

Generally, the debt of a spouse created and/or recognized by a family court associated with a property settlement may be dischargeable in bankruptcy. There are exceptions to this general rule, so consult a qualified bankruptcy attorney with your concerns.

If you enter into a property settlement in which your former spouse will owe you property or will agree to pay a debt for which both of you are responsible, you may be devastated if that spouse files for bankruptcy and has his obligation discharged. In other words, you may lose your ability to collect a debt from your spouse and remain responsible to the creditors for debts that you and your spouse were jointly legally responsible.

## 8. A Bankruptcy May Affect Your Ability to Get a Job

Employers are able to obtain your credit report in order to evaluate your job qualifications. Since October 1997, employers require your consent to investigate your credit history for employment-related purposes.

## 9. Beware of "Bankruptcy Blackmail"

> "I'm not going to be intimidated by his threats of bankruptcy."
> —Tammy B.
> age 35, divorced, two children, physical therapist
> Shreveport, Louisiana

A spouse may threaten to file bankruptcy to gain advantage during a divorce or property-division proceeding. The information given in this chapter equips you with the knowledge that child-support and alimony obligations are not dischargeable. You also are now aware of the potentially detrimental results that can occur if your spouse owes you other debts or property and files for bankruptcy. Now, you are able to work with your attorney to devise a property agreement that will take into consideration the risks of your spouse filing for bankruptcy protection. As with other acts of intimidation, relate all such threats to your attorney.

## 10. Get a Lien or Mortgage

If you are concerned that your spouse may file for bankruptcy and detrimentally affect your property rights, insist that your attorney seek a lien or mortgage on your spouse's property that would be owed to you in a property settlement. If you have a properly recorded lien or mortgage on a property that your spouse is attempting to get discharged, then your attorney can attempt to seize the property pursuant to the lien or mortgage.

Consider bankruptcy from an informed standpoint. After reviewing the above information and consulting a qualified bankruptcy attorney, you may continue to consider taking that large step and decide to file for bankruptcy protection. If you have made an informed decision to file for bankruptcy, know that you are not alone. The number of personal, nonbusiness bankruptcies has steadily increased over the last few decades.

## 11. Review Your Credit Report

Your credit history is kept on your credit report, which is maintained by consumer-reporting agencies/credit bureaus. The Fair Credit Reporting Act was created to ensure that accurate information is maintained on your credit report.

Accurate information on your credit report cannot be removed for seven years. If you file for bankruptcy, information regarding your bankruptcy will remain on your report for ten years.

In order to get a copy of your credit report, send a letter to one of the following agencies requesting the report that includes the following information:

1. your full name (including maiden name)
2. your current address
3. any prior addresses if you are requesting a five-year credit history
4. your date of birth
5. your social-security number
6. your signature

The Three Major National Consumer-Reporting Agencies/
Credit Bureaus

Equifax
P.O. Box 740241
Atlanta, GA 30374-0241
(800) 685-1111

Experian
P.O. Box 949
Allen, TX 75013
(888) 397-3742

Trans Union
760 West Sproul Road
P.O. Box 390
Springfield, PA 19064-0390
(800) 916-8800

## 12. Know Your Rights Pursuant to the Fair Credit Reporting Act

Under the Fair Credit Reporting Act, you have the following rights:

1. You have the right to receive your credit report.
2. You have the right for the credit report to disclose the

identities of entities that have made inquiries about your credit within the last year.

3. You have the right for the credit report to disclose the identities of entities that have made inquiries for employment purposes within the last two years.

4. You have the right to receive a free copy of your credit report after being denied credit. You have sixty days to request the free copy.

5. You may dispute the accuracy of any entry on your report. The consumer-reporting agency/credit bureau must investigate the disputed credit entry.

6. You have the right to submit a written explanation or comment to be supplemented to your record regarding the discrepancy in a disputed credit entry.

(Other than in the instances stated above, a consumer-reporting agency may charge up to eight dollars for a copy of your credit report.)

## 13. Prior to Filing Bankruptcy, Consider Consumer Credit-Counseling Service

Consumer Credit-Counseling Service is a national nonprofit organization sponsored by business interests. This organization will help you work with your creditors to get your financial status under control. Consumer Credit Counseling Service has made remarkable strides in its ability to get creditors to work with you and provide concessions regarding the terms of payment, interest owed, and the extent of the debt. This service assists with budget counseling, debt management, and the correction of incorrect and/or negative information on credit reports. You can find a local office in your yellow pages.

## 14. Take Advantage of the Fair Debt Collection Practices Act

"Every day I get harassing phone calls from bill collectors. Since I filed for divorce, my husband has not paid a single bill."
—Angie A.
age 37, married, one child, unemployed
Kenner, Louisiana

The last thing you need during your divorce, custody battle, or property dispute is to deal with harassing telephone calls and intimidating letters from creditors and collection agencies. The federal government has provided you with some relief from improper collection tactics. Pursuant to the Fair Debt Collection Practices Act (15 USCode 1692), you can severely restrict the ways that a creditor can communicate with you.

Send the creditor and/or collection agency a letter notifying them that you are aware of the alleged debt and inform them that you are asserting your rights pursuant to the Fair Debt Collection Practices Act. Request that they cease further communication with you except at the specific times and places designated by you and for the specific reasons set forth in the federal law. If desired, you may designate a certain telephone number and a specific time period in which you may be contacted. Upon your written request, debt collectors must stop contacting you.

Regardless of whether or not you send a letter to a debt collector, the Fair Debt Collection Practices Act provides you with the following rights:

1. Debt collectors may not harass you.
2. Debt collectors may not use obscene or profane language.
3. Debt collectors may not advertise your debt.
4. Debt collectors may not misrepresent the amount of your debt.
5. Debt collectors may not state that you will be arrested if you do not pay your debt.
6. Debt collectors must properly identify themselves on all telephone calls.
7. Debt collectors must not falsely imply that you have committed a crime.
8. Debt collectors may not contact you at work after they become aware of your employer's disapproval of such communications.
9. Debt collectors can only contact you between the hours of 8:00 A.M. and 9:00 P.M., unless you agree otherwise.

If you have a debt collector who is violating any of these rights, immediately inform your attorney, your state attorney general's office, and/or the Federal Trade Commission.

## 15. Close Joint Credit Accounts

A creditor cannot close a joint credit account merely because you and your spouse are divorced or have filed for a divorce. However, upon the request of either spouse, the account can be closed.

A creditor is not under any obligation to change a joint account into an individual account. You may have to individually reapply for credit once the account is closed. It may be difficult to get individual credit if you do not have sufficient income potential and/or a favorable personal credit history.

Keep in mind that in community-property states (Arizona, California, Idaho, *Louisiana,* Nevada, New Mexico, Texas, Washington, and Wisconsin) you may still be liable for debts incurred during the marriage on individual credit accounts of your spouse. Contact each credit company and inquire how you can terminate any further responsibility associated with your spouse's future use on his individual credit accounts. Speak to your attorney about other actions that can protect your interests.

### 16. Remove Your Name from the House Mortgage if You Are Not Keeping the House

"I promised her that she could have the house when we got divorced."

—Max Z.
age 44, divorced, one child
orthodontist
Metairie, Louisiana

The only way to get your name off the house mortgage is to sell the house or get refinancing purely in the name of the spouse retaining the house. It is highly unlikely that a lender would allow your name to be removed from the mortgage without one of these events occurring. If your name remains on the mortgage note, then your ability to obtain future credit may be detrimentally affected.

Chapter 16

# Discovery Pleadings

## 1. Discovery Overview

Discovery pleadings help your attorney receive information to aid in the litigation of your domestic issues. These pleadings are essential building blocks in your case. You may be shocked by the information you discover through your spouse's answers to the discovery pleadings. Discovery pleadings also include other procedures, such as blood tests and psychological evaluations. The goal is to seek the true financial picture and the factual merits of one's quest for custody, visitation, alimony, child support, property division, and the like.

Typical Discovery Methods
1. Interrogatories
2. Requests for production of various documents and items
3. Depositions
4. Requests for admissions of facts
5. Physical and/or psychological evaluations
6. Inspections

## 2. Interrogatories

Interrogatories are written questions, prepared by your attorney, for whom the other party must provide written answers under oath. Most states limit the amount of interrogatories to twenty-five or thirty-five questions (including subparts). Your lawyer can file a motion requesting to propound in excess of the amount of interrogatories allowed without further court approval.

## 3. Requests for Production of Various Documents and Items

Requests for production of various documents and items are formal requests to the other party to produce, or allow available for inspection, documents and things that are relevant to your litigation. It is wise to use this request for documentary and/or other tangible evidence to support answers to specific interrogatories.

## 4. Depositions

A deposition is the sworn oral questioning of a party. It can be taken with a stenographer and/or by videotape.

Before you are deposed, speak with your attorney and go over the anticipated questions. Be honest, yet answer only what has been asked of you. If you don't know the answer to a question, it's all right to indicate that you don't know or don't recall.

An opposing attorney may attempt to take your deposition at a very inconvenient time. Inform your lawyer of the dates and times of your availability. If your deposition is set at a bad time, don't hesitate to ask your attorney to move the time or date. (The same is true regarding a court date. If the date is inconvenient, or you are otherwise unable to attend on that date, inform your attorney immediately.)

#### Tips on Being Deposed
1. Always tell the truth.
2. If you do not know the answer to the question, do not speculate.
3. Answer only the question asked, and do not volunteer additional information.

## 5. Requests for Admissions of Facts

Requests for admissions are written statements sent to the other party requiring the party to admit, deny, or object to the statement. These requests assist in narrowing the issues in dispute before the court.

## 6. Physical and/or Psychological Evaluations

In domestic disputes, physical and/or mental well-being becomes an important factor during custody and visitation battles. Physicians, psychiatrists, sociologists, and social workers are called on to assist the court in determining what custody and/or visitation arrangement is in the best interest of the children. Drug and alcohol tests assist the court also. Additionally, blood and DNA testing are used to establish paternity.

## 7. Inspections

Your lawyer can make inspections of various locations and things. Inspections are rarely used because one can generally get the information requested from other discovery methods. Notwithstanding the foregoing, requesting that the court order an unannounced inspection of a parent's residence by a custody evaluator may be beneficial in a custody dispute when there is an allegation of neglectful supervision of children or an unsafe living environment.

## 8. Use an Accountant/CPA and a Certified Financial Planner

An accountant who is trained in inspecting business and marital assets can greatly assist your attorney in the discovery of hidden assets and undisclosed income.

Spouses may attempt to hide assets and income in the following illustrative ways:

1. Hide property in remote locations, safety-deposit boxes, and safes
2. Place title to property in another person's name
3. Make an arrangement with his or her employer to defer income
4. Take money out of the bank and/or credit-card advance
5. Lies on tax returns
6. Open a secret checking account at another bank
7. Have wages paid to a third party for work performed by him or her
8. Form corporations or partnerships that assist in sheltering funds
9. Be paid in cash for work performed (or barter)

# Chapter 17

# MEDIATION AND ARBITRATION

"Michael and I probably can work out our differences regarding custody and visitation if we just sit down and honestly look at what is best for the kids."

—Kay B.
age 32, married, two children
pharmaceutical sales representative
Slidell, Louisiana

Mediation and arbitration are two alternatives to allowing a judge to resolve your case. They are intended to reduce the time, cost, and pain of litigation.

## 1. Mediation

Mediation is the process whereby a third person assists both spouses in attempting to resolve disputes regarding child support, alimony, property distribution, and other divorce-related issues. It is a growing means of clearing many issues in the divorce proceeding. In mediation, you and your spouse attempt to settle as many disputes as possible with the assistance of an impartial mediator. This process allows the two of you to explore various options to resolve your dispute. Usually, lawyers are not allowed to attend the meetings; however, it is very common for your attorney to review and seek to revise any proposed agreement.

In order for mediation to be meaningful, effective, and fair, the following should occur:

1. Both spouses should have relatively equal bargaining power. Neither party should be domineering nor controlling.
2. Both spouses should operate in good faith.
3. Both spouses should be mentally and physically able to participate. If either party is too emotional, angry, intimidated, or fearful, then mediation is not appropriate.

4. Both spouses should be willing and able to openly communicate.

5. Both spouses should be fully informed about the existence and value of all relevant issues (i.e., assets and liabilities). All relevant information should be disclosed. Mediation should not be used as a fishing expedition to discover the other side's strengths and weaknesses. Furthermore, in custody and visitation disputes, both parents have fully evaluated each other's abilities and weaknesses, as well as what is in the best interest of the children.

6. The mediator should be neutral, fair, and impartial. The mediator is not your advocate.

7. The mediator should know the divorce laws of your state.

8. The mediator should be aware of the tax consequences of all proposed resolutions.

Mediation may be less expensive than using your attorney to negotiate, yet it can be costly if the mediation is unsuccessful and/or if you have a duplication of costs, as your attorney should review any proposed written agreements.

> "My wife and I met with a court-appointed mediator on four separate occasions. The mediator drafted an agreement that was derived from these meetings. I am relatively comfortable with the provisions, but I want to make sure that I am not giving up other rights that I haven't thought of."
>
> —Dean E.
> age 38, married, one child, speech therapist
> New Orleans, Louisiana

It is prudent to have any proposed, mediated, written agreement reviewed by your attorney and/or tax advisor prior to signing.

## 2. Don't Be Afraid to Walk Away

> "As soon as I walked into the mediation session, I could tell that I wasn't going to like the results. The mediator seemed awfully chummy with Todd. After the first thirty minutes, it was obvious that the mediator was agreeing with everything Todd was saying.
>
> Quite frankly, I don't think that the mediator knew what she was doing. It was also obvious that Todd was lying to the mediator; he was never active in our child's life. Now he pretends to be the father of the year."
>
> —April V.
> age 41, married, one child, pet groomer
> Lake Charles, Louisiana

If the mediation process is not working out, or if you feel that one or more of the factors for fair mediation, stated in section 1, is being violated, then you should not hesitate to end the session and walk away. You can resume the mediation process if any unfair advantage is removed; otherwise, your attorney will be ready and willing to assist you with further litigation.

In the following states, courts can order parents to participate in mediation prior to bringing a custody and/or visitation matter to court:

| | |
|---|---|
| Alabama | Missouri |
| Alaska | Montana |
| Arizona | Nevada |
| California | New Jersey |
| Colorado | New Mexico |
| Connecticut | North Carolina |
| Delaware | North Dakota |
| Florida | Ohio |
| Idaho | Oregon |
| Illinois | Pennsylvania |
| Indiana | Rhode Island |
| Iowa | South Carolina |
| Kansas | South Dakota |
| Kentucky | Texas |
| *Louisiana* | Utah |
| Maine | Virginia |
| Maryland | Washington |
| Michigan | West Virginia |
| Mississippi | Wisconsin |
| Minnesota | |

Mediation can be quite useful; however, it is not a panacea to every case.

## 3. Arbitration

"My ex has proposed that we go to arbitration instead of having our property division heard before the court. Is this a good idea?"

—Keith M.
age 47, divorced, three children, carpenter
Shreveport, Louisiana

Arbitration is different from mediation in that a panel of arbitrators becomes the decision maker. Most arbitration decisions are enforceable in courts of law. Although your attorney is generally present during the process, the decision is nonappealable. Thus arbitration is a less formal and flexible process than mediation. It can save costs and time in an otherwise bogged-down court system.

Chapter 18

# Prepare for Your Court Date

## 1. Successful Steps Takem up until This Point

Your trial date has arrived. With the help of this book, you are prepared because you have accomplished the following goals:

1. You have chosen the right attorney
2. You have made the appropriate fee arrangements with your attorney so that he had enough financial resources to do his job.
3. Your attorney has propounded discovery pleadings and appropriate responses have been given.
4. You have sufficiently tabled your emotions to be as persuasive as possible.
5. You have taken possession of your children, the house, the available money, other valuable documents, and other evidence.
6. Your lawyer has been successful in getting the judge to sign the appropriate restraining orders.
7. You have either attempted mediation or decided that it is not appropriate for your case.
8. You have considered any settlement proposals discussed between the parties.
9. In custody and visitation disputes, you have consciously weighed what is in the best interest of your children.
10. You are ready to fight for your rights and the rights of your children.

If you have read this book in the middle of your domestic litigation, you may not have accomplished all of the goals above. However, your chances of realistically achieving many of these goals is significantly enhanced by your application of the tips found in this book.

Knowing that you have become empowered through your preparation and knowledge, you should attempt to calm your concerns.

Understand that it is natural to be nervous. Rest assured, knowing your spouse is probably nervous as well. Staying focused on your goals for the trial or hearing should channel the nervous energy into pure motivation to get the results you want.

It is always better to negotiate from a position of strength, not weakness! The information you have gained and the preparation you have made with your attorney should place you in a position of strength.

## 2. Before Your Court Date, Watch Your Judge Conduct a Trial or Hearing

As your trial approaches, pick a day to go to court when your judge is presiding over a domestic matter. This will give you a good idea of what you may expect on your trial date. Hopefully, this will alleviate some of your possible courtroom jitters. If you find that being a spectator in the courtroom has caused you more concerns, discuss your concerns with your attorney. Remember, knowledge is power.

## 3. Several Days before Trial, Schedule an Office Meeting with Your Attorney to Go Over Your Case and Ask Any Remaining Questions

## 4. When Appropriate, Entertain Settlement Discussions

A judge does not like to hear that you have not had settlement discussions with your spouse. It may be advantageous for your attorney to tell the judge that you tried to resolve the matter and the other party would not cooperate. On the other hand, if there is no room for negotiations, any attempt to settle could be a sign of weakness and vulnerability. Discuss these issues with your attorney.

It may be possible for you to resolve some issues before the court date. You are ready for trial after the settlement discussions have rendered only partial or no results.

All settlement negotiations should be handled through your attorney. By allowing your attorney to relay settlement proposals and responses to offers, you are lessening the chances for negotiations to break down because of the fragile emotional state of one or more of the parties.

Always negotiate less controversial issues first. By doing so, you are able to eliminate many issues that otherwise would be caught up in the emotional quagmire associated with other, more volatile points of dispute (i.e., agree on who gets the use of which cars, and save the heated dispute on who gets custody of the children for last).

Have a plan and know your bottom line. It is wise to anticipate any settlement proposals your spouse may make prior to going to trial. Many opponents strategically wait until trial begins to throw out a proposal that you would not remotely consider except while under the stress of the moment. By knowing your bottom line, you can undermine these efforts and focus on the trail at hand. By pre-planning a negotiation strategy, you have eliminated a potential plan of attack from a manipulative opponent.

Don't be swayed by emotions; follow your intuition.

## 5. Evidence Used at Trial

Evidence can be elicited in three general ways:
1. By stipulation
2. By testimony
3. By exhibits

Stipulations occur when both parties agree that

1. certain "facts" be admitted into evidence as being true,
2. certain "agreements of the parties" have been made that become a judgment of the court, and/or
3. certain "documents and/or things" are admitted into evidence.

### Who Will Testify?

Once the trial begins, witnesses will be called to testify under oath. Depending on the issues litigated, the witnesses called may include various people whose importance has been discussed throughout the book.

"Lay" witnesses are witnesses who are not experts in the field in which they are testifying. They testify to facts as known through their own personal knowledge. These individuals could include persons such as the following: each parent, teachers, day-care providers, baby-sitters, nannies, coaches, doctors, dentists, priests, rabbis, neighbors, the children (if deemed mature enough), the children's friends (if deemed mature enough), boy-scout leaders, girl-scout leaders, school principals, Sunday-school teachers, guidance counselors, police officers, housekeepers, private investigators, etc. Usually, the court will limit the number of witnesses anticipated.

Expert witnesses are persons that have an expertise recognized by the court. These persons are able to provide expert opinions based on information and/or hypothetical situations that are posed to them. Typically, expert witnesses include persons such as the following: psychiatrists, sociologists, other physicians, social workers, vocational rehabilitation experts, accountants, handwriting specialists, real-estate appraisers, etc.

### When It Is Your Turn to Testify
Here are some general tips to allow you to maximize your courtroom presentation.

#### Attire
- Dress neatly (don't dress in extremes—either too casual or too formal).
- Do not wear a hat in court.
- Do not chew gum.
- Do not smoke.
- Do not wear expensive jewelry.

#### Listen, Wait, Think, and Then Answer
- Be truthful (you have not withheld information from your attorney).
- Be courteous and polite.
- Listen to each question.
- Pause and think of your answer before you respond to each question.
- If you do not understand the question, tell the questioning attorney so and ask that it be restated or rephrased.
- If you do not know or recall the answer, say so.
- Answer only the question asked.

#### Maintain Self-control
- Have good eye contact with the judge (and jury, if one exists).
- Do not swear or make obscene gestures.
- Do not call your spouse bad names (i.e., "that despicable maggot in the blue shirt").
- Do not speak to your spouse in the courtroom.
- Do not let the opposing attorney get you angry and emotional.
- Do not bring your children to court unless and until you have a prior discussion with your attorney.

• Be a gracious winner.

Always maintain good eye contact with the judge. When answering questions asked by either attorney, address your answers to the judge. Good body language and eye contact will reinforce the truthfulness and rightfulness of your position. You want to maintain "good" eye contact. Don't "stare down" the judge or jury!

## 5. Bring All Needed Documents and Things to Court

You should have previously provided all of the documents and things that your lawyer and the opposing attorney have requested. As a precaution, bring all of the relevant documents and things in your possession and tell your lawyer what you have brought.

Lastly, remember, do what is best for your children, then do what is best for you. Hopefully, they are the same.

# AFTERWORD

Now that you have reviewed all of the insights found here, you have the significant advantage of being informed and prepared. You are equipped with the ability to work with your attorney to reach the most advantageous outcome. You can control your emotions and financial security. You have minimized your spouse's chances of taking advantage of you. One of the most dramatic messages found in this book is that you are not alone. In the time that it took you to read this book, thousands more have divorced. The great distinction between you and the literal millions who have ventured these perilous times is that you are prepared for the test.

The ultimate family-law recommendation: **Become prepared and knowledgeable!**

Best wishes

# Appendix A

# YOUR PERSONAL PROFILE

Your name:_____

Your address:_____

_____

_____

Your home telephone number:_____

Your work telephone number:_____

Your pager number:

Can your attorney send mail to or call all of the above addresses and telephone numbers? If not, please explain, and state how you can be contacted:_____

_____

_____

Your social-security number:_____

Your driver's license number (also indicate state): _____

Your date of birth: _____

Your place of birth:_____

Your religious affiliation: _____

Your passport number: _____

Name of person whom your attorney can contact in the case of an emergency or if your attorney cannot locate you: _____

_____

Address and telephone number of contact person: _____

_____

Your relationship to this contact person: _____

Name of prior spouse(s) (if any): _____

Date of divorce, annulment, or death of former spouse: _____

_____

## Marriage Information

Date of marriage: _____

City and state of marriage: _____

Date of separation from your spouse: _____

Date of divorce, if any: _____

Your spouse's full name (including maiden name): _____

_____

Your spouse's current address: _____

Your spouse's current residential telephone number: _____

Your spouse's current work telephone number: _____

Your spouse's social-security number: _____

Your spouse's driver's license number (also include state): _____

_____

Your spouse's date of birth: _____

Your spouse's place of birth: _____

Your spouse's religious affiliation: _____

Your spouse's passport number: _____

Has your spouse previously been married? If so, state to whom, identify when divorce or widowed, and date and place of divorce, if any:

_____

Does your spouse have any children from another relationship?

_____

## Children

### Minor Children of the Marriage or Union between You and Your Spouse

Name of child (1): _____

Date of birth of child (1): _____

Place of birth of child (1): _____

Person with physical custody of child (1): _____

Name of child (2): _____

Date of birth of child (2): _____

Place of birth of child (2): _____

Person with physical custody of child (2): _____

Name of child (3): _____

Date of birth of child (3): _____

Place of birth of child (3): _____

Person with physical custody of child (3): _____

Name of child (4): _____

Date of birth of child (4): _____

Place of birth of child (4): _____

Person with physical custody of child (4): _____

### Minor Children Not Born of the Marriage or Union between You and Your Spouse

Name of child (N-1): _____

Date of birth of child (N-1): _____

Place of birth of child (N-1): _____

Parent of child (N-1): _____

Name of child (N-2): _____

Date of birth of child (N-2): _____

Place of birth of child (N-2): _____

Parent of child (N-2): _____

Name of child (N-3): _____

Date of birth of child (N-3): _____

Place of birth of child (N-3): _____

Parent of child (N-3): _____

Name of child (N-4): _____

Date of birth of child (N-4): _____

Place of birth of child (N-4): _____

Parent of child (N-4): _____

## Adopted Children
### Minor Children Adopted by You and/or Your Spouse

Name of adopted child (A-1): _____

Date of birth of adopted child (A-1): _____

Place of birth of adopted child (A-1): _____

Date of adoption (A-1): _____

Place of adoption (A-1): _____

Person with physical custody of adopted child (A-1): _____

_____

Name of adopted child (A-2): _____

Date of birth of adopted child (A-2):_____

Place of birth of adopted child (A-2): _____

Date of adoption (A-2): _____

Place of adoption (A-2): _____

Person with physical custody of adopted child (A-2): _____

_____

## Adult Children

Name of adult child (Ad-1): _____

Date of birth of adult child (Ad-1): _____

Name of adult child (Ad-2): _____

Date of birth of adult child (Ad-2): _____

## Your Parents' Information

Father's name:_____

Father's address: _____

_____

Father's telephone numbers: _____

Is father living?_____

Father's date of birth: _____

Is your father a favorable witness for you? _____


Mother's name: _____

Mother's address: _____

_____

Mother's telephone numbers: _____

Is mother living?_____

Mother's date of birth: _____

Is your mother a favorable witness for you? _____

## Sibling Information

Your brother/sister's (1) name: _____

Your brother/sister's (1) address: _____

_____

Your brother/sister's (1) residential telephone number: _____

Your brother/sister's (1) work telephone number: _____

Is brother/sister (1) living? _____

Brother/sister's (1) date of birth: _____

Is your brother/sister (1) a favorable witness for you? _____

Your brother/sister's (2) name: _____

Your brother/sister's (2) address: _____

_____

Your brother/sister's (2) residential telephone number: _____

_____

Your brother/sister's (2) work telephone number: _____

Is brother/sister (2) living? _____

Brother/sister's (2) date of birth: _____

Is your brother/sister (2) a favorable witness for you? _____

Your brother/sister's (3) name: _____

Your brother/sister's (3) address: _____

_____

Your brother/sister's (3) residential telephone number: _____

Your brother/sister's (3) work telephone number: _____

Is brother/sister (3) living? _____

Brother/sister's (3) date of birth: _____

Is your brother/sister (3) a favorable witness for you? _____

Your brother/sister's (4) name: _____

Your brother/sister's (4) address: _____

_____

Your brother/sister's (4) residential telephone number: _____

Your brother/sister's (4) work telephone number: _____

Is brother/sister (4) living? _____

Brother/sister's (4) date of birth: _____

Is your brother/sister (4) a favorable witness for you? _____

(Attach additional information for other siblings written on a separate sheet of paper.)

## Financial Information

### Your Monthly Income/Deductions and Employment Information

Earnings: $_____

Income: $_____

Deductions: $_____

Minus the following deductions:

Federal income tax/FICA withheld: $_____

State income-tax deduction: $_____

Insurance-premium deductions: $_____

Any child-support garnishments: $_____

Other garnishments/deductions: $_____


Net earnings

Net monthly wages (after deductions): $_____


Employer

Name of your employer: _____

Address of your employer: _____

_____

_____

Your employer's telephone number: _____

## Your Spouse's Monthly Income/Deductions
## and Employment Information

Earnings
Spouse's gross salary (before deductions): $ _____
per (month /year/not applicable)
Spouse's overtime: $_____
Spouse's commissions: $_____
Spouse's bonus(es): $_____
Spouse's interest income: $_____
Spouse's trust income: $_____
Spouse's dividend income: $_____
Spouse's spousal support: $_____
Spouse's social-security benefits: $_____
Spouse's retirement benefits: $_____
Spouse's worker's compensation benefits: $_____
Spouse's income/earning from any other source: $_____

Deductions
Minus the following deductions:
Federal income tax/FICA withheld: $_____
State income-tax deduction: $_____
Insurance-premium deductions: $_____
Any child-support garnishments: $_____
Other garnishments/deductions: $_____

Net Earnings
Net monthly wages (after deductions): $ _____

Employer
Name of spouse's employer: _____
Address of spouse's employer: _____
Spouse's employer's telephone number: _____

## Your Expenses
(*Note:* Your children's expenses are listed separately.)

Housing Expenses
>  Housing (rent or mortgage payment): $_____
>  Property insurance and taxes: $_____
>  Condominium assessments: $_____
>  Furniture payments: $_____
>  Household supplies: $_____

Utilities
>  Electricity: $_____
>  Gas: $_____
>  Heating oil: $_____
>  Water/sewerage: $_____
>  Garbage collection/recycling service: $_____
>  Telephone: $_____
>  Long-distance telephone: $_____
>  Cable: $_____

Housing Maintenance
>  Maid expense: $_____
>  Household cleaning supplies: $_____
>  Lawn and garden maintenance: $_____
>  Exterminator expense: $_____
>  Plumbing expense/repair: $_____
>  Major-appliance expense/contract/repair: $_____
>  Electrical expense/repair: $_____
>  Painting: $_____
>  Firewood: $_____
>  Snow removal: $_____
>  Miscellaneous housing maintenance: $_____

Household Accommodations
>  Furniture purchase/rental expense: $_____
>  Appliance purchase/rental expense: $_____
>  Other household purchases/rental expenses: $_____

Food

    Groceries: $_____

    Meals eating out (work/school lunches): $_____

    Liquor/cordials: $_____

    Catered special events: $_____

Clothing and Personal Grooming

    Your clothing: $_____

    Dry cleaning/laundry: $_____

    Alteration/tailor expense: $_____

    Shoe repair: $_____

    Special equipment: $_____

    Fur storage: $_____

    Miscellaneous clothing expense: $_____

    Haircut/styling/coloring: $_____

    Manicures/pedicures: $_____

    Facials/waxing/massages: $_____

    Health club/spas: $_____

Medical (not covered by insurance)

    Medical expenses: $_____

    Dental expenses: $_____

    Orthodontic expenses: $_____

    Chiropractic expenses: $_____

    Prescriptions: $_____

    Nonprescription medication: $_____

    Copayments/deductibles: $_____

    Eye examination/glasses/contacts: $_____

    Contraceptives: $_____

    Physical therapy: $_____

    Other miscellaneous medical expenses: $_____

    Children's medical expenses: $_____

Transportation

    Car note/lease: $_____

    Gasoline: $_____

    Car maintenance: $_____

    Parking: $_____

    Toll: $_____

    Taxi/bus/train/ferry: $_____

Oil change: $_____

Tires: $_____

Repair: $_____

Registration/inspection fees: $_____

Car rental: $_____

Auto-club expense: $_____

Towing: $_____

Other transportation expenses: $_____

Insurance

Health/medical: $_____

Automobile: $_____

Life: $_____

Disability: $_____

Funeral/burial: $_____

Homeowner's/renter's: $_____

Fire: $_____

Flood: $_____

Theft: $_____

Travel: $_____

Other insurance: $_____

Education (for yourself)

School/lessons/tutoring/fees: $_____

School loans: $_____

Books/supplies: $_____

Extracurricular/military uniforms: $_____

Miscellaneous education expenses: $_____

Entertainment/Recreation

Restaurants (not listed in food category): $_____

Theater/opera/symphony/movie/movie rental/concert:

$_____

Sporting events: $_____

Vacation expense: $_____

Club dues: $_____

Hobby expense: $_____

Other entertainment expense: $_____

## Child-Care/School Expenses
Tuition/school/education: $_____
Uniforms: $_____
School lunches: $_____
Day care/before- and after-school care/baby-sitting: _____
$_____
Tutoring: $_____
Children's clothing: $_____
Children's allowances: $_____
Children's books and supplies: $_____
Children's room-and-board expense: $_____
Children's travel expense: $_____
Lessons: $_____
Camp: $_____
Extracurricular/military/sports uniforms and equipment:
$_____
Child's transportation expenses (not previously listed in transportation category): $_____
Miscellaneous child-related expenses: $_____

## Other Legal Obligations
Child support for other children: $_____
Spousal support to a former spouse: $_____
Taxes (federal and state) (not previously listed in housing category): $_____
Other taxes: $_____

## Legal Expenses
Attorney fees: $_____
Court costs: $_____
Legal expenses: $_____
Expert-witness fees: $_____
Other legal expenses: $_____

## Miscellaneous Expenses
Pet/pet supplies: $_____
Nursing-home care: $_____

Professional licenses and dues: $_____

Union dues: $_____

Religious tithes: $_____

Gifts and donations (include holidays): $_____

Children's gifts to others: $_____

Other debts_____

Specify creditor: $_____

Specify creditor: $_____

Specify creditor: $_____

Specify creditor: $_____

Finance/Investment Charges

Accounting fees: $_____

Brokerage fees: $_____

Bank finance charges: $_____

Credit-card interest charges: $_____

Tax preparation services: $_____

Known Future Expenses Not Listed Above: (specify)

_____

_____

_____

_____

Children's Medical Expenses: $_____

**Total Monthly Expenses:** $_____

## Summary of Your
## Income and Expenses

Total Gross Monthly Income: $_____

Minus (-)

Total Monthly Expenses: $_____

Equals (=)

**Your net monthly income: $_____**

### Summary of Your Spouse's
### Income and Expenses

Total Gross Monthly Income: $_____

Minus (-)

Total Monthly Expenses: $_____

Equals (=)

**Other spouse's**
**net monthly income: $_____**

## Your Annual Gross Income
(for last five years)

This year's year-to-date gross income: $_____

Last year's gross income: $_____

Your gross income two years ago: $_____

Your gross income three years ago: $_____

Your gross income four years ago: $_____

Your gross income five years ago: $_____

## Your Spouse's Annual Gross Income
(for last five years)

This year's year-to-date gross income: $_____

Last year's gross income: $_____

Spouse's gross income two years ago: $_____

Spouse's gross income three years ago: $_____

Spouse's gross income four years ago: $_____

Spouse's gross income five years ago: $_____

## Bank Accounts

Name of bank/savings and loan: _____

Address of bank/savings and loan: _____

Type of account (checking/savings/certificate of deposit): _____
_____

Account number: _____

Name (or names) in which the account is/was listed: _____
_____

Amount in the account as of (date): $_____

Name of bank/savings and loan: _____

Address of bank/savings and loan: _____

Type of account (checking/savings/certificate of deposit): _____
_____

Account number: _____

Name (or names) in which the account is/was listed: _____

Amount in the account as of (date): $_____

Name of banking/savings and loan: _____

Address of bank/savings and loan: _____

Type of account (checking/savings/certificate of deposit): _____
_____

Account number:_____

Name (or names) in which the account is/was listed: _____
_____

Amount in the account as of (date): $_____

## Your Ownership Interest in Business

Name of business: _____

Address of business: _____

Telephone number of business: _____

Type of business: _____

Form of business_____

(sole proprietorship, corporation, joint venture, partnership, etc.):

_____

Position held (if any):_____

## Real Estate

PRESENTLY OWNED

Address/location: _____

Date acquired: _____

Purchase price: _____

Down payment: _____

Equity: _____

Debt still owed: _____

First mortgage holder and amount: _____

Second mortgage holder and amount: _____

Other mortgages: _____

Liens: _____

Persons/entities named as owners on the act of sale or donation:

_____

PREVIOUSLY OWNED WITHIN LAST THREE YEARS

Address/location: _____

Date acquired: _____

Date sold by you/your spouse: _____

Purchase price: _____

Purchase down payment: _____

Price sold: _____

Any owner financing, if so amount and terms: $_____

_____

Persons/entities named as owners on the act of sale or donation:

_____

# Appendix B

# LOUISIANA COURTHOUSE MAILING ADDRESSES

Acadia Parish Clerk of Court
P.O. Box 922
Crowley, LA 70527
Phone: (337) 788-8881

Allen Parish Clerk of Court
P.O. Box 248
Oberlin, LA 70655
Phone: (337) 639-2030

Ascension Parish Clerk of Court
P.O. Box 192
Donaldsonville, LA 70346
Phone: (985) 473-9866

Assumption Parish Clerk of Court
P.O. Drawer 249
Napoleonville, LA 70390
Phone: (985) 369-6653

Avoyelles Parish Clerk of Court
P.O. Box 196
Marksville, LA 71351
Phone: (318) 253-7523

Beauregard Parish Clerk of Court
P.O. Box 100
DeRidder, LA 70634
Phone: (337) 463-8595

Bienville Parish Clerk of Court
100 Courthouse Drive, Room 100
Arcadia, LA 71001

Phone: (318) 263-2123
Bossier Parish Clerk of Court
P.O. Box 430
Benton, LA 71006
Phone (318) 965-2336

Caddo Parish Clerk of Court
501 Texas Street, Room 103
Shreveport, LA 71101
Phone: (318) 226-6780

Calcasieu Parish Clerk of Court
P.O. Box 1030
Lake Charles, LA 70602
Phone: (337) 437-3350

Caldwell Parish Clerk of Court
P.O. Box 1327
Colombia, LA 71418
Phone: (318) 649-2272

Cameron Parish Clerk of Court
P.O. Box 549
Cameron, LA 70631
Phone: (337) 775-5316

Catahoula Parish Clerk of Court
P.O. Box 198
Harrisonburg, LA 71340
Phone: (318) 744-5497

Claiborne Parish Clerk of Court
P.O. Box 330

Homer, LA 71040
Phone: (318) 927-9601

Concordia Parish Clerk of Court
P.O. Box 790
Vidalia, LA 71373
Phone: (318) 336-4204

De Soto Parish Clerk of Court
P.O. Box 1206
Mansfield, LA 71052
Phone: (318) 872-3110

East Baton Rouge Parish
Clerk of Court
P.O. Box 1991
Baton Rouge, LA 70821
Phone: (225) 389-3960

East Carroll Parish Clerk of Court
400 First Street
Lake Providence, LA 71254
Phone: (318) 559-2399

East Feliciana Parish Clerk of Court
P.O. Box 559
Clinton, LA 70722
Phone: (225) 683-5145

Evangeline Parish Clerk of Court
P.O. Drawer 347
Ville Platte, LA 70586
Phone: (337) 363-5671

Franklin Parish Clerk of Court
P.O. Box 431
Winnsboro, LA 71295
Phone: (318) 435-5133

Grant Parish Clerk of Court
P.O. Box 263

Colfax, LA 71417
Phone: (318) 627-3246

Iberia Parish Clerk of Court
P.O. Box 12010
New Iberia, LA 70560
Phone: (337) 365-7282

Iberville Parish Clerk of Court
P.O. Box 423
Plaquemine, LA 70764
Phone: (225) 687-5160

Jackson Parish Clerk of Court
P.O. Box 370
Jonesboro, LA 71251
Phone: (318) 259-2424

Jefferson Davis Parish Clerk of
Court
P.O. Box 799
Jennings, LA 70546
Phone: (337) 824-1160

Jefferson Parish Clerk of Court
800 Second Street
Gretna, LA 70053
Phone: (504) 364-2900

Lafayette Parish Clerk of Court
P.O. Box 2009
Lafayette, LA 70502
Phone: (337) 233-0150

Lafourche Parish Clerk of Court
P.O. Box 818
Thibodaux, LA 70302
Phone: (985) 447-4841

La Salle Parish Clerk of Court
P.O. Box 1372

Jena, LA 71342
Phone: (318) 992-2158

Lincoln Parish Clerk of Court
P.O. Box 924
Ruston, LA 71270
Phone: (318) 251-5130

Livingston Parish Clerk of Court
P.O. Box 1150
Livingston, LA 70754
Phone: (225) 686-2216

Madison Parish Clerk of Court
P.O. Box 1710
Tallulah, LA 71282
Phone: (318) 574-0655

Morehouse Parish Clerk of Court
P.O. Box 1543
Bastrop, LA 71220
Phone: (318) 281-3343

Natchitoches Parish Clerk of Court
P.O. Box 476
Natchitoches, LA 71457
Phone: (318) 352-9321

Orleans Parish Clerk of Civil
District Court
401 Loyola Avenue
New Orleans, LA 70112
Phone: (504) 592-9104

Ouachita Parish Clerk of Court
P.O. Box 1862
Monroe, LA 71210
Phone: (318) 327-1444

Plaquemines Parish Clerk of Court
P.O. Box 129
Pointe a la Hache, LA 70082

Phone: (985)333-4377

Pointe Coupee Parish
Clerk of Court
P.O. Box 86
New Roads, LA 70760
Phone: (985) 638-9596

Rapides Parish Clerk of Court
P.O. Box 952
Alexandria, LA 71309
Phone: (318) 473-8153

Red River Parish Clerk of Court
P.O. Box 485
Coushatta, LA 71019
Phone: (318) 932-6741

Richland Parish Clerk of Court
P.O. Box 119
Rayville, LA 71269
Phone: (318) 728-4171

Sabine Parish Clerk of Court
P.O. Box 419
Many, LA 71449
Phone: (318) 256-6223

Saint Bernard Parish Clerk of Court
P.O. Box 1746
Chalmette, LA 70044
Phone: (985) 271-3434

Saint Charles Parish Clerk of Court
P.O. Box 424
Hahnville, LA 70057
Phone: (985) 783-6632

Saint Helena Parish Clerk of Court
P.O. Box 308
Greensburg, LA 70441
Phone: (985) 222-4514

Saint James Parish Clerk of Court
P.O. Box 63
Convent, LA 70723
Phone: (985) 562-7496

Saint John the Baptist Parish
Clerk of Court
P.O. Box 280
Edgard, LA 70049
Phone: (985) 497-3331

Saint Landry Parish Clerk of Court
P.O. Box 750
Opelousas, LA 70570
Phone: (337) 942-5606

Saint Martin Parish Clerk of Court
P.O. Box 308
St. Martinville, LA 70582
Phone: (337) 394-2210

Saint Mary Parish Clerk of Court
P.O. Drawer 1231
Franklin, LA 70538
Phone: (337) 828-4100, ext. 200

Saint Tammany Parish
Clerk of Court
P.O. Box 1090
Covington, LA 70434
Phone: (985) 898-2430

Tangipahoa Parish Clerk of Court
P.O. Box 667
Amite, LA 70422
Phone: (985) 549-1610

Tensas Parish Clerk of Court
P.O. Box 78
St. Joseph, LA 71366
Phone: (318) 766-3921

Terrebonne Parish Clerk of Court
P.O. Box 1569
Houma, LA 70361
Phone: (985) 868-5660

Union Parish Clerk of Court
Courthouse Building
Farmerville, LA 71241
Phone: (318) 368-3055

Vermilion Parish Clerk of Court
P.O. Box 790
Abbeville, LA 70510
Phone: (337) 898-1992

Vernon Parish Clerk of Court
P.O. Box 40
Leesville, LA 71496
Phone: (318) 238-1384

Washington Parish Clerk of Court
P.O. Box 607
Franklinton, LA 70438
Phone: (985) 839-7821

Webster Parish Clerk of Court
P.O. Box 370
Minden, LA 71058
Phone: (318) 371-0366

West Baton Rouge Parish
Clerk of Court
P.O. Box 107
Port Allen, LA 70767
Phone: (985) 383-0378

West Carroll Parish Clerk of Court
P.O. Box 1078
Oak Grove, LA 71263
Phone: (318) 428-2369

West Feliciana Parish

Clerk of Court
P.O. Box 1843
St. Francisville, LA 70775
Phone: (985) 635-3794

Winn Parish Clerk of Court
P.O. Box 137
Winnfield, LA 71483
Phone: (318) 628-3515

# Appendix C

# SAMPLE DISCOVERY PLEADINGS

### Interrogatories

EMPLOYMENT/INCOME

Please state the name, address, and telephone numbers of any and all of your employers. In so doing, state the date that you commenced your employment with present employer(s); your present rate of gross monthly pay; the date on which that rate was established; the frequency with which you receive your pay; and for each of your last twelve pay periods, state your gross pay, net pay, and the amount and purpose of each deduction from your gross pay.

Please state your total gross income for the last three years, and state, with particularity, the components, with dollar values undersigned, of each year's gross income.

Does your employer pay for or reimburse you for meals, entertainment, travel, automobile, and/or other expenses? If so, state how you are reimbursed, what expenses are reimbursed, and whether you or your employer keeps records of these expenses and reimbursements.

Have you had your employment terminated within the last twelve months? If so, state whether you quit or were fired.

RETIREMENT

Please list and describe each pension, retirement plan, profit-sharing plan, stock option, 401(k) plan, or similar type of fund in which you have a present or future interest of any kind, stating for each fund, the name of the fund, the legal entity that maintains the fund, the amount of your vested and nonvested interest in that fund as of the date that you received these interrogatories, and the name, address, and telephone number of the administrator of the fund.

## SCHOLASTIC AND VOCATIONAL DOCUMENTS
Please identify any and all scholastic and/or vocational diplomas, awards, and/or degrees that you have received.

## EXPENSES
Please itemize, with numerical particularity, any and all of your expenses on a monthly basis. Include, with specificity, the amount of money expended each month for each of the following categories: housing, property insurance and taxes, household repairs, furniture payments, household supplies, utilities, telephone, cable, food, automobile expense/travel, clothing purchases, laundry, personal grooming, education, pet supplies, union dues, recreation, gifts/donations, medical insurance, medical expenses not covered by insurance, and miscellaneous expenses.

## LIABILITIES/DEBTS
Please list each liability/debt owed by you or your spouse as of the date you received these interrogatories, stating for each the name, address, and telephone number of each creditor; the amount owed; the monthly payment required; the date on which the obligation was incurred, and the purpose for which the obligation/debt was incurred.

## BANK ACCOUNTS
Please list each checking, commercial-banking, savings, credit-union, and/or other depository account of every nature in which you have an interest, showing as to each such account the name and address of the institution, account number, the name(s) listed on each account; and the amount in the account as of the date you were served or otherwise received these interrogatories. For each withdrawal, indicate the date, amount, and purpose; and for each deposit, state the date, amount, and source of funds deposited.

## BUSINESSES
Do you have an ownership or equitable interest in any business entity of any kind? If so, please state the name, address, and telephone number of each business and your percentage interest therein, the form of that business operation (i.e., a sole proprietorship, joint

venture, partnership, corporation, etc.), and whether any other person has an ownership or equitable interest in that business.

## FINANCIAL STATEMENTS

Please state whether you have prepared any financial statements during the last three years or if any have been prepared for you. If so, please state whether you have furnished any financial statements to any banks or other lending institution(s) within the past three years. In so doing, state the date on which the statement was furnished and the name of the bank or institution to which the statement was furnished.

## SECURITIES

Please list any and all stocks, bonds, certificates, options, or other securities of whatever nature owned by you or by someone on your behalf for the last three years. State the location of each security.

## REAL ESTATE

Please list any and all real property in which you have, or had, a legal or equitable ownership interest for the last three years, stating for each such property the acquisition date; purchase price; initial down payment; whether each property has been sold or donated, and if so, for how much, to whom, and when; if not sold or donated, what mortgages are outstanding on each property. For each such mortgage, state the mortgagor's name and address.

## PROPERTY

Please describe in detail any property that you allege to be your separate (nonmarital) property. State for each property the description; location; date of acquisition; method of acquisition, including source of funds used to acquire the property; and the facts relied on to support your allegation that the property is your separate (nonmarital) property.

Please describe in detail any property that you allege to be your community property. State for each property the description; location; date of acquisition; method of acquisition, including source of funds used to acquire the property; and the facts relied on to support your allegation that the property is community property.

## VEHICLES

Please list all motor vehicles, boats, motorcycles, motor homes, trailers, and/or airplanes owned by you or by someone on your behalf, stating for each the make, model, and identification number, purchase price, and (if any) down payment; the chattel or mortgage holder and amount of any note and amount remaining unpaid; and the amount of monthly payments of each note and/or chattel mortgage, and the identity of the registered owner(s).

## JEWELRY AND OTHER VALUABLES
Please list each piece of jewelry and other items of personal property owned by you, having a value in excess of $100.

## CONTENTS IN SAFETY-DEPOSIT BOXES/SAFES
Do you maintain a safety-deposit box and/or safe? If so, state as to each such safety deposit box and/or safe the institution in which the safety-deposit box is maintained, the address of that institution, the number or other identification for the safety-deposit box, the description of the contents of the safety-deposit box and/or safe, and the signatories for the safety-deposit box.

## TRUSTS
Are you the beneficiary of any trust? If so, for each please state the date that the trust was established; the name, address, and telephone number of the trustee(s) and/or administrator(s); the amount of money and/or description of property held in trust; and the income or funds received by you or someone on your behalf during the past three years, specifying the dates and amounts of each transaction.

## PRIOR SPOUSES/CHILDREN
Have you been married to someone other than your present spouse? If so, state the name, address, and telephone number of each prior spouse; the names of all children born of that union; the birth dates of all children; and whether you are under a court order or agreement to pay alimony and/or child support to any other person. If so, state the amount of alimony/child support owed.

## CHILD SUPPORT
Please provide any and all bases for which you aver should be made for a deviation from the state child-support guidelines.

## DAY CARE/TUITION
Please state the cost of any day-care, child-care, tuition, camp,

and/or educational expenses for the children of the parties. In so doing, provide the name, address, and telephone number of each school and/or provider of child care.

## INSURANCE

Please list every type of insurance policy (whether life, health, disability, liability, automobile, or other) owned or purchased by you or your spouse, stating for each policy the name of the insurer(s); the policy number; the date of issuance; the type of insurance policy; the face value (if any); the current cash-surrender value (if any); the name, address, and telephone number of each beneficiary; and whether there is a loan on the policy, and if so, what is the amount of the loan, who obtained the loan(s), and for what purpose.

## FAULT

If you are alleging that any fault should be placed on any party who lead to the breakup of the marriage, please state with specificity any and all allegations regarding the alleged fault of any party.

## WITNESSES

Please identify the name, address, and telephone number of each witness you may call at the trial of this matter or any incidental proceeding.

## EXHIBITS

Please list any and all documents and things that you may introduce into evidence or use as demonstrative evidence at the trial of this matter or any incidental hearing.

### Requests for Production of Documents and Things

## EMPLOYMENT/INCOME:

- Any and all paychecks, pay stubs, federal tax returns, state tax returns, cash-register receipts, contracts for work, accounts-receivable records, appointment calendars, cash-register tapes, purchase receipts, tax refunds, and/or daily log of cash receipts

- Any and all documents regarding reimbursements and/or payments for the past three years, including but not limited to travel, automobile, meal, health-club, country-club, and entertainment expenses

- Any and all employment records for the past three years

RETIREMENT:

- Any and all documents and things regarding pensions, retirement, profit-sharing plans, stock options, 401(k) plans, and/or deferred compensation

SCHOLASTIC AND VOCATIONAL DOCUMENTS:

- Any and all of your scholastic and/or vocational diplomas, awards, and/or degrees

EXPENSES:

- Any and all documents and things referencing the expenses of either you or your spouse within the past three years, including but not limited to invoices, canceled checks, checkbook registries, and the like, for the following categories: housing, property insurance and taxes, household repairs, furniture payments, household supplies, utilities, telephone, cable, food, automobile expense/travel, clothing purchases, laundry, personal grooming, education, pet supplies, union dues, recreation, gifts/donations, medical insurance, medical expenses not covered by insurance, and miscellaneous expenses

LIABILITIES/DEBTS:

- Any and all documents and things referencing each liability/debt owed by you or your spouse within the past three years

BANK ACCOUNTS:

- Any and all documents and things regarding each checking, commercial-banking, savings, credit-union, and/or other depository account of every nature in which you have had an interest within the past three years

FINANCIAL STATEMENTS:

- Any and all financial statements rendered by you or on your behalf for any purpose, within the past three years

SECURITIES:

- Any and all stock certificates, bonds, options, and other evidence of securities that you had or have a legal or equitable interest within the past three years

- Any and all documentation concerning the valuation of any and all securities, including but not limited to stocks, bonds, and/or mutual funds, within the past three years

BUSINESSES:

- Any and all documents and things regarding your business interests, including but not limited to articles of incorporation, initial reports, annual reports, minute books, stockholder subscriptions, partnership agreements, counter letters, and/or other documents, concerning any entity in which either spouse has or had an ownership interest within the past three years

- Any and all state and federal tax returns filed by you or on your behalf for the past three years

- Any and all financial statements, balance sheets, profit and loss statements, and income statements of any and all proprietorships, joint ventures, partnerships, realty trusts, corporations, or other business interests that you had or have a legal or equitable interest within the past three years

TRUSTS:

- Any and all evidence of trusts and/or custodial accounts in which you are a trustee, administrator, and/or beneficiary

PRIOR SPOUSES/CHILDREN:

- Any and all birth certificates, adoption decrees, affidavits of acknowledgment, divorce decrees, paternity/DNA test results, and/or decrees of emancipation regarding your children and/or any child made subject to this litigation

INSURANCE:

- Any and all insurance policies that you have or had within the past three years

MEDICAL EXPENSES:

- Any and all medical bills regarding any party to this litigation and/or the minor children thereof

CHILD SUPPORT:

• Any and all documents and things indicating that you have paid and/or received child-support payments within the past three years

DAY CARE/TUITION:

• Any and all documents and things evidencing that day-care, child-care, tuition, camp, and/or educational expenses were paid and/or incurred and are associated with the children of the petitioner and defendant

REAL ESTATE:

• Any and all documents and things concerning any appraisal of any and all real estate owned by either party to this litigation

• Any and all mortgages, notes, titles, deeds, acts of sale, acts of donation, or time-share contracts, associated with any property that you had or have a legal or equitable interest within the past three years

FURNITURE/OTHER PROPERTY:

• Any and all documents and things concerning any evaluation of the worth of the furniture and/or furnishings owned by either party to this litigation

• Any and all documents and things concerning the sale and/or acquisition, within the past three years, of any property by either party to this litigation

VEHICLES:

• Any and all titles, acts of sale, acts of donation, and/or registrations to any vehicle, boat, motorcycle, motor home, and/or airplane owned by either party to this litigation within the past three years

• Any and all documentation concerning the appraisal of any vehicle boat, motorcycle, or airplane owned by either party to this litigation within the past three years

GIFTS:

• Any and all records of any gifts given to and/or received by you within the past three years

CONTENTS OF SAFETY-DEPOSIT BOXES/SAFES:

• Any and all documents and things in your safety-deposit box(es) and/or safe(s)

ATTORNEY FEES:

• Any and all invoices of your attorney of record paid with marital property

PRENUPTUAL/POSTNUPTUAL AGREEMENTS:

• Any and all prenuptial or postnuptial agreements between the parties to this litigation

SURVEILLANCE:

• Any and all surveillance reports in your possession, custody, and/or control pertaining to any party to this litigation

COUNSELING:

• Any and fall documents and things concerning counseling and/or psychological evaluations of any party to this litigation and/or of the minor children thereof

FAULT:

• Any and all documents and things, including photographs and recordings, relating to any allegation of fault that should be placed on any party who lead to the breakup of the marriage

WITNESSES:

• Any and all resumes and/or curriculum vitaes of any witness whom you may call as a witness at the trial of this matter or any incidental hearing

EXHIBITS:

- Any and all documents and things that you may introduce into evidence or use as demonstrative evidence at the trial of this matter or any incidental hearing

# STATE RESIDENCY REQUIREMENTS IN AMERICA

| | |
|---|---|
| Alabama | Six months |
| Alaska | No residency requirement |
| Arizona | Ninety days |
| Arkansas | Sixty days |
| California | Six months |
| Colorado | Ninety days |
| Connecticut | One year |
| Delaware | Six months |
| Florida | Six months |
| Georgia | Six months |
| Hawaii | Six months |
| Idaho | Six weeks |
| Illinois | Ninety days |
| Indiana | Six months |
| Iowa | No residency requirement |
| Kansas | Sixty days |
| Kentucky | 180 days |
| Louisiana | No residency requirement |
| Maine | Six months |
| Maryland | One year |
| Massachusetts | No residency requirement |
| Michigan | Six months |
| Minnesota | 180 days |
| Mississippi | Six months |
| Missouri | Ninety days |
| Montana | Ninety days |
| Nebraska | One year |
| Nevada | Six weeks |
| New Hampshire | One year |

| | |
|---|---|
| New Jersey | One year |
| New Mexico | Six months |
| New York | One year |
| North Carolina | Six months |
| North Dakota | Six months |
| Ohio | Six months |
| Oklahoma | Six months |
| Oregon | Six months |
| Pennsylvania | Six months |
| Rhode Island | One year |
| South Carolina | Three months |
| South Dakota | No residency requirement |
| Tennessee | Six months |
| Texas | Six months |
| Utah | Ninety days |
| Vermont | Six months |
| Virginia | Six months |
| Washington | One year |
| Washington, DC | Six months |
| West Virginia | One year |
| Wisconsin | Six months |
| Wyoming | Sixty days |

# INDEX